THE LIFE OF YOUR AVERAGE AIRCRAFT SALESMAN

Book 2

An autobiography of
Leslie V. Hubbell

4-14-07

To: Don Atkins

From: Leslie Hubbell

ISBN 0-9747147-6-3

Published and Distributed by:
MK Publications
420 E. St. Germain
St. Cloud, MN 56303
www.yourbookpublisher.net
800-551-1023

Printed in the United States of America by
MK Group, St. Cloud, Minnesota.

Forward

I was first introduced to Leslie Hubbell by my interest in aviation. I am an old Huey crew-chief who flew in Vietnam and was recently involved with a documentary film call "In the Shadow of the Blade" which deals with that great icon from the Vietnam War. I flew for almost 3 months across this nation (Some 11,000 miles) in an old restored UH-1D Helicopter, affectionately known as a Huey.

My son, who is a California Highway Patrol Officer and a part-time flight instructor, is very interested in anything that flies. So, when I saw the the cover of Leslie's first book called, "The Life of Your Average Aircraft Salesman-Book One" - which featured a photo of Leslie standing in front of an older model Cessna 310 - I wanted to get his book and share it with my son.

Little did I realize that this book was so much more than just air-craft stories. This unfolded to become one very unique and inter-esting auto biography. I found out that Leslie-the self proclaimed "average aircraft salesman" was anything but "average" and his life story expressed much more depth and insight on life than I thought I would find within those pages. I was left wondering what ever happened to the author and where did his life take him after he shared the first part of his life with me in his book.

The mystery of where and what happened to that "average air-craft salesman" continues on with his second volume-Book Two. We are introduced once again to the aerial adventures and trials of Leslie Hubbell, as his life journey pushes ahead several more years and many more air miles. His love of flying is almost an obsession. He is one who lives as much in the sky and the heav-ens as most people live on the terra firma. His spirit soars as he truly lives his life within the clouds and in those vast blue skies. He is not one to be satisfied sitting earth bound and feels free only when he is flying as close to heaven as he can.

For those reading his life story who also love to fly, this may make you very jealous. I know there is a part of me full of envy. Sit back and read what is far from an average book about an average man–this is an adventure story and you are about to soar into the heavenly skies with one very readable and enjoyable book. Fasten your seat belt and put your trays in the upright position–you are about to take off on an aviation adventure!

W. H. McDonald Jr.
Award Winning Author, Poet, & Lecturer.
Director of the American Authors' Association

Books: A Spiritual Warrior's Journey", "Purple Hearts"
"Sacred Eye–Poetry in Search of the Divine"

Contributing author: "Angels in Vietnam – The Women Who Served" "Spinning Tales – Helicopter Stories"

Documentary Film: "In the Shadow of the Blade" www.intheshadowoftheblade.com

Book Two

Chapter One

A Lot More Guts Than Sense

The next day after passing my ATP check ride I was back in a Cessna 150 with Lew Gibbs doing slow flight, stalls, and touch and goes over at Cloquet and back to Duluth for a total of 1.8 hours. Then it was another 1.2 hours with Bailey Crawford doing more slow flight, chandelles, emergency landings, 1080's and steep 720's. After that, I spent an hour with Earl King doing touch and goes, at Duluth and signed him off to take his check ride and hung it up for the day. The next few days I flew with Al Pitocia, Walt Ellis and Tom Buchanan.

On March 20th, 1972, I had a flight for the Goldfine Company with Monnie and Erv. The Duluth weather was marginal, so I filed IFR to Grand Rapids. We were in Grand Rapids for an hour and then IFR on out to Grand Forks. We arrived in Grand Forks about 10:30 and as usual I had 46Quebec put in a heated hangar and I called the Holiday Inn and got me a heated room for the day too! It always felt good to take a hot tub, have lunch, take a nap and wait for a call from Monnie. He called about 2:30 to tell me they'd be ready to go by 3:30. Early for a change, I thought!

And sure enough, they were right on time as usual! As we were taxiing out Monnie asked me how the weather was back in Duluth. I said, "It's been below minimums all day and they've had some freezing rain, but Hibbing has been holding 500 ft and a couple miles and forecast to stay that way."

He asked, "What if we can't get into Duluth?" I said, "We'll land at Hibbing and rent a car and drive to Duluth, but I'll wait and make that decision over Grand Rapids." We departed Grand Forks IFR and broke out on top about eight thousand feet and went up to nine thousand. About 10 miles west of Grand Rapids I called Duluth, approach control and asked what the weather was doing? They came back with an RVR (runway visual range) of 1800 ft. We needed an RVR of 2400 to land, so I changed our destination to Hibbing, which was still 500 and 2.

There was a North Central DC9 in the holding pattern over Pikla intersection at the time and about halfway to Hibbing I heard approach call the 9 to tell them the RVR was up to 2400ft and did they want the approach? The 9 pilot said, "Yes they did." and approach cleared him for the ILS 9 approach. I had a lot more guts than sense, so I figured if North Central can get in, so can I! I guess I forgot that I was on a part 135 charter flight plus the only de-icing equipment 46Quebec had was pitot heat, and the sweat that might run out from under my arms! So I called approach and said, "46Quebec would like the ILS 9 at Duluth." "Roger 46Quebec, turn right to 180 and descend to 3,100 ft" approach said. Well at least I had learned by now that I'm not getting down into any icing conditions any sooner than I have to! So I said, "46Quebec would like to stay on top until we intercept the glideslope." The 9 made it in and reported light to moderate icing. I thought, Hmmm, light to moderate icing on a DC 9 is probably severe times 2 on a 310!

But I had gotten myself into a situation where the whole upper mid-west was marginal, so if I had to make an approach someplace it might as well be at Duluth I figured. At least I was very familiar with the area and the ILS 9 approach down to the 10,000-foot long runway! We intercepted the localizer and I told Monnie, "Now Monnie don't talk to me anymore." He asked, "Why?" I said, "Because by the time we cross the outer marker (five miles from the runway) we're probably going to have so much ice that this airplane ain't going to be able to climb back up out of it. So the first approach has to be right down the middle and I won't have time to tell you what I'm doing." Monnie never said a word after that.

When we intercepted the glideslope, I just trimmed the nose down and kept the power where it was. I had decided I was going to keep the airplane, clean and fast, no flaps and no gear, until I had the runway in sight. We were descending at about 200 mph and you could see the ice building rapidly on the tip tanks and leading edges. By the time we crossed the outer marker we had two inches of ice and building!

One thing I had always noticed, the worst the conditions got, the better I kept the needles centered and I had the localizer and glideslope nailed! I was thinking though, hmmm how much ice, can an antenna have on it before it breaks off?

I asked approach for a mile fix off the runway, I couldn't see anything and then a half a mile fix off the end of the runway, nothing. I had turned all, of the defroster I could get on the windshield but that wasn't doing much good either. I couldn't see anything ahead. I figured when we broke out I might be able see a little bit ahead and to the left.

I had also decided by now that I had 10,000ft of runway to get stopped in, so I'm not going to use any flaps either so as not to blank out the horizontal stabilizer and elevators. I figured, if there's 3 inches of ice on the wings, there's probably more than that on the horizontal stabilizer! As we were descending, I had backed the power off now and then so as to just maintain a cruise power setting of about 23 inches of manifold pressure and 2350 rpm. By now 46Quebec had at least 3 inches of ice on the leading edges and tip tanks. Worse yet, there had been freezing rain in the Duluth area earlier in the day and the 9 pilot had reported, nil breaking. And I had a wind of 20kts out of the North, a direct left cross-wind, great stupid, I thought.

Finally I started seeing the flashing of the rabbit lights in the fog and then the runway lights, which I had asked approach to turn to high. I throttled back a little and raised the nose of 46Quebec just a little until the airspeed got within 10mph of gear speed and lowered the gear and then increased the power to maintain that speed.   I flew 46Quebec right down to about two feet off the runway before I reduced the power a little and flared just enough to touch the main gear first, followed by the nose gear a nanosecond later, still doing about 150 miles per hour!

So far so good I thought! Except we were sliding sideways down the runway at about a 30degree angle because of the crosswind and the glare ice runway! I'm thinking, I hope there isn't a bare spot out here or I'll wipe the gear off! I slowly backed the power off the right engine enough to get 46 Quebec straightened out and then brought both throttles slowly back to idle, and I still made the mid-field turn off! Monnie said to me, "I wouldn't do that with anyone but you Les." I said, "I ain't sure if I want to do that with me again!" When I pulled up and parked in front of Halvair, all the other pilots came out to see how much ice was on that airplane, maybe 3 1/2 inches?

I had done everything right, except for the most important thing, not deciding to stay in Grand Forks for another day or until the Duluth weather had improved considerably.

On the drive home I said, "thank you God for watching over me again." And, I thought, I must be the luckiest kid in the world! And I made a mental note to, not cut it that close anymore.

There were two benefits for me from that approach though. Before that, every normal ILS down to 200 feet was, somewhat stressful. After that approach, a normal ILS was a walk in the park! And I learned that I don't panic when things get tough. I believe good pilots and good swimmers die if they panic.

And after that flight I had my instrument students fly the ILS down to 200 feet and call out the DH. Then go down to 100 feet and later down to 50 feet as they got better, and then until they felt the main gear of the 172 on the runway, before I recommended them for their flight checks. I'd tell them on final, "Oh no, fog has moved into the whole upper mid-west! Every place is below minimums, it's almost "00" and we're low on fuel. In fact, we've only got enough for one approach! What are we going to do"? I figured if my students could do that, a normal ILS would be a walk in the park for them too!

Chapter Two

A Medical Flight to Portland, Oregon

On the 22nd of March 1972, I was assigned to fly a medical flight to Portland, Oregon in 46Q. The mechanics had taken the two left side and right rear seats out and made room for a stretcher along the left side of the airplane. About 9:00am an ambulance arrived and our Line Manager, John Cartier, had him drive into the hangar so they could place Mr. Conroy into 46Quebec without him getting cold. Mrs. Conroy was a nurse and she sat next to him, just behind the co-pilot seat.

Cartier had asked me if he could go with and I was glad to have his company and help with Mr. and Mrs. Conroy. We took off IFR out of Duluth about 9:45 am and about 2 hours and 30 minutes later we landed in Minot, North Dakota for fuel and a bathroom stop. John had made up a nice in-flight lunch for Mrs. Conroy and us so we had plenty of goodies to eat and drink along the way! I don't know what was the matter with Mr. Conroy, but I assumed he was in very serious condition because he didn't talk or move hardly the whole flight. I was thankful that the air was smooth for him and Mrs. Conroy. After another 2 hours and 30 minutes we landed in Kalispell, Montana, again for fuel and a break for Mrs. Conroy. The weather couldn't have been better for the flight, clear all the way, and smooth. We had come this far at eight thousand feet but now we had to cross the Rocky and

Cascade mountains, so when I filed IFR out of Kalispell, I filed for 12 thousand feet. Even though Mr. Conroy was on oxygen, I had decided to not take him any higher than necessary. This leg of the flight was about 550 nautical miles so we were going to be about another 3 hours and 15 minutes before landing in Portland.

With about eight hours and fifteen minutes of flight time, and another hour and a half of ground time, and the two hour change in time zones, it was about 6:30 PM local time when we landed in Portland. I had called ahead about 50 miles out for an ambulance to meet us at the FBO and it arrived just as we were shutting down out front. John and I said goodbye and good luck to Mr. and Mrs. Conroy. We went in and made arrangements to fuel and park 46Quebec overnight and called a close-by motel to come get us.

After we got checked in and put our bags in the room, we walked a short distance from the motel to a restaurant and had supper and a couple of beers and called it a day. I had been up since 6 am and it was now about 7:30 pm my time so I was very tired. I called home and talked to the wife and kids for a while and I think it took about 2 minutes after my head hit the pillow to fall asleep.

The next morning we were up bright and early and walked back to the restaurant and had breakfast, no beers though! It was a nice warm sunny morning in Portland and the grass was green even! I took a styrofoam cup from the motel and filled it with green grass and when we got to the airport I put it behind my seat.

I filed IFR from Portland to Glasgow, Montana and we departed about 7am local time, 9am our time. We were in the clouds all the way and as we got closer to the mountains, center sent us up to thirteen thousand feet. When we reached thirteen thousand, just the windshield and prop tips of 46Quebec were out of the clouds! John and I laughed at that! It wasn't very long and we had cleared the mountains and shortly thereafter I started a descent on into Glasgow, Montana. We landed and had lunch and refueled 46Quebec, de-fueled ourselves and visited the gift shop. I bought a pottery cup for a souvenir from Glasgow.

The weather was CAVU (ceiling and visibility unlimited) all the way to Duluth, so I offered John the left seat, which he eagerly accepted! We departed Glasgow VFR and climbed up to nine thousand five hundred feet. After about thirty minutes, I'm looking back at the stretcher and thinking, hmmm, I could sure use a nap. John was doing a good job of flying so I said, "wake me up over Grand Rapids, Cartier" and went back and laid down on the stretcher. The airplane was swaying back and forth and up and down a little and with the drone of the engines I felt like a baby in my mother's arms. I must have fallen asleep in two minutes and didn't hear a thing until John was hollering that we were over Grand Rapids. I don't think I've ever slept better than I did in 46Quebec on that flight! I watched as John made a nice landing on runway 9 back in Duluth. We filled out our paper work and stopped by the Afterburner Club down under the tower and had a couple of beers to celebrate a successful trip.

When I got home I spread the green grass on the two feet of white snow in front of the house.

As usual, the kids and Ginger were glad to see me. The wife was doing the laundry. She said, "The kids have been acting up all day and I told them that they are going to get it when you get home!" I said, "Don't do that to me. I don't want these kids living in fear of me when I get home. When you're here, you discipline them if they need it. When I'm here and I see they need disciplining, then I will talk to them." I liked my kids being happy to see me. I sure didn't want them to be afraid of me when I got home and I thought it was unfair for the wife to use me in that way.

Chapter Three

I Meet The Luckiest Kid in the World

For the next week or two I was pretty much a flight instructor. On March 23rd, 1972 I flew the 150 N50185 with Lew Gibbs and Al Pitoscia doing private maneuvers. On the 24th Russ Johnston was back over from Ashland, Wisconsin and we did a few hours of ground school. And I told him about my trip back from Grand Forks and approach into Duluth with 46Quebec a few days earlier. Then I told him that from now on to call the DH at 200 ft and then go on down and call 100 feet and go missed. Then we flew for an hour and a half, starting out with an "ITO" (instrument take-off) off runway 9. I knew that deep down in his heart, Russ loved ITO's. We went straight out for the back course 27 approach, from there straight out to do the ILS 9 front course. Just outside the outer marker I told Russ, "Oh no, the Duluth weather just went below minimums and we've only got enough fuel for one approach! Oh my God, what are we going to do?" Russ gave me that same look that he had several times before, like, "how the hell did you ever get an instructor rating?" There was no wind to speak of and Russ was right on the localizer and the glide slope so I talked him through his first, 00 landing! He called 100 feet, then 50 feet and then touchdown! He was proud as hell when he found out he could do that! I had told the tower we'd be a touch and go and as soon as Russ felt the main gear on the runway he went to full throttle and climbed straight out to 3,000ft and then a right turn to the VOR and into the holding pattern. Russ had the holding pattern nailed after the second time around so we went right into the VOR 31 approach and landed. Russ was happy. He had flown a good flight! We had a couple of beers at the Afterburner Club and he headed back to Ashland, and I went home.

The next day, March 25th, I started Mike Gardonio on his multi-engine rating in the 310 N3285X. That afternoon I flew with Tom Buchanan in the 150 N1621Quebec. On the 26th I flew again with Al Pitoscia in the 150 doing crosswind and normal landings. On the 27th I flew with Mike Gardonio again in the 310 N3285Xray for 1.1 hours doing VMC demos, normal takeoffs and landings, slow flight and a few stalls, and some single engine work. Mike was doing his usual good job. On the 28th I flew with Vic Thompson for 1.1 hours doing turns around a point, S turns, and normal and soft field landings in the morning and after that I returned Bill Jeans 182 back to the Anoka County airport for the sales manager. When I got back I flew with Bailey Crawford reviewing all the takeoffs and landings.

On March 29th Mike and I spent a couple of hours of ground school in the morning and then flew the 310 N3285Xray for an hour making an instrument X country to Hibbing and a VOR approach. At the missed point I gave Mike a heading and altitude back to Duluth. After we got to altitude and he had everything pretty much going his way, I feathered the left engine. He gave me that "you jerk" look again but did a good job of coping with the situation, so I let him restart the left engine and do a VMC demo. Then we went back to Duluth approach and then to the tower and he made a nice ILS 9 approach, so we called it a day.

After lunch a brand new Cessna Citation landed and pulled up front of Halvair. It was a factory demo airplane! The pilot's name was Bob Phizer. He was giving demo flights in it and after Roy and Tom Halvorson, Terry Anderson, Fred Winship and Jim Nelson flew it, I got a chance to fly it! I hollered at a couple of line kids and secretaries to get in and Bob gave me the left seat! He coached me through the start up, pre-flight checks and takeoff and away we went! After we got up and leveled off about seven thousand feet he had me put it into a 60 degree bank and put my hands in my lap and feet on the floor. The Citation was so stable he said, that it would just keep going around and around like that until it ran out of fuel! We came in and I landed it back on runway 27 and taxied in. I thought it flew just like a 182, faster though! It was the first jet I had ever flown and the most comfortable airplane I have ever flown for the first time!

The next week was pretty much routine flying with Al Pitoscia, Craig Taft, Mike, Dave Hedin, Jennifer Church, Lew Gibbs, Don Hudson, and then a trip to International Falls in the 210 N9471Mike, with the Retail Clerks of Duluth. And Earl King passed his private check ride on April 4th! We of course had to celebrate with a couple of beers down at the Afterburner Club!

On April 5th life got a little more interesting again. I was flying with Lew Gibbs in one of our Cessna 150's N1621 Quebec. We were in the pattern at Duluth doing normal take-offs and landings, first on runway 27 and then I had switched to runway 31 for some crosswind takeoffs and landings. There was, also one of 3M's new G2's in the pattern doing takeoffs and landings on runway 27. It was a pretty gusty day and we had made two takeoffs on runway 31 and were doing our second landing which was going to be a full stop and taxi in. We were cleared to land and we were about halfway from the approach end of runway 31 to the intersection of runway 27. Lew was having trouble getting the airplane onto the runway because of the gust and I was probably sitting there thinking, hmmm, I'm glad I ain't flying this little orange crate. We were down about six feet over the runway and being knocked around pretty good and all of a sudden I thought, hmmm, where did that G2 go? I looked over to my right and there was the G2 in the flare for 27! I told Lew, "I've got it" and went to full throttle and a steep climbing left turn! The G2 pilot must have seen us at the same time so he decided to go around too! I think we missed the G2 by about fifty feet and about the same for the control tower! I got a "Cleared to land on runway 27," which I did. And when I got into the office, I called the tower for a change! I said, "This is the IP (instructor pilot) of 21Quebec. What the hell are you doing up there?" The controller said, "Well, it would have worked out ok if you guy's had landed." I said, "When I'm cleared to land that whole runway is mine! I sure the hell didn't expect to see a G2 landing on 27!" I added, "This ain't Chicago, there's no reason you should ever have to get two airplanes within three miles of each other here in Duluth, Minnesota!" Lew and I went over to the Afterburner Club and celebrated still being alive. I should have sent the bill to the tower!

The next few days were pretty routine flying the 150's with Vic Thompson, Bill Radke, Al Pitoscia, and then Russ in the 172 again on April 8th doing an NDB holding and an approach over at Cloquet. Russ was getting pretty good at this instrument flying so we headed back to Duluth and I had him ask approach for the ILS 9. I had told Russ about my flight back from Grand Forks in the 310 with the Goldfine's and how I had landed with the windshield iced over, etc. So as we were flying back to Duluth from Cloquet, and Russ is still under the hood and I said, "You know what Russ? The weather has really gotten bad, I can't see the wing tips anymore. I can't even see the ground anymore! And we're getting some ice! And I just heard that Duluth and everything within 500 miles is 00! (0 visibility and 0 ceiling) And, we've only got enough fuel for one approach! Oh my God, what are we going to do?" Russ gave me that, "how the hell did you ever get, an instructor rating" look again. But I knew, deep down in his heart he loved doing OO landings! And he made another good one! Russ headed back to Ashland and I gave an intro ride to David Hayns for another half hour.

The wife had asked me earlier in the week if I'd take her out dining and dancing on Saturday night and tonight was the night so I headed home! I never wanted to miss the chance to get her about half drunk so I could take advantage of her! I had learned a long time ago that, candy's dandy, but liquors quicker!

A friend had a bar and dance hall out west of Cloquet on the Big Lake Road so after we had supper at the Highland Supper Club in Duluth we drove out there. Was I ever surprised when we walked in! The wife had reserved the place and had arranged a surprise ATP party for me! The, dance hall was decorated with congratulations banners and balloons and all my friends, including Russ were there! We had a great time and when we got home, I let the wife make love with me. What could I do I figured, one good deed deserves another!

On the 12th I had another flight for the Goldfine Company. I guess Monnie and Erv must have figured if I found the runway on that last flight it must be safe to fly with me again. Or else they just enjoyed living on the edge. I've always figured, if you ain't living on the edge you're taking up too damned much space! We flew down to Mankato, up to Willmar, over to Minneapolis and then back home to Duluth in 46Quebec. I loved flying 46Quebec! And I liked flying for Monnie and Erv Goldfine.

On the 13th and 14th I rode shotgun with Carl Lucas in the 421, N8043Quebec, with numerous stops around the upper mid-west and landing back in Duluth about 11:30 am on the 14th. The, 421 was nice, pressurized, quiet and it was different for me to be up in the twenties instead of down in the eight to twelve thousand foot altitudes.

During the afternoon of the 14th I made a cross, country flight with three students from East High, Dale Swanson, Brad Sieverson and Jeff Hammerston, in the 172 N7490Xray. We went from Duluth, to Hibbing, to Eveleth and back to Duluth. We did a combination of dead reckoning, VOR and ADF. We had spent an hour plotting the course on the map and then calculating the wind correction angle subtracting the variation and applying the deviation to come up with our compass heading. It was fun to see them learn how it worked! And for good measure, when we got back to Duluth, I showed them how an ILS works too!

On the 16th I did my examiner act with Vic Thompson getting him ready for his private check ride. Vic was doing a good job, but I still had fun preparing him for the examiner! I'd ask him a question and if he didn't know the answer I'd say, "Why don't you know that? I know your instructor taught you that so don't blame it on him!" My students couldn't believe what a jerk I could become in just a few minutes! (And they hadn't even talked to the wife!) I've got to admit though, I enjoyed transitioning them from the nice flight instructor, to the examiner who didn't care nothing about them except, did they know the regulations, the manual and could they fly the airplane! But, none of my students ever failed a written or the flight check!

Russ came back over from Ashland so I flew with him after Vic and I finished. We made an ITO (I knew, deep down in his heart, that Russ liked "ITO's") off runway 27 and made a right turn out toward Hibbing. I had him do steep turns, left and right, stalls, partial panel, whatever I could think of. Then we went direct to Hibbing and entered the holding pattern for a couple of turns and then the ILS 31. Same thing, "Gee's Russ, I just heard the weather at Hibbing is 00 and worse yet, the whole upper mid-west is 00! And worse yet, we've only got enough fuel for one approach! My God, what are we going to do!" Of course Russ would always look at me with that, "How the hell did you ever get an instructor rating" look, but now I could tell it was also the, "And I drove all the way over here from Ashland for this" look. We made a full stop landing and taxied back for takeoff. I was going to let him take off VFR, but when we rolled out on the runway he stopped and said, where's the hood? I was right, deep down in his heart Russ loved ITO's! And he had gotten very good at doing them! He was becoming a very good instrument pilot, so I covered up his vacuum instruments and made him, needle, ball, airspeed, compass and altimeter it back to Duluth for a PAR (Precision Approach Radar) to Runway 9. He did a good job. I knew I was getting close to recommending him for his check ride. We called it quits for the day and stopped by the Afterburner Club for a couple of beers. Russ and I were going to be flying again in the morning so I had invited him to stay at my house. The wife had made a nice pot roast supper and we had a nice visit with Russ.

The next morning, April 16th, we did an hour of ground school and then Russ preflighted the 172, N4231Quebec. We flew all of the approaches at Duluth and ended up in the VOR holding pattern for a few turns and then a VOR 31 approach to a full stop landing. Russ was getting close.

On the morning of the 17th I had another cross country flight with three more Hermantown school students, Greg Cullen, Steve Eberling and Mark Haugen, from Duluth to Hibbing, to Eveleth and back to Duluth. In the afternoon I made the same trip again with three more Hermantown students, Don Johnson, Steve Carlson and Keith Burcar.

On the 18th, I had a charter flight in 46Quebec, for US Steel out over Lake Superior and up toward Isle Royal. We departed Duluth about 8 am. There was a lot of ice out in the lake yet and they had a couple of ore boats stuck in the ice. They had handheld radios and were directing the coast guard cutter, Woodrush toward what looked like the best path through the ice to the Duluth harbor. And they were also talking to their own boats and giving them headings to steer. We spent about three hours slowed up to 130 miles an hour doing that and then returned to Duluth in time for lunch. I had fun!

After lunch I had another cross country navigation flight with three more Hermantown students, Bret Wargin, Jerry Olson and Brian Kellerhuis, from Duluth, to Eveleth and back to Duluth.

The morning of April 19th I had another DLH, HIB, EVM and back to DLH cross country navigation flight with three more Hermantown school students, John Kwidloz, Doug Pierson and Lee Palm. In the afternoon I did the same thing with three more East High school students, Mark Ellefson, Steve Kossett and Mark Roman. I was even getting pretty good at this cross, country navigation stuff myself!

On the 19th I flew with Lew Gibbs, Al Pitocsia and Roy Larson and on the 20th I soled Lew Gibbs before lunch!

After lunch, Newt Peyton, who owned the Pioneer National Bank in West Duluth, called me and told me he had bought a Twin Comanche from someplace down in southern Minnesota. He said the instructor had signed him off for his check ride but he didn't feel like he was ready. He asked if I'd fly with him, being I had owned a Twin Comanche? I thought, hmmm, I might need to borrow some money from him someday? So I said, "Sure I will, come on up!"

Newt was at the airport within the hour and we visited for a while and I looked over his logbook. Then we went out and pulled his Twin Comanche out of his hangar and I watched as he did a pre-flight. He seemed to know what he was doing and very familiar with the airplane. We got in and he started up using his checklist and we taxied out and took off from runway 27. So far he was doing great I thought! I had him do a couple of stalls and a VMC demonstration. So far he was doing OK. Then I had him simulate a takeoff with full takeoff power and gear down. I closed the left throttle, bad move on my part! That Twin Comanche rolled inverted to the left! I looked over, and Newt's eyes were the size of saucers! I never did ask him if mine were too! I simultaneously closed the right throttle and continued the left roll until we were back to a normal, upright flight attitude. Luckily we were at about 4,500 feet so we had some room to play with. I looked down and saw the Hibbing airport about five miles ahead so I said to Newt, "Newt lets go land at Hibbing and do some ground school work for a while."

So we landed and went in, sat down, and talked about single engine procedures, airspeeds, etc. for a while. Then we took off and climbed back up to 4 thousand feet and reviewed all the maneuvers we had discussed. We didn't even roll it this time!

That same afternoon (after I changed my shorts) I flew with Bill Radke doing cross wind and accuracy landings for an hour. The next morning I flew with Newt again for an hour and a half. After lunch I did my Jekyll and Hyde routine on Vic Thompson. Then we flew for an hour and I signed him off for his check ride with Gordy.

I happened to be out in the lobby about 10am one morning and noticed a Navajo taxing up the ramp. I thought something looked different about it so I waited until he parked out front. I went out and walked around the airplane while the pilot was shutting down and got out. He had all kinds of damage to the airplane! I asked him what had happened and he said he had shot the approach into Grand Marais and gotten a little low and barely got it back out of the trees. I would-

Damaged Navajo.

n't have believed it would still fly if I hadn't seen it taxi in! Now I know, I'm not the luckiest kid in the world, that kid is!

The next morning I flew the Duluth, Hibbing, Eveleth and back to Duluth cross country navigation flight with three East High School students in the 172. That afternoon I did the same thing with Al Pitocsia in a 150 for his dual cross country, flight for 1.8 hours and then did my examiner routine with Bill Radke for an hour reviewing private pilot maneuvers.

On the 25th I made the Duluth, Hibbing, Eveleth and back to Duluth cross country, navigation flight with three more East High School students. I did it again on the morning of the 26th! I was getting where I could make that flight with my eyes closed! I also was getting where I needed a long charter trip in 46Quebec!

On the 26th I played the examiner again with Bill Radtke and signed him off to go take his check ride with Gordy and the next day he passed!

On the 27th I made the DLH, HIB, EVM, and back to DLH navigation flight with East High school again! Now I'm thinking, I don't have to go, the 172 could do it by itself!

Just like the horses we had back on the farm! We had a 20 some year old stud horse, Dick was his name. My Dad and us boys were cutting tamarack down in the tamarack swamp on weekends during the winter to sell to the paper mill. Dad was probably doing that for two reasons, to keep us out of trouble and so we could earn some spending money. Being I was the runt of the bunch I was the cat skinner, or horse rider. My Dad and younger brother would be in the woods with a chain saw cutting down the tamarack and cutting the limbs off. Then I'd ride Dick, with a harness on consisting of a collar, hames, whippletree, and of course, a bridle with a bit in his mouth and reins etc into the woods. My Dad and brother would hook me up to two or three tree lengths and then Dick and I would pull them the 1/4th mile down the trail to the landing where my older brother would unhook them. Then I'd turn around and take the same trail back into the woods. In the meantime my older brother would cut the tree lengths into 8ft long pieces and stack them up.

Dick would have to almost break into a trot to keep three tree lengths moving along nicely. Once in a while though one of the tree lengths would hit a stump along side the trail and that would break the leather strap holding the hames together in the collar and the whole works would end up in my lap! And then the whole works and me would end up on the ground watching Dick go down the trail!

Dick was a really well mannered gentle horse. In fact, so well mannered and gentle, that after making the trip in and out of the woods about 30 times I thought I'd automate this job. I made a few trips in and out of the woods one Sunday morning and then I told my older brother, "The next trip I'm going to start Dick down the trail and then I'm going to bail off and have a cup of coffee. When he gets out here you just unhook the logs, turn him around and give him a little pat on the rump and send him back down the trail to me." So, I got Dick hooked up to three tree lengths and we headed down the trail. I bailed off next to my lunch box and poured myself a cup of coffee and watched Dick go out of sight down the trail. I thought, "why the hell didn't I think of this a long time ago!" I leaned back against a stump and drank coffee and ate a roll for about twenty minutes, looking down the trail now and then for Dick to come back. I waited 25 minutes and then 30 minutes and about now I'm wondering, "where is Dick?" So I walked out to the landing and there sat my brother, having a cup of coffee and eating a roll. I said, "where the hell is Dick?" He said, "He went by here at a full gallop! You'll probably find him up at the barn!" So I walked 3/4ths of a mile up to the barn and sure enough, there was Dick standing at the back door looking for his hay and oats! He was sweating a little from the run so I gave him a bucket of water and some oats too! I guess he figured, if I wasn't going to work, he wasn't working either!

I remember when I married the wife. Right after the reception we headed out to Niagara Falls on our honeymoon. We didn't make it fifty miles out of Cloquet before I stopped at a motel. I went in and told the guy behind the counter that we were on our honeymoon and needed a room. He said, "do you want the bridle" I said, "nope, I'm just going to hold her by he ears!"

Another time, my school friend, Roland Okerstrom asked me if I'd bring Dick down to his house and skid some poplar out of the woods that he had cut down. Okerstrom lived about two miles from our farm. So one Saturday I rode Dick down there and pulled about 40-50 tree lengths out for him.

Mrs. Okerstrom made us a nice lunch when we were done so I ate and headed home with Dick. I figured, Dick didn't need me to help him get home so I turned around and laid, down on his back with my head between the hames and crossed my arms over my chest. Several cars pulled up along side and laughed. The only trouble was though that the closer we got to the farm the faster Dick wanted to go, so the last 1/4 mile I had to sit up and rein him in to slow him down a little. Later Dad, also bought a big mare, Bessie was her name. One time I was riding her back to the barn after a day of pulling logs out of the woods. The closer we got to the barn the faster she'd start going too! I was thinking I'd get her stopped before we got to the barn, I always had before. But she wasn't thinking that, and she ran into the barn at a good trot. The only problem was the old log barn door was only six inches higher than her back so I got wiped off against the barn wall and ended up on the ground again! When I got in the barn she was just standing there eating some hay. She looked at me, like she was saying, where'd you go? I don't know how I survived growing up on the farm without ever breaking any bones!

Chapter Four
My Good Friend, Russ Johnston

On April 27th, 1972 I flew with Newt Peyton again in his Twin Comanche and signed him off to go take his check ride with Gordy. Finally on the 28th I got a charter for Wahls Department store in the 210 N9471Mike, down to Fort Dodge, Iowa. The 210, wasn't a 310 but I still enjoyed flying it for 4.6 hours instead of a 150 or 172 for a change! But the next morning I was back in a 150 with Dave Hedin for the Duluth, to Hibbing, to Eveleth, and back to Duluth cross, country navigation flight!

That afternoon Russ was back over from Ashland and after an hour of ground school he preflighted the 172 and we taxied out to runway 27. Russ had learned by now that every takeoff, unless there was a significant cross wind, would be an ITO so he'd just take the hood and put it on without giving me the "you jerk" look anymore. So he made an ITO off runway 27 and we departed to the southwest. I had him do some slow flight, standard rate turns, steep turns, partial panel and then over to Cloquet for the ADF approach there. Russ was doing great. After the ADF approach at Cloquet, I had him go direct to the Duluth VOR and enter the holding pattern for a couple of turns and then into the VOR 31 approach. When he called the missed approach point I had him look up because he was, right on the money and I wanted him to enjoy that moment.

I know I always felt good (and sometimes lucky!) when I broke out of the clouds and there, just like magic was the runway! I had him go missed and direct to Pikla intersection, which was the outer marker for the ILS 9 approach. I had him do the whole approach, procedure turn and back on the localizer, then intercept the glide slope, descend down to the DH (decision height) of 200 ft above the runway. Then call it out, keep going down to 100ft, call it out, call 50ft and then put the main landing gear of the 172 on the runway without looking up. Russ had gotten good at doing 00 landings and he was proud of himself when he did this one so good! I had told him when we first started doing 00 landings that they are just like doing glassy water or night landings on floats. You establish an airspeed with full flaps that gives you a bit of a nose up attitude and use power to adjust the rate of descent and just wait for the floats or wheels to touch. I wanted Russ and all my instrument students to know how and to have the confidence to make a 00 landing. I figured, just in case they ever get themselves into a situation where the weather had gone to hell or were low fuel for some reason, if they could get on an ILS they could find the runway and land on it. And besides, Russ was one of my best friends so I wanted to do my very best for him, just like I did for all my students! I was proud of Russ too! So I signed him off to take his instrument check ride!

I called Gordy Newstrom over in Grand Rapids and he was available the next morning to give Russ the exam.

I had planned on flying with Russ the next morning anyhow so I invited him to stay overnight at my house again.

After supper we went down to the family room and I did the oral "examiner" act with him again. He was ready for his checkride.

The next morning I had him file an IFR flight plan to Grand Rapids and of course an ITO off runway 27 again and then the VOR 34 approach into Grand Rapids when we got there. I introduced him to Gordy and went and got a cup of coffee and something to read while Russ and Gordy talked and went flying. The oral lasted about an hour and the flight check was another hour and when they got back, Gordy gave Russ his instrument rating! Russ was happy! While Russ, was out pre-flighting the 172 for the trip back to Duluth, I asked Gordy how he had done and was there anything I had overlooked? He said Russ had done a good job and he didn't find anything to trick him up on so I must have done a good job too! Now I was happy! When we got back to Duluth, Russ and I had a couple of beers at the Afterburner Club and then he took the wife and me out for supper at the Highland Supper Club! After supper the wife and I went home and Russ drove back to Ashland.

Chapter Five
Getting Checked Out in the 402 with Gordy

For the next week I was busy with my students and charters. I flew with Lew Gibbs the morning of May 3rd, 1972. Then I had a charter to International Falls in the 172 with Al Haynes from the Duluth Retail Clerks union in the afternoon. The next morning it was the DLH, HIB, EVM, and DLH cross country navigation trip with East High students and then 1.1 hours doing private maneuvers with Al Pitoscia in the 150 N6822Golf. The 5th I flew with Bailey Crawford doing commercial maneuvers for 1.5 hours. On the morning of the 8th I had a charter in the 210 71Mike for the Gustafason Equipment company to Minneapolis and back, for another 2.2 hours. When I got back I started John Hagen on the private pilot course for another 1.2 hours, while Vic Thompson was taking his check ride with Gordy Newstrom. Vic passed so we went over to the Afterburner Club and celebrated with a couple of beers and then we both went home.

As usual the kids and Ginger, were glad to see me, the wife was, to busy to say anything.

I was also getting a little bored with instructing and finding myself working six long days every week and once in awhile seven days. I had told myself when I sold Sunnyside that I'm not working 7 days a week anymore! But I am. And I wasn't making any money either. I had hoped that when I passed the ATP rating that I'd get a raise but apparently that wasn't going to happen. And I didn't like dipping into my savings account to pay monthly bills. I thought about applying with North Central Airlines a few times but I didn't want to be away from the wife and kids fifteen days out of every month. (Besides, I needed to make love with the wife every day, morning and night, and maybe a nooner on weekends!) Hmmm, I wonder if that's why the wife isn't as glad to see me, as I am to see her?

At least since we moved from the country to Duluth Heights on Stanford Avenue, the wife and I weren't as busy taking the kids here and there for school, etc. In fact the kids had made a lot of friends with the North's, Karnowski's, and Taranoski's kids and other kids in the neighborhood. And the wife and I enjoyed visiting with the parents now and then too. I had built a beautiful, old brick, recreation room in the basement and we'd have the neighbors over for a drink or two once in a while in the evening.

For the next three weeks I was in and out of 150's and 172's with the exception of a 210 charter up to International Falls on May 24th and 2 hours of scenic rides over the Duluth harbor on June 1st in the 210!

Thank God Monnie Goldfine called and scheduled a charter in the 310 for two days! He told me there would be him and Erv and a guy and his son from New York. He also told me both the guy and his son were 200 lbs each or more so I left 46Quebec light on fuel for the trip. On June 5th we took off promptly at 07:30 for Mankato and spent a couple of hours there and then went on to Grand Forks and spent the night. Monnie had also told me the guy and his son would be getting on an airline at Grand Forks the next day and going back to New York. We were scheduled to leave Grand Forks right after lunch, returning back to Duluth. When I checked weather, Duluth was down to minimums as usual as well as the whole upper mid-west again. So I had 46Quebec topped off, mains, aux's, everything in case I had to go to an alternate airport and maybe then some! Just after lunch Monnie and Erv arrived and along with them the guy and his son from New York! Monnie told me they needed to go down to Fargo for a meeting for about an hour and then bring the guy and his son back to Grand Forks to catch their plane. I said, "Monnie can I talk to you a minute over here?" He said, "Of course Les, what's up?" I said, "The Duluth weather and in fact the whole upper mid-west is down to or below minimums so I filled 46 Quebec with all the fuel she'll carry thinking these two guys weren't coming back." Monnie said, "What problem does that present for us Les?" I said, "Well, first of all it means that if we lose an engine on takeoff, we're probably going to be landing in that corn field out there north of the runway. And second, I'm going to have to get in the airplane first, then the kid will have to get in a back seat. And then Erv and the other guy get in, and all this time, Monnie, you're going to have to be up on the wing standing by the door as far forward as you can get or the tail is going to be on the ground." I added, "and that isn't going to look good to the guy's over there in the flight service station. And third, if I get slower that 125mph on the landing approach and right down to the runway at Fargo, the tail is going to fall out from under us." Monnie said, "Well, it can't be as bad as that approach into Duluth a couple of months ago, you can do it, let's go." So I got in, Monnie stood by the door as far forward as he could on the wing, the kid got in the back, Erv and the guy got in and then Monnie got in and locked the door. I started both engines and had to hold full forward elevator and a little bit of brakes to keep the tail from dragging on the way to the runway. On the takeoff roll I just let 46Quebec accelerate until she was telling me she was ready to fly and then some before I gently rotated a little. She flew off as nice as could be! On the landing approach into Fargo I kept the speed up to 125mph and only used 1/3 flaps so as not to blank out the elevators any and landed doing 125mph. Monnie said, "I knew you could do that Les." I said, " I know I can do it, but the fed's probably wouldn't be real happy with me for doing it." They had their meeting for about an hour. We hadn't burned off much fuel going from Grand Forks to Fargo so I had to do the same thing going back to Grand Forks! We got back to Grand Forks without incident and the guy and his son from New York left. So I had 46Quebec topped off with fuel, all the way across again, and we departed on an IFR flight plan for Duluth. The weather was perfectly clear until about Bemidji and then we were on top at nine thousand feet. The weather was normal for Duluth, 200 and 1/2 with light drizzle. At least it was June so no ice! As usual I hand flew 46Quebec down the ILS 9 and got the lights right at the DH (decision height). I always got a thrill out of popping out of the soup and seeing those beautiful rabbit and runway lights! I always thought, there isn't anything prettier than an ILS runway fully lit up at night or in the fog! (I never told the wife that though) I did my paper work and went home.

The next morning I was back out to the airport early for a 7:30 takeoff in the 210 with Dick Wilson from Aero Industries going to Langdon, North Dakota. Langdon is about 275 nautical miles northwest of Duluth. It was gener-ally about two hours going bucking a headwind and a little less than two hours coming home with a tailwind. It was a nice charter in the 210 but a long haul in the 172 now and then! I always enjoyed visiting with Johnny Robertson in Langdon though in any case. Sometimes he'd be there, sometimes he'd be out spraying or instructing, etc. But he always left the keys in his pickup and had told me I could use it anytime to go to town for lunch if I wanted to. I had let the wife sleep in so I used Johnny's pickup and went to town for breakfast. Dick had said he'd be returning right after lunch, which he did and we were back in Duluth about 3:30. It was a nice flight with nice weather for a change!

The next morning I had an early charter down to Hayward, Wisconsin in the 172 N4313Quebec. We were only there for an hour and then back in Duluth by 11:30, just in time for lunch! There was a restaurant, the "Chalet," just off the airport to the east a couple of blocks. Most of the time a few of us instructors and students would go there for soup and a sandwich.

After lunch I spent an hour of ground school with Rick Alston planning an instrument cross, country flight in the 172 N4231Quebec. Rick had also gotten where he knew every takeoff was going to be an ITO, wind permitting, so when he pulled out on runway 27 he just put the hood on and away we went! Rick was doing a good job and I knew he was getting close to his check ride also. I had told all my students, "at first I talk a lot, as you progress I don't talk a lot, when you start making flights and I don't say much, your getting close! So the way to shut me up is to do what I've told you and shown you!" I flew with Rick again the next morning for an hour and a half doing all the local approaches. I had the next day off! On June 11th I had a charter to take eight people to Hayward, Wisconsin and leave them there. That meant two trips in the 210! The next morning I flew the 210 down to St Paul for a gear check and after that I flew over to the Crystal airport and picked up Vic Thompson and brought him back to Duluth. He had taken the 172 down to Crystal Shamrock for some radio work. The morning of June 14th I flew with Joe Nelson for 1.2 hours and signed him off to go take his commercial check ride with Gordy. Joe passed his commercial on June 20th! In the afternoon I had a charter in 46Quebec up to Baudette, MN and back. (I still loved flying 46Quebec!) When I got back, I flew with Rick Alston in our IFR equipped 150 N6822Golf for 1.4 hours. The next morning, June 15th, my 35th birthday, I flew again with Rick Alston doing every approach in Duluth including a no gyro PAR approach to runway 9. That afternoon I had a pop up charter in the 210 to Minneapolis St Paul airport for North Central Airlines and return. Being it was my birthday, I went home a little early. The wife's parents had come over from Cloquet and had brought some nice T-bone steaks, so I fired up the grill. The wife had made some potato salad and beans and I had a very nice birthday party!

The next morning I flew with Rick Alston again and we ended up at Grand Rapids. I signed him off for his instrument check ride and he passed that with Gordy Newstrom a couple of hours later! Rick flew the 150 back and I brought the 172 N4334Quebec back to Duluth. It was late by the time we got back so I ended up doing a night check out with Dave Hedin in the 150 N6822Golf. On June 18th I did my, Jekyll and Hyde routine with Dave Hedin, doing the oral and private pilot check flight and signed him off to take his check ride. Gordy was in Duluth the next day and Dave took his check ride and passed! On the morning of June 19th I returned a 182 N7382Quebec to Grand Rapids.

Monnie had called me to schedule a charter flight for two days from Duluth to Eveleth, back to Duluth, to Minneapolis to Willmar, back to Minneapolis, back to Willmar, then to Mankato, to Aberdeen and to Fargo staying overnight there. And the next morning to Grand Forks then to Minneapolis, back to Grand Forks and back to Duluth. He said there would be six people plus me, which made seven people! I thought, hmmm, 46Quebec only holds six people, looks like a 402 trip to me. The only problem was I hadn't ever flown a 402, let alone being, part 135 current in it! The 402 was kept in Grand Rapids for Blandin Paper Mill trips so by returning the 182 to Grand Rapids I could take a 135 ride in the 402 with Gordy, so I could fly the trip for Goldfine's. I spent an hour reading through the manual reviewing performance charts, fuel system, turbo system, emergency procedures, etc., looking over the airplane and then Gordy and I went flying. The nice thing about Cessna's, I thought, they all fly about the same! The 402, other than the increased performance of the turbo's felt just about the same as a stretched, 46Quebec. The biggest difference was you got in the back door, not the front door, as far as I was concerned. After take-off Gordy handed me a hood and gave me a heading to the northwest. (I didn't give him the, "you jerk" look, like my students always gave me though.) We went out about ten miles and did some steep turns, stalls, and then he feathered the left engine. We did some turns, etc. and I re-started it. I had taken several check rides with Gordy so I was comfortable with him. Finally he said, "Let's go home and do the VOR 34 approach." So I dialed in the GPZ VOR and centered the needle with a "to" indication and headed for the VOR. We were off to the northwest of Grand Rapids so when I crossed the VOR I dialed in the 130degree radial and flew that out about four miles and made a turn to the right and intercepted the 154degree radial inbound. I crossed the VOR, extended the landing gear, went to full flaps and descended to the missed approach point and looked up, saw the runway and landed! We taxied in and shut down and got out and went in and got a cup of coffee. Gordy was kind of quiet, which was unusual for Gordy. Finally he said, "Hubbell, you did a good job of flying the airplane but you didn't intercept the outbound radial and make a procedure turn on that approach. What kind of approach do you call that?" I said, "I don't have to intercept the outbound radial and make a published procedure turn Gordy. I can do anything I want as long as I stay within ten miles of the VOR and above 3000 ft on the procedure turn side of the approach." Gordy said, "Are you sure about that Hubbell, I've never heard about that before?" I said, "Yes I'm sure of that Gordy." He said, "Well I've got to admit that it worked good and saved some time so I'll take your word for it. In fact I'm going to start doing that!" So I flew the 402 back to Duluth!

The next morning at promptly 7:25 am, Monnie, Erv and four other guys were climbing aboard the 402 N7808Quebec. We took off from Duluth and went to Eveleth. An hour later we flew back to Duluth and picked up another guy and went to Minneapolis. After an hour we went to Willmar. An hour later we went back to Minneapolis. An hour later we went back to Willmar. After another hour we went to Mankato, and an hour later we went to Aberdeen, SD. We were there for a couple of hours and departed for Fargo and spent the night there. I already had 6.5 hours in the 402 the first day I flew it! The next morning we departed for Grand Forks. A couple hours later we went back to Minneapolis. A couple of more hours later, we went back to Grand Forks. After a couple of more hours we went back to Duluth! I had gotten another 4.7 hours in 08Quebec, and I liked her!

The next morning I had a charter in 46Quebec for the University of Minnesota Duluth. I flew Dr. Darland, Dr. Carter, and another Doctor down to the Anoka County airport in Minneapolis and returned. In the afternoon I had another charter in 46Quebec for Hanna Mining from Duluth, to Hibbing, to St Paul and back to Duluth.

The next morning I was back in a 150 doing the, DLH, HIB, EVM, and DLH dual cross country flight with Bruce Smith. That was it! I need a vacation! So I took a week off!

Chapter Six

Vacation time!

I spent a couple of days getting some things done around the house, spending time with the kids, the dog, Ginger and the wifc (not necessarily in that order either!). And visiting the neighbors! Then we loaded up the wife's station wagon and headed out to visit my oldest sister and her family over in Grand Rapids, Michigan. We headed south down through Wisconsin on hwy 53 to Chippewa Falls and hung a left on Hwy 29 over to Manitowoc, Wisconsin. It was kind of fun to drive for a change. We had reservations to catch a 1 pm ferryboat out of Manitowoc across Lake Michigan, to Ludington, Michigan. From there it would be about an hour drive down to Grand Rapids. We should get there about, suppertime I had told my sister. We were within four blocks of the ferryboat when a guy ran a stop sign and I "T-boned" him. By the time the police arrived and filled out their report, and it took about another hour to go to a body shop and get my bumper and fender pulled ahead so I could steer without the tire rubbing on the fender, we missed our reservation. Never the less, we were thankful that nobody got hurt and we got in line for the next ferryboat in three hours. I called my sister and told her to go ahead and eat without us because of the delay. There were several hamburger stands, etc. within walking distance so we had hamburgers and malts while we waited. It was still daylight when we got on the ferry and didn't get dark until we were about halfway across the lake. It would have been more fun for the kids, and me too, if we could have seen what was going on when they docked the ferryboat. But that's the way she goes sometimes, I figured. We drove down to Grand Rapids and my sister and brother-in-law met us at a pre-arranged service station on the northwest side of town. After a bunch of hugs we followed them to their house. We got there on Friday night and planned on leaving Monday morning. (I had heard that company and fish start to stink after three days so I didn't want to be guilty of that!) My sister and brother-in-law had five girls. My brother-in-law is a dyed in the wool hunter and fisherman and here he gets five girls! I had told him once that if you want boys, you have to plant them a little deeper! After all, I was an expert on that subject! When I married the wife I knew I'd be on Okinawa when she gave birth and I figured she'd like to have a little baby girl to play with first. So I gave her a little girl. When I came back from Okinawa, I figured, hmmm, I bet she'd like to have a little baby boy next, so I planted that seed a little deeper, and she got her boy. Then next, another girl and then another boy! Nothing to it! I thought I was being a great husband and father so I couldn't figure out why she wasn't ever glad to see me! If it was because she had wanted another girl instead of a boy, all she had to do was tell me! And then I got "neutered"!

We left Grand Rapids Monday morning after a nice visit. We thought it would be fun to cross the Mackinaw Bridge so we headed north! In a few hours we had crossed the bridge and headed west on Hwy 2. About mid-afternoon we found a cabin in a little town on the shore of Lake Michigan. Everyone put on their swimsuits and we had fun swimming and walking the beach for a while. Then we walked into town and found a hamburger stand and had supper. The next morning we just followed hwy 2 until it intercepted hwy 53 just south of Superior, and were back home by late afternoon. We had left Ginger with one of the neighbors and she was sure glad to see us come home! (I always wondered, why is my dog always happier to see me than my wife is when I get home?)

I had a couple of more days of vacation time, so we drove over to Cloquet and visited the wife's parents and some friends.

I went back to work on July 10th, 1972 by starting out where I had left off, flying with Joe Nehring reviewing commercial maneuvers. Joe was getting close. The morning of the 11th I had an overnight charter to Rockford, Ill in the 182 N7382Quebec. We got back mid-afternoon on the 12th and I left again on the morning of the 13th on a charter in the 210 N9471Mike to Minneapolis, for the day. The 14th was a slow day. I spent a couple of hours of ground school with Al Pitoscia reviewing all the private maneuvers, and then flying with him for about an hour.

On July 15th I flew pipeline patrol with Ray Wells from the Lakehead Pipeline Company in Superior. We flew from Superior to Pembina, North Dakota and back in the 172 N4213Quebec. That was about 290 miles at 300 ft above the ground! We had lunch in Pembina and then flew back at about 300 ft again! I put 5.3 hours in 13Quebec that day! Before I went home I saw the general manager alone in his office, so I took advantage of that opportunity and asked him if I could plan on a raise anytime soon? He said the company was losing money and there wouldn't be any raises for anyone until that changed. That was very disappointing for me to hear, especially since I was working about 60 hours a week!

I had a day off on the 16th, and on the 17th I was back in the 310 N1133Quebec with Mike Gardonio reviewing multi-engine procedures. Mike was getting close too. I spent an hour of ground school with Joe Nehring on the morning of July 18th and then we flew for an hour and I signed Joe off to go take his commercial check ride with Gordy. Right after that I took off in the 310 N1133Quebec, with the aircraft sales manager, Gene Berg to go demo it to a guy in Princeton, Minnesota. We returned about mid-afternoon. Then I flew with Mike for two more hours in 33Quebec doing multi-engine procedures. I got home late and was tired. I had flown 5.7 hrs and did 3 hours of ground school that day. I was even thinking on the way home, I hope the wife won't demand sex tonight because I'm, to tired. But then, I didn't have to worry about that. She never had to ask me, I was always asking her! "Hmmm, I wonder if she was getting like my Dad and the flight engineers at Bolling AFB?" My Dad said he almost hated to come home from work, because all he would hear was, "Can I get a car Dad, can I get a car Dad, can I get a car Dad." And the flight engineers, "Can I start it, can I taxi it, can I start it, can I taxi it?" etc, etc. Hmmm, was the wife getting where she wasn't happy to see me come home because all she would hear was, can we make love now, can we make love now, can we make love now? Maybe I wasn't that bad. And actually I don't remember the wife ever turning me down either!

On July 19th I flew my favorite airplane, 46Quebec on an all day charter down to Rochester, Minnesota and back!

The next morning I did my, examiner act with Mike Gardonio for an hour of multi-engine review and then an hour of in-flight review in the 310 N1133Quebec. We ended up in Grand Rapids and I signed Mike off to go take his check ride with Gordy Newstrom, who was standing 10 ft away! I had called Gordy the day before and scheduled Mike for his check ride. I knew Mike wouldn't have any trouble with the oral or the check ride and he didn't! His oral only lasted about 30 minutes and the flight an hour and they were back! Gordy gave Mike his multi rating and we shook hands and went out and Mike preflighted the 310. I told him, "I'm just a passenger now so have fun and take me back to Duluth!" Mike had fun and did his usual great job of flying. Even now, every once in a while I'd think, I wish I could hold heading and altitude as good as Mike can! I rationalized it though that he wasn't an overworked, underpaid and stressed out flight instructor with 4 kids to feed like I was! (It worked for me!) Mike took me over to the "Chalet" and bought me lunch and when I got back I spent the afternoon flying with three more students in a 150 and then took a couple of days off!

Russ was back over from Ashland on the morning of the 23rd and I spent a couple of hours with him studying the 310 manual and multi procedures. Then we spent another 45 minutes getting familiar with N1133Quebec and went flying for 2.5 hours. We headed northwest, doing turns, slow flight, stalls, VMC's, single engine work, etc., and then made a few landings at Hibbing and taxied in and had a coke and candy bar and discussed what we had done. Russ was, doing really good! I had worked Russ pretty hard, so as we were walking back out to 33Quebec, I said, I'll shut up on the way back to Duluth so you can practice what you've learned." Russ gave me what I think was his, "thank God for small favors" look. And he did a good job of flying 33Quebec back to Duluth. I had lunch with Russ and he headed back to

Ashland, and I got in a 150 for another 1.5 hours, plus the ground school.

Chapter Seven

It Don't Pay to be Perfect, Sometimes!

On the morning of July 24th, 1972, I had a flight with Dr. Don Swenson up to International Falls. Don had bought 33Quebec from Gene and was leasing it back to Halvair and I was checking him out in the airplane. He already had a multi and an instrument rating, so I was just getting him familiar with 33Quebec. The weather was IFR in Duluth and all the way to International Falls, so I watched as Don prepared and filed an IFR flight plan. Then he preflighted 33Quebec and we started up and took off heading for Hibbing and on up to International Falls on Victor 129. The weather in the Falls, as we called it, was about a 500 ft ceiling and a mile visibility. Don did a good job in route and on the ILS 31 and even the landing! He said he'd be about three hours doing surgery at the hospital and then be back. When he got back we checked the weather and Duluth and Hibbing had some broken clouds with tops about 6,000 ft and the Duluth radar was out of service. The Falls was just about like it was when we got there. I had Don file another IFR flight plan at 5,000 ft to give him some more instrument time and we departed and headed down Victor 129 to Hibbing and then on to Duluth. About 5 miles north of Hibbing we started popping in and out of the clouds now and then. Over Hibbing the airways makes a 10 degree turn to the left towards Duluth. Don had made a 10 degree left turn but we were just paralleling the airway. We weren't getting back on the centerline and we were about five miles from the Hibbing VOR. I was just about to tell Don that he should have turned left another 10 degrees so as to have intercepted the airway and be well established on the centerline within three miles from the Hibbing VOR. (The VOR needle was off course about I/4 of an inch.) We were in the clouds when I was going to tell Don this and all of a sudden we popped out into a hole less than a 1/2 mile in diameter. We were heading southeast on the south side of the hole and a North Central Convair was descending through the north side of the hole going Northwest! We were level wingtip to wingtip! I said, "Don, look at that!" I couldn't believe it! I called Duluth approach and asked, if they had a North Central Convair IFR to Hibbing? Approach said, "No we've got one VFR." I said, "VFR hell!" Approach asked what I meant and I said, "I'll call you when we get on the ground." When we landed I called approach and told them what had happened. I thought, Hmmm, God must have been looking down at me again or I must be the luckiest kid in the world! If I had been flying 33Quebec I would have been on the centerline of the airway, or if I had been the, perfect flight instructor, we would have been on the centerline and met that Convair nose to nose. And I imagine the papers would have written it up as, little airplane hits big airplane! I thought, Yup, it don't pay to be perfect sometimes!

I wasn't out of the 310 for an hour and I got into the 210 N9471Mike and took John Grinden and three other people for a scenic ride over the Duluth-Superior harbor and up the north shore a few miles and back to the Duluth airport. John was the airport director. When I got back I was happy to learn that Joe Nehring had passed his commercial check ride with Gordy! But on the way home I was disappointed because I hadn't gotten a raise since I started at Halvair and I knew I wasn't going to be able to maintain the lifestyle of living that I was, accustomed to, by instructing and chartering, even though I enjoyed it. As usual, when I got home the kids and Ginger ran out to meet me! The wife was making supper and rinsing some dishes off in the sink. I nibbled her neck and rubbed her ass a little hoping to start a fire for later. After supper we went for a walk and I told her about the near miss with the Convair. She didn't have much of any reaction, one way or the other. I'm starting to wonder just what it is that I love about this woman, other than sex!

The next morning I had a charter in my favorite airplane, 46Quebec! I took Monnie and Erv down to Mankato for the day. For once we left about 9:30 in the morning, and got back about 3:30 in the afternoon!! I always appreciated how punctual Monnie and Erv were. You could set your watch by those two guys! Again, though, on my way home from the airport I'm thinking, I'm having a lot of fun but I'm not making very much money and if I ever figured out how much an hour I was making, I'd come out better having a paper route.

July 26th was an easy day. I did my examiner routine on Al Pitoscia for an hour of ground school and then we went and flew the 150 N1621Quebec for 1.2 hours doing a practice, private pilot check flight. Al was ready so I signed him off to go take his check ride with Gordy. I took the next day off.

Chapter Eight
Quitting My Job!

The next morning, July 27th 1972 I had a 9 am charter in the 172 N4213Quebec to take Mr. Law up to Grand Marais. It was a beautiful Saturday morning. My oldest son Tim, who was about 14 years old, followed me out the back door and asked, "Do you have to go to work again today Dad?" I said, "Yes I do, but I'll get back home before lunch and we'll do something." It bothered me on the way to work that the kids were growing up fast and I wasn't getting much time to spend with them.

I was in the pilot's office getting ready for the flight when the sales manager, Gene Berg came in and asked me where I was going and when would I be back? I told him I had to take a guy up to Grand Marias at 9 o'clock and drop him off and I'd be back about 11-11:15, maybe if I don't get lost. (I couldn't help throwing that in.) Gene said, "How the hell can you get lost? You just have to follow the north shoreline!" I said, "Yes, but what if I get confused and follow the south shoreline?" Gene said, "Well, if you do find your way up there and back, will you go with me to demo the 310 33Quebec to the Hoover Construction Company in Eveleth?" I said, "Gee's, I'm sorry Gene, Tim followed me out of the house this morning and had asked me if I had to go to work today? I told him that I had to fly a guy up to Grand Marias and drop him off and I'd be home about noon and we'll do something." Gene reached in his pocket and took out a hundred dollar bill and said, "Will this buy me a few hours of your time?" I could always use a hundred bucks so I said it would. I took Mr. Law up to Grand Marias in the 172 and on the way back I thought, when I land this 172 back in Duluth, I'm going to turn in my resignation. (It didn't even consider that I had a wife, four kids, a dog and a big house payment!) When I got back to the office I found a yellow legal size tablet and started writing out my resignation. Gene came into the office and started telling me about the company that we were going to be showing the 310 to. I said, "How do you spell, regretfully?" He spelled it and actually I had it right and by now he's standing behind me reading my resignation. He said, "You can't quit, you told me you'd go demo that 310 with me." I said, "I will, but I'm going to give this to the chief pilot on the way out the door and when we get back I'm done." "Why?" Gene asked. I said, "I'm tired, I'm getting up at 5:30 to make 7:30 takeoffs and then not getting back here until about 6:30 or later at night and shooting approaches down to minimums. I'm flying six long days a week and they'd make it seven if I let them. Plus, I'm not making any money. And then when I do have a day off, usually on Sunday, I'm so tired I don't feel like doing much with the kids or anything else."

I called Tim and told him I wasn't going to get home until later and we'd do something then. I went out and preflighted the 310 N1133Quebec and Gene and I flew up to Eveleth. Gene had told me we were going to be showing 33Quebec to the Hoover Construction Company from Eveleth. When we got there the president of the company, Mr. Peter Johnson and his brother were waiting for us. Gene showed them around the airplane and then he asked me if we could make a short flight in it. Gene and the brother got in the back seats and I and Mr. Johnson, sat up front. I had asked Mr. Johnson if he wanted to fly 33Quebec but he said for me to fly it and then he could look at all the equipment. I flew up to Ely and made a landing there and taxied back for takeoff and then we headed back toward Eveleth. I let Mr. Johnson fly it for a while to get the feel of it and then we landed back at Eveleth. Gene was busy showing the airplane to Mr. Johnson again and after about ten minutes or so I invited the brother to go inside and get a cup of coffee. About twenty minutes later Gene and Mr. Johnson came in and Gene told him, "We'll make those changes on the airplane and Les will bring it up and check you out in it." We said good-bye to Mr. Johnson and his brother and got back in 33Quebec and I started up and taxied out for takeoff. Gene said, "That was beautiful the way you got the brother away!" I said, "I could see you needed that." He said, "You're going to work for me!" I said, "No I'm not." About now I was taking off so I was kind of busy for a little while. After I leveled off and got things set up Gene said, "What are you going to do?" I said, "I don't know yet, all I know now is that I'm going to spend a month catching up on my sleep and family time." We landed in Duluth and Gene said, "Let's go over to the Officers Club and have a couple of drinks and talk." Gene was a retired Air Force Major, so we went over to the Officers Club and had a couple of drinks and talked. After a while I told Gene, "I won't go to work for you, I'll go to work with you. If I take an airplane out to sell it, I'm not going to call you and ask you what you want to do. I'll either sell it or I'll bring it home!" Gene said, "Good, I'm tired of babysitting these guys!" "And I'm not working weekends anymore, I need some time with my family." Gene agreed with that. "And I'm still going home for a month, but when 33Quebec is done I'll take a day and go check Mr. Johnson out in it."

On the way home I decided I couldn't just drop my students like that. The next morning Gene got approval from the Halvorson's for me to transfer into aircraft sales with him. I met with the chief pilot, Fred Winship and told him I'd finish working with the students I had that were getting close to their check rides and take the charters that I had on the schedule for the next month. The next day was Sunday so I had a day off! Monday morning I had an all day charter in the 210 up to Bemidji and back. The next morning I started Joe Nehring on his instrument rating. Then Joe Nelson and I went on his instrument cross country to Minneapolis and back in the 172 N4231Quebec. When I got back from that and de-briefed Joe, I got back in 31Quebec and took Gene Basgen, from Basgen Photography on a photo flight up to Hoyt Lakes. The next morning, August 1st, Gene Basgen and I got back in 31Quebec at 8 am and flew another photo flight to Eveleth, Ely, Grand Marias and back to Duluth for another 6.2 hours! When we got back I did my examiner act with Al Pitocia for an hour of oral exam and then flew the 150 N1621Quebec for just about another hour. Al was doing a good job and getting close. The next morning I flew with Ross Peterson in 21Quebec doing some short field and soft field takeoffs and landings. Then I had a scenic flight over the Duluth-Superior harbor in the 210. After lunch I flew with Joe Nehring for another 1.2 hours doing an ITO off runway 9 with a left turn to the northwest. When we were out of Duluth's airspace I had Joe do some slow flight, climbs, descents, turns to headings, partial panel, and ending up with a ILS 9 back into Duluth. Over the outer marker I told Joe, "Oh no, I just heard the Duluth weather is 00 with fog and we've only got enough fuel for one approach! What are we going to do?!" I had him call the DH at 200 feet and then go on down to 100 feet and call that and then look up and land. I hadn't explained how to make a glassy water landing to Joe yet so thought I'd wait until the next lesson before I had him make a 00 landing.

On August 3rd I had an all day charter in the 210 to Oshkosh, Wisconsin. It was late by the time we landed back in Duluth. I had the line crew top 71Mike off with fuel and vacuum it out for an early charter in the morning. I put another 4.6 hours in 71Mike the next day! On August 5th I was an instructor again flying in the 150, N1621Quebec, doing an intro flight with Jim Stover and another intro with Horace Kalbaugh and started Mike Gardonio on his instructor rating. I suppose Mike figured if they gave me an instructor rating, anyone can get one! I had Sunday off and Monday morning I was back in a 150 again, but at least a different one, N5667Golf. I did my examiner act with Al Pitocia. This was the second or third time I had done this with Al and he did a good job so I signed him off to take his check ride with Gordy. Al passed his check ride, the next day! In the afternoon I flew with Dale Torgerson doing private maneuvers. On August 8th I flew with Joe Nehring doing an instrument cross, country flight in the 172 N4231Quebec down to Cambridge and back. Then I flew with Mike again for 1.2 hrs and Joe again for another 1.3 hours in the 172 N4213Quebec. That was enough for one day! Thank God I had a charter with Monnie and Erv down to Mankato for the day on August 9th! I needed to get out of 150's and into 46Quebec for a day! I loved 46Quebec and I liked flying with Monnie and Erv! The next morning I had a charter up to Winnipeg in 71Mike to drop three people off and come back empty. The customs agent was giving me a hard time because I had left from Duluth and our Canadian charter documents showed Grand Rapids as our designated departure point only. Luckily I had actually read the document once and I remembered that someplace it said Grand Rapids and or Duluth. After reading it again I found that sentence in very small print and showed it to the Customs Agent. He still wasn't totally convinced but let me go! When I got back to Duluth I flew with Dale Torgerson in the 150 N1621Golf for another 1.2 hours doing slips and cross wind takeoffs and landings at Duluth.

The next morning I had another charter in 46Quebec for the Hal Company to Rhinelander, Wisconsin, Alpena, Michigan, back to Rhinelander and back to Duluth for 4.5 hours. After lunch I did an hour of ground school and then flew .7 hrs with Dale Torgerson again in the 150. When I got back from that I checked Joe Nehring out in the 210 N9471Mike and we did a instrument cross country to Grand Rapids and back after a VOR 34 approach into Grand Rapids. And then I took a week off before I started in the sales department!!

Chapter Nine
My Seventh Career Change

On August 24th, 1972, I demo'd my first airplane! We had a brokered Aircoupe N2767Hotel and I demo'd it to Gary LeeDahl. I had never flown an Aircoupe before and neither had Gary. But I'd always had the theory that airplanes are just two wings, some control surfaces, some wheels, and an engine and propeller. And if you look at the airspeed indicator it pretty much shows you everything you need to know to fly it. So Gary and I read through the aircraft manual, got it started and taxied out to runway 27. After a run up and takeoff clearance, Gary taxied onto the runway and applied full power. I'm thinking, it isn't a race horse but neither is a 150. But after a while the airspeed needle started nibbling on the green arc so I told Gary to raise the nose a little. It ran along on the main wheels for a while and became airborne! We climbed straight out until we had 500ft and made a left turn toward Cloquet and leveled off at 2,500ft. After a minute or so Gary adjusted the throttle to cruise power to see what it indicated. Then we did some stalls, turns left and right, and we headed back to Duluth. I think both Gary and I thought it was a pretty good little airplane for the money! Gary was thinking of putting in a strip at home but didn't know if he'd have enough room, being the Aircoupe didn't have any flaps. I said, "that's no problem! We'll just get behind the power curve a little bit and when we're about 100 feet above the runway, just lower the nose a little to increase the airspeed and then apply a little power when you flare to arrest the rate of decent." (It sounded good to me!) So we got a clearance to land on runway 21 from the tower and on short final I had 67Hotel just behind the power curve a little and she was settling in, just perfect! About 100 feet in the air I lowered the nose and increased the airspeed. So good so far I thought. Then I flared and applied some power to arrest the rate of descent, but there wasn't any power there! The engine just "burped" a couple of times! I had 67Hotelon the runway on her main gear and nose high! The only problem was when the nose gear dropped onto the runway, kind of hard, it didn't taxi straight anymore! It had a single side brace nose fork and it had bent a little! So on my first demo, I had dinged the airplane! I wrote it up in my logbook as a P.P. landing. (Piss Poor landing). I blamed it on the weak nose fork though! I'd had 150's hit harder than that and not hurt anything! Gene just laughed about it. I offered to pay for the fork but he wouldn't hear of it. He even bought me a couple of drinks at the Officer's Club to celebrate my first demo, and to calm my nerves. I like working with Gene!

The next morning I got on an early North Central flight to Minneapolis and caught another flight to Wichita, Kansas to pick up a new 210 N2CR that Gene had sold to Carl Roseaun, which explains the "CR". Five hours after takeoff from the Cessna factory, I was landing back in Duluth! On the 27th I took our Cessna 150 N5667Golf down to Rice Lake and demo'd it. On August 30th I flew the 210 N9471Mike down to Minneapolis and demo'd it. So far though I've demo'd three airplanes and haven't sold anything yet, but at least I hadn't dinged anything else either! I'm thinking, maybe I ain't going to be able to live in the manner I'm accustomed to, doing this either! On the morning of the 31st I took a 150

N5667G to Grand Rapids and brought the 172 24Golf back to Duluth. After lunch I had a charter in the 210 N9471Mike to Hibbing for a couple of hours and back with Steve Harvey.

On September 5th I flew my favorite, 46Quebec down to Wichita, Kansas for some re-painting. I left 46Quebe there and got into a new Cessna 150 N18063 and made it as far as Red Oak, Iowa before I called it quits for the day. I called home and talked to the wife and kids to let them know where I was and that I'd see them tomorrow and then went and had a beer and a hamburger. The next morning I left Red Oak by 7 am and was back in Duluth at 10am. I got out of 063 and right into another 150 N5667Golf and flew that up to Grand Rapids. I got out of the 150 and preflighted a Cessna 185, which I'd never flown one before, and flew that down to Amery, Wisconsin. Then I preflighted a Cessna 180 N3874Charlie on EDO 2870 floats, which I'd never flown one of those before either, and flew it down to Stevens Point, Wisconsin to demo it to Dr. Klasinski. We had arranged to meet at the boat landing in the park on a peninsula jutting out into the Wisconsin River on the west side of town. I had no problem finding that and Dr. Klasinski was there, waving me in. When I got out I saw a thin streak of oil coming out of the cowling on the left side of the airplane. I shook hands with Dr. Klasinski and told him about the oil leak. He found a couple of screwdrivers in his trunk and helped me take the top cowling off. It turned out the oil leak was coming from the oil pressure line at the elbow in the crankcase. I knew that there was a very small orifice in the elbow and the leak looked a lot worse than it actually was and explained that to Dr. Klasinski. So I put a little gas on a rag and wiped the streak of oil off the side of the airplane and put the cowling back on. Dr. Klasinski got in the left seat and I got in the right seat and we flew it. I was impressed that Dr. Klasinski did a very nice job flying it and seemed to like it. We weren't up more than thirty minutes and Dr. Klasinski parked her back on the boat landing. I said, "Well, I think you like 74Charlie Dr. Klasinski, shall we put it in writing?" He said, "Yes I do like it, but can we talk price a little?" We agreed on a price and I went to the airplane to get the clipboard that I had a purchase order on, only to discover that I had left it in the 185 back in Amery! I asked Dr. Klasinski if he had a tablet in his car, but he said he didn't have anything. I reached in my pocket and the only thing I had was a matchbook full of matches. (I'm ashamed to admit that I smoked then.) I tore the matches off and asked Dr. Klasinski if I could use the pen he had in his shirt pocket. He gave me the pen and I wrote up a purchase order for N3874Charlie with EDO 2870 floats and wheels, on the matchbook. I asked, "Do you have a check for $500.00 dollars on you doctor?" He said, "No, I don't even have my checkbook with me." He reached into his pocket and said, "All I've got is a twenty dollar bill." I said, "That's close enough," and I wrote $20.00 on the match-book cover and handed it to Dr, Klasinski to sign. He was laughing as he signed it. I said, "I'll take it back home and get the oil leak and a couple of other small discrepancies fixed." And Dr. Klasinski said, "We might as well take the floats off being the season is almost over." So I flew it back to Grand Rapids and landed it in the pond and flew a 150 back to Duluth. Gene was still in the office when I got back. He said, "How'd it go?" I said, "I sold it," and showed him my purchase order and the, twenty dollar bill. Gene said, as he laughed, "You're going to do well Hubbell!" He took me over to the Officers Club and we celebrated my 1st sale with a couple of drinks. I was excited to tell the wife about it when I got home, but she didn't have much of a reaction, one way or the other. I'm really starting to wonder if I'm married to the right woman or not?

On September 22nd I flew a Cessna 172 N3885Romeo over to Cloquet and had the pleasure of doing business with one of my former 170 partners, Doctor Byron Backus!

On October 6th, 7th and the 10th I checked Carl Roseaun out in his new 210 N2CR! Boy was that a nice airplane, I thought.

Gene came into the office one morning and asked me if I'd take a new Cessna 172 that he had sold and deliver it to a guy up in Ely and bring the trade-in back home. I said, "Sure I'll do that for you," and as he was walking out of the room I asked, "By the way, what is the trade-in?" Gene turned around and smiled, and said, "A Cessna 190." Gene was a good pilot but he wasn't comfortable with tail draggers. And, I think he knew that I'd like the chance to fly a 190. So I flew the 172 up to Ely and checked the buyer out in it. I asked him to go around the patch with me once in the 190 just to make sure I understood the fuel system, starting procedure and any other idiosyncrasies it might have. We made one takeoff and landing and I dropped him off and flew the 190 back to Duluth. When I got back to Duluth I had to pick up some paper work off my desk for a listing I was getting on an airplane up in Grand Rapids. I had the 210 N9471Mike signed out for doing this, but I liked flying the 190 so much, I cancelled the 210 and took the 190 instead! In fact that 190 was my favorite transportation until we sold it to a guy from Green Bay for $4,500.00 about a month later!

Chapter Ten
Watching Two People Burn in a 182

I was sitting at my desk in the office about 10 am the morning of November 8th, 1972 working on a quote for a new Cessna 182 for someone when I started to hear an approach controller on the lobby speakers talking to someone. He was saying, "You're drifting right of course turn left, you're still drifting right of course turn further left, you're to far off course abandon the approach and turn left to a heading of 360 degrees and climb to 3,100 feet." I went back to working on my quote. About 15 minutes later my attention was again drawn to the overhead speakers out in the lobby. The approach controller was telling the pilot again that he was drifting right of course on the ILS 9 and for him to turn left and then, "You're still drifting right of course turn further left." I went out to the lobby and looked out the window. It looked like the ceiling was about 200 feet and the visibility wasn't bad, a mile or more I figured. Mike Gardonio and Gene Berg were listening to this too. The approach controller was still saying, "Turn further left, you're still drifting right of course", and then, "You're to far off course abandon the approach and turn left to a heading of 360 degrees and climb to 3,100 feet." Then I heard this high, pitched voice say, "I can't, I've got a heavy load of ice." Then the approach controller tried calling him a couple more times and got no answer. The control tower called a couple of times and got no answer. I said to Gene and Mike, "Let's get in my car and get down there, he's in the woods!" The three of us ran out and got in my Mustang and we drove west until the Ugstad road and turned north on that. We went about a half mile and I could see smoke off to our right in the woods. I pulled over and we all started running toward the smoke. I was the first one on the scene. The 182 was, nose down at about a 45degree angle and burning fiercely! The pilot had been thrown threw the windshield and was up against a tree about twenty feet in front of the airplane. I looked at the burning airplane and could see the silhouettes of two people burning. There was nothing I could do for them. I put my suit jacket around the pilot mostly to protect him from the heat of the fire. Mike and Gene arrived but there wasn't anything we could do but watch the airplane burn. Fred Winship had jumped in a 150 and was circling overhead and must have informed the tower because soon we heard the sirens of the fire trucks and an ambulance coming. I suggested to Mike and Gene that one of them run back out to the road and the other stop halfway to direct the emergency crews to the accident site. After a short while the fire and ambulance crews arrived. There wasn't anything they could do for the two people in the airplane either, but to extinguish the fire. Then they put the pilot on a stretcher and carried him out to the ambulance.

I saw the approach controller who was working that 182 a few days later. I asked him, "Why didn't you send that guy up on top at five thousand instead of 3100 feet after the first bungled approach to get him out of the ice and maybe to think about it? Or to go back to St Paul or something if he can't fly a simple ILS?" He said, "It isn't up to me to fly his airplane." I said, "That's true, you've got your procedures to follow. But after that first approach and knowing the icing conditions I would have declared an emergency for him and sent him back up on top to think it over." Chances are he left St Paul with full tanks and a 182 has enough fuel to fly from St Paul to Duluth and shoot a approach and back to St Paul and still have an hour or more reserve. The only problem with him declaring an emergency though, is now he has taken responsibility and liability for the outcome of the flight. A big responsibility I agree. And, the pilot is the pilot in command of his airplane. I remembered the time I came back from Rice Lake, Wisconsin in 34Y when I was flying for Northland Homes. I was on top at eight thousand feet, FDAH and when I got handed off to Duluth approach and got a decent to 3100 feet about ten miles out and started getting ice before I leveled off at 3100 feet. It didn't take me long to figure out that I was going to get too much ice to go out for the whole approach. So I told approach control about the ice and requested and got a turn directly to the outer marker and down the ILS 9 to a landing. There's no doubt in my mind that if I hadn't done that, we'd been in the woods about three miles west of the outer marker. I was lucky that I did what I did and I lived to learn that the controllers have their procedures, but you don't have to follow them! I used to think you had to do what a controller said! Most controllers aren't even pilots. They are looking at a map superimposed on a radar screen with routes and altitudes and that's what they go by. I was lucky that I had learned, before it was too late, that you can do almost anything you want to do, as long as you coordinate it with the controller. Like, stay on top until the last minute and slam dunk the approach if you want, or change your route, as long as you ask them so it doesn't cause a conflict with other traffic.

I didn't, sleep very good for a long time after that. All I could see was the silhouettes of the two people burning in that airplane. That scene of the burning 182 with the silhouettes of the two people in it and the pilot up against the tree will forever be engraved in my mind and I hope I never see another one like it.

Chapter Eleven

Delivering My First New Cessna

On November 13th 1972 Gene sent me down to Kansas Aircraft Sales in Olathe, Kansas to bring back a Cessna 180 N6000Lima that he had bought from them. That was the first time I met Michelle Stauffer, Amy Heaven and Conrad Jones. I called Gene and told him 6000Lima looked good to me and he said he'd have the money wired to them as soon as possible. Michelle took me to lunch and when we got back the money had arrived, so I preflighted 6000Lima and headed back to Duluth. I liked 6000Lima! Four hours later I was landing in Duluth! It was about 6 pm when I landed and Gene was still there. He thanked me for bringing 6000Lima home and handed me an envelope with $100.00 in it! I was getting to like Gene too!!

On November 27th I demo'd and sold a 172 N46621 to Don Miller out in Parshall, ND.

On the 28th I flew the 210, 71Mike over to Appleton, Wisconsin and picked up John Dietz and Glen Gruett and brought them back to Duluth. The next morning we flew commercial from Duluth to Minneapolis and then Wichita, Kansas to the Cessna factory to pick up their new 182 Skylane, N999DG that they had bought from me! They accepted delivery of 999DietzGruett, we had lunch, and I checked them out in it on the way back to Duluth! They were like two kids in a candy store! I was happy for them. They were nice guys and had a nice airplane!

Les :

It is a pleasure to make up This book to show you our appreciation on all the fine service you have given us.

We have taken many trips business and pleasure in our new Skylane 182 and we all have enjoyed it to the fullest extent. Thank you again.

John G. "Dietz
Gene H. "Truett

One day in mid December Gene asked me if I would deliver a 185 on floats to Florida? I said, "Sure, when next spring?" Gene said, "No, as soon as possible," and he smiled. He told me he had sold the airplane to Jerrie Cobb and she was going to use the airplane down in South America on the Amazon River for missionary work. I recognized her name. She was the first woman qualified for the space program. Then he said, "In fact, the airplane is up at Grand Rapids right now and they are installing a 50 gallon barrel with a wobble pump plumbed into the right wing tank in place of the back seats." Then he said it was strictly up to me when I wanted to go weather wise, etc. So I started doing some flight planning, etc. and it looked like the first open water, other than the Mississippi River, was going to be near Lake of the Ozarks, Missouri, about 550 nautical miles away! The airplane had 84 gallon fuel tanks and I figured we'd get 45 gallons in the 50 gallon barrel laying on it's side, for a total of 129 gallons. I figured I'd probably be burning about 15gph, so that's a good eight hours and thirty minutes of fuel. And truing out about 120kts, that's just about four and a half, hours in route with no wind. And even if I encounter a hell of a head wind, I've pretty much got Lake of the Ozarks made anyway. And I wasn't too worried because I figured if I got into a low fuel situation for one reason or another, like if the wobble pump broke or something, I'll just land along side of a plowed runway, unless I'm south of the snow belt. Then they could drive a fuel truck right out to it! Otherwise, there are lots of frozen lakes and fields along the way. Piece of cake I figured and my kind of flying!

One day John Cartier came into the office. He had heard that I was taking the 185 on floats to Florida and wanted to know if he could go with? I said, "Gee I don't know John, it's on a ferry permit so I'll have to check with the feds down at

GADO (General Aviation District Office) in Minneapolis."
Later in the day I did a little research on ferry permits and
the next morning I called down to the GADO office. Bill
Stewart answered the phone. I said, "Mr. Stewart, Hubbell
here, you're just the guy I need to talk to!" I said, "You know
that 185 that you signed the 50 gallon barrel installation off
on last week?" Stewart said, "Yes I do, why?" I said, "Well
as you know I got volunteered to fly it to Florida, and you
know John Cartier, our line manager, well John would like to
go with me, can you approve that?" Stewart said, "No I can't
Les. That's on a ferry permit and that's only good for one person." I said, "Stewart, I've been studying these ferry permits
a little and it says, minimum crew, and I think as pilot in
command it's up to me to determine minimum crew."
Stewart kind of laughed a little bit and said, "I guess your
right Les, but for what reason do you need a co-pilot?" I
said," Well, Stewart this is going to be the first time I've taken
a float plane off the snow. And I don't want to be looking
inside at the airspeed indicator and have one float in a foot
of snow and maybe the other one plowing into three feet of
snow. I need Cartier to call out the airspeeds, just like the
airliners do, so I can keep my eyesight outside the airplane
Stewart, or I could lose directional control." I was sure that
when I mentioned, "just like the airliners do," that it would
be a done deal, but Stewart said, "No, I think you can do that
ok, Les." Then, he said, "Do you have anything else Les, I'm
kind of busy?" I said, "Well this is going to be a long trip
Stewart, I need Cartier to talk to and to pour the coffee." He
said, "No, I think you can handle that too." Then he asked,
"Is there anything else Les, I'm really busy." I said, "Well,
Stewart I could sure use Cartier to help me navigate." He
said, "Didn't you tell me last week when I was up there that
you were just going to follow the Mississippi River to the

Gulf and cut across to Tarpon Springs?" "Oh ya, that's right I guess," I said. He said, "Les, I'm really busy, is there anything else I can help you with?" "Well, Stewart you know, I'm going to have to run that right tank down to about a quarter tank and then someone's going to have to get on the wobble pump and pump it full again, and you know Stewart, that's co-pilots work!" He said, "That's the only thing you've said so far that makes any sense so I'll approve it for that reason." I said, "Thanks Stewart," and hung up before he changed his mind! Cartier was glad to hear that he was going with! I was thinking, hmmm, I should be charging Cartier for all these trips I take him along on! First to Portland, Oregon and now to Florida! But actually Cartier was good company and a lot of help always! Hmmm, maybe I should have been paying him to go with me?

On December 7th I flew the 180 N6000Lima down to Pine City and demo'd it to Dr. Eck. He liked it and said he'd talk to his bank! A few days later I called Dr. Eck to see how things were going and he said he really wanted the airplane but the bank wouldn't finance it for him. I asked him, "How's your credit?" He said, "it should be very good." I said, "Well what you've got then is a small town bank that hasn't ever financed an airplane and they don't know what to do with it, so the easiest thing for them is to say, no!" I said, "Let me make a call and I'll get right back to you." I called my old banker in Cloquet, Ted Micke, and asked him if he wanted to finance an airplane for a dentist down in Pine City? He said sure, so I told him to expect a call. I called Dr. Eck back and gave him Ted's number. The next morning Ted called me and said, "he's as good as gold, I'll do it". I called Dr. Eck and told him we'd fly up to Cloquet and have lunch with Ted and do the paper work! Dr. Eck was happy, I was happy, and Ted was happy! And I think even 6000Lima was happy! And on the 16th I spent five hours with Dr. Eck checking him out in 6000Lima. And he did a very good job of flying 6000Lima!

On December 21st I delivered a 182 N9351Golf down to Forrest Lake and Gene came and picked me up in 71Mike! I was on a roll! I was getting to like being an aircraft salesman! Although I always told people a used aircraft salesman is, about two rungs down the ladder, below a used car salesman!

We picked up Ron Annis from Altair Floats in Forest Lake and flew to Grand Rapids so he could inspect the floats before I left. That was the first time I had seen the 185 N5842Joliet with the 50gallon barrel in it and the Altair floats. Ron said the floats had about 20 layers of fiberglass and nine, watertight compartments in each float. The 185 and floats looked good to me. Of course, anything that flies would probably look good to me!

I took off a week for Christmas! We always went to the wife's folks for Christmas Eve. There would be about 25-30 relatives there and everyone brought something for the smorgasbord and the mother-in-law always put a roast and ham in the oven. It was always like a royal feast and with plenty of drinks too!

Chapter Twelve

Taking a 185 on Floats Off the Snow and Delivering it to Florida

I had decided to leave for Florida with the 185 N5842Joliet on Altair fiberglass floats on January 1st 1973. Gene flew John and I and our duffel bags up to Grand Rapids in 74Mike early that morning. They had left 42 Joliet in the heated hangar where we could load all our stuff in it and I could preflight it. Thank God because, it was about zero outside! We loaded everything we had on top and around the 50 gallon barrel and put the maps, munchies and coffee between the two front seats. I preflighted the airplane and the floats and said to pull her out the door. They had the tractor

The author standing on the floats.

hooked to the float dolly and lifted 42 Joliet just enough to get it up off the floor, but not so high that the vertical stabilizer wouldn't clear under the hangar door. When we got 42Joliet out the hangar door Cartier and I got in before we froze our butts off! Then they pulled us out to the approach end of runway 16 and set us down on the runway. They unhooked us and used the tractor to dig a hole through the, five foot high snow bank with the front end, loader. Once they got the hole cut through the bank they hooked back on to the float dolly and lifted 42 Joliet back up and pulled us through the hole and set us back down and pulled the dolly out and away from the airplane. I had asked Grand Rapids to not plow the grass runway, which was someplace out in front of us so that I'd have a fairly smooth field to takeoff from. The wind was out of the northwest at about 10 knots. My, plan was to head southeast and then make a sweeping left turn back to the northwest and takeoff. The windows were starting to get pretty well frosted up by now so I told Cartier to quit breathing! We had already opened the windows and John found a rag and we cleared the windshields as best we could and then, we hollered good-bye to everyone! After confirming that there was nobody anywhere near the prop I started 42 Joliet up. So far so good I thought! Being she had sat in the heated hangar for a few days I didn't need to let it warm up very long. I only let her run for about a minute or so and we had good oil pressure and starting to indicate temps already, so I did a run up and cycled the prop once and, put the power to her. Just enough though to get her taxiing nicely on the snow. I'd flown my Dad's champ on skis but that had been a long time ago. Actually 42 Joliet felt just like she was on the step in the water! She handled very nice I thought! I came out of the turn heading northwest and went to full throttle and she came off the

Circling Grand Rapids after takeoff.

snow just as if she was on skis! We circled the airport once and everything looked and felt good so we headed southeast!

I, just knew, that Cartier and I were going to have one hell of a fun trip! And I was glad to have him with! We went up to 5,500 feet and actually the outside temperature warmed up about ten degrees, so we had plenty of cabin heat too! I was planning on intercepting the Mississippi River at St Paul and kind of staying near it. When we flew over St Paul, Cartier and I were laughing at what the people on the ground must be saying or thinking as they looked up at us flying by in a floatplane on January 1st, 1973! Like, how the hell far north were those guys? Or, Boy, are their wives going to be pissed when they get home!

42 Joliet was purring along as nice as could be so just on the, west side of St Paul I decided to turn south and head straight for the Lake of the Ozarks, Missouri. We had taken

off from Grand Rapids about 9:30 am it was going to be about 4 hours and 30 minutes before we got to the Lake of the Ozarks I figured. We had a tailwind so we were making good ground speed and it was a beautiful clear day! My wife had made us a bag of my favorite, chocolate chip cookies too! So I gave the controls to Cartier and told him to follow that fence line down there and it will take us right to the Lake of the Ozarks! I poured myself a cup of coffee and sat back and enjoyed the coffee and about a half dozen chocolate chip cookies! Then I took the controls back and Cartier almost ate the rest of them! I gave serious thought to landing on a frozen lake and kicking him out for that!

We arrived over the Lake of the Ozarks about fifteen minutes earlier than planned because of the nice tailwind. About five miles north I called the Tan -Tar-A Resort and seaplane base on unicom and announced our position and said we'd be landing in a few minutes. I had called them about a week earlier and made reservation for us.

We noticed there was a little ice around the edges of the lake as we were letting down. I was set up for what I thought was going to be a nice landing, but when we touched down we skipped about three times! That was a surprise to me. I've never had a float plane skip on landing before! We taxied into the bay and I called Tan-Tara- unicom and asked them where we could park this thing for the night. The guy said to pull up alongside one of the sailboat buoys and tie up to that and he'd send a boat out to get us. I said, "Thanks!" The bay had a lot of ice in it about 1/4 to 1/2 inch thick. Cartier had gotten out on the right float and said, "A little to the left Hub, OK, straighten it out, kill it." I had pulled the mixture back and was turning switches off when all of a sudden I heard, "SPLASH!" I looked over to the right and down, and there's Cartier in the water! I hollered, "What the hell

are you doing in the water Cartier!" I was impressed though
how fast he got out of the water and back up on the float! He
got out so fast that his wallet didn't even get wet! I wanted
to take a picture of Cartier in the water but he wouldn't stay

In the boat crunching through the ice to the lodge.

there long enough for me to get my camera out of my bag! I
said, "What happened?" He said, "I put my foot on the buoy
thinking it was concrete to stop us, but it was Styrofoam!"
We tied a rope around the prop and to the buoy so 42Joliet
could weather vane into the wind if need be, providing she
didn't get frozen in! They were there with the boat about
then, so we threw our duffel bags in and were soon inside the
lodge and checked in so Cartier could get some dry clothes

on. I just knew we were going to have a lot of fun on this trip!

After Cartier took a warm shower and got dressed, we went looking for a place we could get some medicine for Cartier and to calm our nerves! And to also celebrate the safe and successful completion of the first leg of our trip! I was glad Cartier hadn't drowned or I wouldn't have been able to celebrate because I don't like to drink alone! We didn't have to look very far to find some medicine for Cartier to take in case he might be suffering with the onset of hypothermia. Just to be safe, I figured I should take some medicine too in case it's contagious! In fact, I think every other room in that resort was for taking medicine in! We took our medicine and then found a restaurant and had something to eat. By now it was about 6 pm so we went back to the room and I called home and told the wife we had made it to the Tan -Tar- A Resort and of course, about Cartier ending up in the water! She wanted to know if he was OK, and I said, "he's taking some medicine to ward off hypothermia." And I said, "I was taking some too in case it was contagious." I think she said something about, "the blind leading the blind," whatever that meant? I talked to the kids for a while and then back to the wife to remind her to call Gene about our progress after hanging up. Then I looked at Cartier and he was looking kind of blurry to me, so I figured he must need some more medicine so we went back and medicated ourselves a little more, just to be on the safe side we rationalized. We'd had a long and fun day but we were both tired so we turned in about 10:30.

The next morning we were up bright and early and in the restaurant as soon as the doors opened. We checked out about 8 am and threw our bags in the boat and got a ride back out to 42Joliet. We threw our bags in the airplane and as I prefighted 42 Joliet John took the paddle and broke up the ice up around the airplane. I asked the boat driver to make a couple of turns around the plane to break up the ice enough so I could get turned around and he did. I noticed there was also about a 1/4 inch of frost on the wings too so that presented another problem of how to get the frost off! I asked Cartier if he could walk on water with a push broom to sweep the frost off, but he said he couldn't. A lot of help he is, I

The ice breaking up behind 42Joliet.

thought! But then I guess he had already proved that yesterday! I liked Cartier and he was fun to have with!

I got in and Cartier untied the rope from the prop and buoy and when he got in I started 42 Joliet. She fired right up. I let her idle for a few minutes and then increased the rpm's about to 1000rpms and held the wheel all the way back and we crunched through the ice. I told Cartier, "You can tell it's getting to be near the end of the float flying season when you taxi out in the morning breaking up ice." Cartier just laughed and said, "Yes, I suppose that would be one indication!"

I didn't know yet how we were going to get frost off the wings and we needed to get some fuel too. I knew there was suppose to be fuel available over on the east side of the lake someplace, but that was about ten miles away. I was thinking, hmmm, maybe by the time I taxi over there and get some fuel the sun will have taken care of the frost problem.

We had crunched through the ice for about a half a mile or so and were heading north toward the bigger part of the lake, hoping it wouldn't be frozen over, when I looked off to the right and there was a lady out raking her yard! Plus, the lit-

Co-pilot Cartier sweeping frost off the flaps.

tle bay along the north side of her house was, ice free! I told Cartier, I bet that lady has a broom and a ladder too! I pulled in and beached 42 Joliet and we went over and introduced ourselves to the lady and told her where we had come from and where we were going. I asked her if she might have a ladder and push broom we could borrow. She did! Then I told Cartier that sweeping the frost off was co-pilot's work, so he put the ladder against the leading edge of the wing, being careful to position it so as not to damage the leading edge and started sweeping the frost off! Then we turned 42Joliet around so he could sweep the frost off the flaps and ailerons. I liked Cartier! But then I felt a little guilty so I traded off with him and we got the frost off! We put the ladder and broom back in the ladies garage and thanked her. Then we pumped the floats and mostly just sucked air but it was nice to know they were dry. We got in and I started 42Joliet up and taxied as far as I could to the east, end of the bay. It looked to me like we had plenty of open water heading west out of that bay to get airborne, and besides, there was another long narrow bay across the main channel. I did a thorough check of the controls, fuel selector, cowl flaps, wing flaps, checked the mags, cycled the prop and asked Cartier if he had said his prayers. He said he had so I poured the coals to 42 Joliet. This was my first takeoff in a 185 on floats, off the water that is. She got up on step pretty much like I expected she would, but then she wouldn't accelerate! The airspeed was glued on 40 miles per hour! I put a little bit of nose down pressure, and then some back pressure to try and find an attitude where she'd accelerate, but she wouldn't, she was stuck on 40 mile per hour! I wondering, what's wrong? I knew the floats were dry, we'd swept all the frost off and we're low on fuel so were light and the rpm's were at red line. Hmmm, why ain't this thing accelerating? We were heading into the narrow bay across the main channel and I'm just about to abort when we hit some ice and 42Joliet leaped into the air! That was great but I've still only got 50 miles an hour of airspeed! So I needed to lower the nose and get some more airspeed because we're in a box canyon with a big hill ahead of us and trees on both sides of us and not enough room to turn around or to get stopped! I kept the nose down so we were just skimming the ice and at the last possible second I pulled the nose up and did a wing over to the right and cleared the trees on the long narrow point of land running out into the lake. I still didn't have enough airspeed to stay airborne so I let 42 Joliet settle back onto the water, still at full throttle and finally after horsing it off the water a couple of times I got enough airspeed to stay airborne again!

We found the re-fueling dock on the east side of the lake and tied up to it. We got out and looked the airplane over for anything that might explain why she wouldn't get out of the water. Then I called the telephone number on the sign to get

At the fuel dock.

Cartier refueling 42Joiliet

fuel. While we waited for the guy to arrive we pumped the floats again to make sure they were dry. Then we even opened up the covers to make sure some of the pump out hose's hadn't dropped off and we had a lot of weight we didn't know about. They were all dry?

It took an hour for the fuel guy to get there and then he tried for another hour to get the pump to turn on but couldn't because of some electrical problem. I was anxious to get the show in the air because we had another 525 knots to go! And I'm thinking already, that it's going to be getting pretty late by the time we make Eufaula, Alabama.

I looked at the map and saw the Linn Creek airport a few miles away next to the lake. I used the phone on the dock and called them and they said to fly over there and they'd have a little yellow fuel truck waiting for me on the beach! So we started up and taxied away from the dock and I poured the coals to 42Joliet and again she got up on step, and stuck on 40mph again! I horsed her off the water three more times before I got enough airspeed to stay airborne and we flew down and found the Linn Creek airport and the little yellow fuel truck! And again when I landed she skipped three times before she stayed on the water! And I don't know why the hell she's doing that! And I'm sure Cartier is wondering if I know what the hell I'm doing, too!

We topped off the tanks and taxied out for takeoff. There wasn't much of any wind but I took advantage of what little bit there was. I asked Cartier if he was ready and he said, let's go, so I pulled up the water rudders, dropped some flaps and slowly applied full power. She got up on step nicely, but again the airspeed was glued at 40miles per hour! Again I rocked back and forth feeling for that, pencil point, of the step. I noticed the nose of the airplane seemed a little lower than I thought it should be when I felt like I was on the step though? I've never experienced this problem with any other airplane before, I'm thinking. Finally, I just pulled the wheel back abruptly again and horsed 42 Joliet off the water! We still didn't have enough airspeed to stay airborne and we settled back onto the water. But at least we were doing 45 miles and hour now! So I horsed her off the water again, and we still didn't have enough airspeed to stay airborne, but now at least we've got 50 miles per hour! I told Cartier, "One more time and I think she'll fly!" So I horsed her off again and we just barely stayed in the air. I had to keep easing off the back, pressure as she gained airspeed until I got enough airspeed to climb out. I expected to see Cartier checking the bus schedules about now, but he wasn't. I told him, "Hey, if you ain't living on the edge you're taking up to much f---king space!" We both laughed! We headed direct to Lebanon, Missouri to get south of a restricted area, and then we had a straight shot right between a couple of MOA's and right into Eufaula, Alabama.

I had called the Eufaula airport a week or so earlier and talked to Roy McLain about a place to park the airplane and getting some fuel. It turned out Roy ran the airport and the marina downtown too! As I looked at my map he described where to land in the Chattahoochee River to get to the marina. He described some bridges and a Holiday Inn to look for. Roy mentioned that he had just won the T6 race in Reno a few months earlier! It was getting pretty late by the time we got to Eufaula. Cartier spotted the Holiday Inn and then I recognized the bridges that Roy had described and then the finger of water where the marina was! I did a "U'ee" just past the Holiday Inn and turned the landing lights on and flew down and landed on the Chattahoochee River! Again 42 Joliet skipped three times on landing! I was puzzled as to why she was skipping? And Cartier kept looking at me like, what the hell, are you doing Hubbell? We taxied up to the marina and found the boat ramp that Roy had told me I could park on for the night. We found the pay phone also right where Roy said we would and called the Holliday Inn. By the time we got our bags out of the airplane, locked it, and tied it off to a couple of trees, the van from the Holiday Inn was there to pick us up. We checked in and we both called home to report in. John was complaining that he still felt a little chilled from being in the water the afternoon before. He thought he should take some more medicine to prevent hypothermia from setting in. I told him that I've always believed in prevention medicine so I better take some more medicine too in case it's contagious. We laughed and headed to the restaurant! We both had Cajun style fish and a few shots of medicine. Again it had been a long eventful day and we were tired so we took our medicine and turned in early, which was about 10 pm our time.

The next morning we were up early and having breakfast in the restaurant. There were two couples at the next table and one of the guys said to the other people, "did you see that floatplane last night? He came right over the Holiday Inn and made a sharp left turn and a steep decent and landed right down there on the river," as he pointed to the window. "Boy that guy sure knew what he was doing!" he added. Cartier and I had all we could do to keep from laughing! I'm not sure we really knew what we were doing, we just needed a place to park for the night! We had a nice breakfast and checked out and the Inn gave us a ride back down to the marina. I had called Roy from the Holiday Inn and told him we were just leaving for the marina and it wasn't very long and he was backing his fuel truck up to 42 Joliet. We paid and thanked Roy for the great service and taxied out. Again I had to horse 42 Joliet off the water three times before she'd stay in the air! We headed south down the Chattahoochee River toward Lake Seminole.

This was going to be an easy day because we only had about 300 knots to go! I didn't get much higher than 300 feet it was so pretty! We followed the Chattahoochee river down to Lake Seminole and took the Apalachicola river south out of there. Cartier and I were just enjoying the hell out of this. I'm only about 300 feet in the air just kind of winding along with the river. We were surprised how many stilt houses there were! But it appeared most of what we were seeing was swamp country, so they needed to build their houses on stilts.

It was strange looking country to a couple of guys who had just taken off from the snow a couple of days ago! We thought later, we were probably lucky we didn't get some buckshot thrown at us! They might have thought we were revenuer's flying that low! When we got to the Gulf we just headed directly across to Tarpon Springs at 500 feet above the water! Was that a sight out over the Gulf too! We saw several large ships and numerous small fishing boats and a lot of water! I told Cartier, "Isn't this a time warp? A couple of days ago we took off from Grand Rapids, Minnesota on the snow and it was 0, and now we're flying over the Gulf of Mexico and its 70 degrees!" I'm wondering, hmmm, what do people do that don't fly?

I called the maintenance facility on unicom, that Jerrie had told me to, about fifty miles out and said, "we'll be there in about twenty minutes." They instructed me on where to land on Lake Tarpon and said they'd give me vectors when we were on the water, to where they wanted us to park. I thought, I've never had it so good! I tried something differ-

Jerrie Cobb, John Cartier and the author in front of 42Joliet.

ent on the landing this time. Instead of flaring, I flew 42 Joliet right onto the water, and she didn't skip! About the time I was nudging 42 Juliet up on the shore a car arrived. It was Jerrie Cobb! It was a real honor to meet her! Gene had told us that she was one of the original Mercury 13 astronauts and was the first woman to be certified for space flight! She was very humble. I thought, hmmm, if I ever become famous I'm going to be very humble too! But then I thought, fat chance of that ever happening!

Jerrie asked how the trip had gone and if there were any problems with the airplane. I told her 42Joliet was perfect and then told her about the floats skipping etc. She said that she was going to put 42Joliet on EDO 3430 floats anyway so that wasn't a problem. I was glad to hear that!

Pretty soon a truck and trailer and a crane arrived. We hardly had time to get our belongings out of the airplane and

they had it hooked to the hoist and had lifted it out of the water.

I was curious about the floats, so I looked them over pretty close while it was sitting on the trailer before they drove away.

It was pretty obvious to me why 42Joliet wasn't getting out of the water like she should and why she was skipping on landing! I told Jerrie and Cartier what I thought the problem was and they agreed with me. I said a silent "thanks for the nice ride 42Juliet" as they hauled her away to the avionics shop to put in a HF radio and whatever else Jerrie wanted them to do.

I just couldn't figure out why Gene would have passed up such a great trip as this had been!

Jerrie drove us to her house over in Fort Lauderdale and we completed the paperwork that Gene wanted done. I asked about a nearby hotel or motel and she said she had a lot of room and we were welcome to stay at her house.

She had a large living room with all kinds of artifacts from down in the Amazon jungle where she had spent most of her life flying missionary service. She had spears, shields, bows and arrows, blow guns and darts, everything! I was curious about the blowguns and asked her how accurate they were? Jerrie picked one off the wall, along with a dart. She warned Cartier and I to not touch the tips of any of the darts or spears because they could have some poison on them that could still be fatal if you cut yourself. She put a dart in the blow-gun and said, "See that little piece of wood up there on the wall," as she pointed to a piece of wood about three inches wide and five inches long, about thirty feet away. She blew into that blowgun, and not all that hard either, and that dart hit that small piece of wood just about in the center. I said, "That was good!" And she said, "If you think that was good, just think how accurate the Amazon Indians are!" I remember her saying that when the Trans Amazon highway was being built, every time a white man sneezed, a hundred Indians died. They weren't immune to our viruses like we are.

Jerrie took Cartier and I out for supper and we had a nice visit with her. She asked me, if I would like to fly the 185 down to the Amazon basin for her and she'd put me up in a hotel for a week and pay my expenses and then she had a Beechcraft Baron she'd like me to deliver to Michigan. Boy that sounded interesting! We talked about the route, etc and I was interested! I thought, wouldn't that make the trip of a lifetime, to take off from the snow in northern Minnesota and end up, down on the Amazon river someplace. I called Gene when we got back to Jerrie's and said, guess what? He said, "You ain't coming back are you? I knew she'd offer you a job." I said, "How about if I just don't come back for a couple of weeks?" And I told Gene about Jerrie wanting me to fly 42Joliet down to the Amazon and staying a week, all expenses paid, and bringing a Baron back to Michigan! Gene said, "I know that sounds like fun Les, but I need you back here! In fact I need you to pick that 182 up right there in Ft Lauderdale, and drop Cartier off in Wichita to bring a new 172 home for us. And a couple of days after you get back I need you to go back to Wichita and bring a new 210 home! So I let Gene talk me out of flying 42 Joliet down to the Amazon. Well, that and the fact that I hadn't had any sex for five days now either and I wasn't used to that! The next morning Jerrie drove us over to the Ft Lauderdale airport. We said good-bye to her and that it had been a real treat to have met her and spend some time with her!

I inspected the 182, N381LA and called Gene and told him it looked OK to me. He said he'd wire the money for it and for me to bring the bill of sale back. It was ten o'clock my time before the wire arrived. We had 381LimaAlpha all loaded, fueled, preflighted and ready to go so as soon as the seller said he had the money and gave me a bill of sale we shook hands and left! We were off the ground at 10:15 and had 1100 nautical miles to go to Wichita, Kansas! With the 182 truing out about 130kts that's about eight hours of flying time I figured, not including the almost certain headwind we'd have! It turned out we had the usual 10-15 knot headwind going northwest and about the time we got near Memphis we decided to call it a day and landed at West Memphis for the night. It was a totally uneventful arrival. I didn't skip the airplane three times and Cartier didn't even fall out or nothing!

We found a motel near the airport and checked in and then walked a few blocks to a restaurant and had supper along with a couple of drinks. I called the wife and told her where we were and turned in early. And we got up early! We had another 375 nautical miles to go to Wichita with an hour or hour and a half on the ground and then another 575 miles to Duluth. We just grabbed a couple of Cokes and some candy bars from the machine at the airport and left! We were off the ground by 8:30! Two and a half hours later we were looking at Wichita, Kansas! I had been there several times already so I knew where to land and where to park. It didn't take long to get Cartier together with the 172 and we borrowed a car and went to lunch at a nearby diner. The weather was "CAVU" all the way to Duluth and we were even going to have a tailwind! The 182 had enough fuel to make Duluth non-stop but Cartier was going to have to land someplace, so I gave him the company credit card. The 172 also didn't have any radios! I said, "See you back in Duluth Cartier," and we taxied out and made a formation takeoff out of there about 1:00 pm and headed northeast! I went up to 7,500 and was making 150kts over the ground and landed in Duluth four hours later, about 5:00 pm! Beats walking, I thought!

Gene was there and said, "Welcome back from a safe trip!" I liked Gene. He was always so enthusiastic and wanted to hear how everything had gone. I figured Cartier was going to be about an hour and a half behind me so I called the tower so they would be expecting him and know he'd be going to Halvair. Gene invited me to go to the Officers Club and debrief, so I called the wife and told her I was back and that I'd be home in an hour. We went and had a couple of drinks to celebrate a safe trip and I told Gene it had been a great trip too! I told him about how I had to horse those floats out of the water and how they skipped on landings and what I thought was causing it. He agreed with my theory too. I said I was going to call the guys at Altair and tell them what I thought also. I was anxious to get home and see my family, so after two drinks I headed home.

It was only about a fifteen minute, drive from the airport home. As usual the kids and Ginger were glad to see me! The wife was making supper and barely acknowledged that I was home. I wondered what I had hurried home for?

Chapter Thirteen

I took a couple of days off and just stayed home and caught up on my family time. I did talk the wife into taking a nap together one day! I don't know if the kids ever figured out what that meant? I think Ginger did though. She could probably hear me breathing hard from her rug down in the kitchen! I figured that's probably why she'd have her paws over her ears, and looking up at me like, shame on you, once in a while when I'd come down to the kitchen to get a drink of water.

The first morning I was back to work I called Altair and talked to Rod Annis, one of the owners. I had met Rod about a week before I had taken off for Florida with the 185. I told Rod that I'd had a hard time getting the 185 out of the water on takeoff and that if you made a normal flared landing, it skipped like a flat rock about three times. I said, "When they lifted the 185 out of the water down there in Tarpon Springs, I could see what was the matter." He asked what I thought it was? I said, "Your floats are nose up compared to the cord of the wing. So when I flare the airplane and have about 15 degrees nose up, the floats have about 25 degrees nose up and they skip like a rock when they hit the water!" And I said, "Conversely, on takeoff, when the floats are on the step, the aircraft has a nose down attitude of maybe 10 degrees. That forces the floats deeper into the water the faster you go and the airplane won't accelerate. And when I apply back pressure to lift off, the tails of the floats are dragging further keeping it from accelerating." I said, "Rod, as I see it, you need to lengthen your front float struts or shorten the rear struts a couple of inches and also put something on the bottom of the floats to break up the surface tension." He said, "That's exactly what I've been telling the other guy's but they don't agree." I said, "Well I sure ain't no aeronautical engineer or nothing so that's all I can tell you."

On January 10th I took the airlines back to Wichita again to pick up a new Cessna 210 N22816. I dropped it off in Grand Rapids so they could put some King radios in it at the radio shop there. I took a 172 N39105 back to Duluth.

On January 13th I spent a couple of hours checking Dr. Eck out on skis in his 180 N6000Lima. On the 23rd I demo'd an M35 Bonanza to Marv Nafie from Duluth. I hadn't flown one of those before either but this time I didn't wreck anything!!

That afternoon I had a call from Pastor Johnson and he wanted to come up and look at one of our 150's N5667Golf, that the company had decided to sell. I told him it was buried outside in a snow bank and I'd need to get the line department to dig it out and get it in the hangar overnight to thaw out. I said it cost the sales department $50.00 a night to put an airplane in the heated hangar, but I'd be glad to do that if you're a serious buyer. He said he was, so we made an appointment for the next morning at 10 am. I notified the line department to dig it out of the snow and put it in the hangar. It was going to be 20 below zero that night so hangar space was at a premium!

Pastor Johnson arrived about 10 am and we went out into the hangar and looked over the 150 and then came back into the office and looked over the logbooks. He still seemed very interested so we did a preflight and I had the line crew put it outside. We jumped in before it had a chance to get cold because it was still 20 below zero and blowing about 10-15knots! Colder than a mother-in-laws kiss I figured! We went and flew it for about a half hour and came back in. I said, "Shall we put it on paper, Pastor Johnson?" He said, "Well not yet. I'll have to have my wife come look at it first." "Can you call her and have her come look at it now," I asked. He said, "No, she can't come today, it will have to be tomorrow." I said, "OK, I'll have the line department put it back in the hangar tonight and we'll see you in the morning." The next morning he and his wife arrived and we went out in the hangar and showed her, the 150. She wanted to ride in it before she could make a decision, so I had the line crew pull it out again and I took her for a ride. We flew it for about a half hour and came back in. She seemed to like it, so I asked Pastor Johnson again, "Shall we take it off the market then?" (I had learned that line from Gene!) Pastor Johnson said, "Well not just yet. We're going on vacation for a week and we'll pray on it." I said, "Maybe you should put a little deposit on it so it will be here when you get back though." He said, "No, if God wants us to have it, it will be here when we get back." I said, "OK."

It just happened that a guy called from Syracuse New York the next day about the 150. He liked it and said he'd get on a jet and be in Duluth tomorrow if I'd hold it for him. I said, " I'll hold the airplane for you, just be sure to bring a cashiers check." He said he would! Sure enough the next day about mid-morning he arrived via North Central Airlines and I drove over to the terminal and picked him up. I had left the airplane in the heated hangar overnight again. It was love at first sight for him! He looked it over and we went through the logbooks. He was impressed with how the airplane had been maintained and I told him I had instructed in 67Golf and she flies nice and straight and everything works. I asked him if he wanted to take it out and fly it? He said, "No, I know it will fly just like you say it does Les, so let's get the paper work done because it's cold out there and I've got a long ways to go!" We did the paper work and the line crew pulled the airplane out front and topped it off with fuel and he was gone!

Just about a week later to the day, Pastor Johnson called me to tell me that they were back and that they had prayed on it and God wants them to have the 150. I said, "Pastor Johnson, I'm sorry to have to tell you this, but God wanted a guy in Syracuse, New York to have the 150 more than he wanted you to have it." He said, "Do you mean it's gone?" I said, "Yes, it's gone." I actually felt bad for Pastor Johnson because he had done what was right for him. The only thing he didn't know though, in the airplane business, the early bird gets the worm.

On January 27th Gene took his son Scuffy and I took my son Tim, and we flew up to Baudette, Minnesota ice fishing on Lake of the Woods for the day. I flew the M35Bonanza N9922Romeo up to Baudette and Gene flew it back. The weather was CAVU but colder than a well driller's ass, as the saying goes! And the fishing wasn't any hotter either! But we had a good father son trip never the less!

The month of February was so cold and miserable that I didn't fly all month! It was March 5th, before I demo'd another airplane! It was a Twin Comanche, N7847Yankee, so I was right at home in it! I flew it out to Fargo and showed it to a couple of guys. That was a waste of my time! But on the 12th I flew it down to Charles City Iowa and sold it to Roy Nelson! The shop there did a pre-buy for him and then we flew it. We went to town to have lunch and then Roy stopped by his bank and got a cashiers check. We went back out to the airport and I completed the paperwork and Roy gave me a ride back to Duluth! I thought, why can't, they all go this easy! But then I always figured if they all went that easy everybody would be selling airplanes! But I really appreciated an easy deal once in a while for all the times that I did a lot of work for nothing!

On March 27th I jetted back down to Wichita to pick up a new Cessna 337 Skymaster N1890Mike, that Gene had sold to the Lake Superior District Power Company over in Ashland, Wisconsin. It was a, "no radio" airplane, which I liked because then I don't have to talk to anyone! Basically I'm a bashful farm boy anyway! I flew it into Grand Rapids to have King radios installed at our avionics shop there. It was an easy 3.5 hr non-stop trip back! I flew a 172 back to Duluth.

On March 29th, 1973 I flew a Cessna 180 N5200Echo down to Eau Claire, Wisconsin and demo'd it to Tom and Becky Prior. I liked Tom and Becky from the start! Tom was the swimming coach at the University of Wisconsin and Becky was a RN nurse and they were both pilots. Actually, Becky was a, six month pregnant RN nurse and pilot with their first child! They were both so appreciative of me for bringing 5200Echo down for them to see!

And a few days later on April 6th, I flew back down to Eau Claire in 71Mike and picked up Tom and Becky and we flew back up to Baudette, Minnesota to look at a pair of floats for 5200Echo.

They brought along a grocery bag half full of trail mix, peanuts, fruit, and some fruit drinks. Now I really liked them!

The weather was VFR for most of the trip, except from Hibbing north to Baudette it was snowing lightly, but not enough to be of any concern to an aircraft salesman needing a house payment!

We looked at the floats for about 30 minutes and decided to head back to Eau Claire. It was getting dark by now and snowing lightly with huge snowflakes but you could still see the stars! I asked if either one of them wanted to fly the 210 back to Eau Claire? Becky raised her hand! I thought that was really neat! I also thought it was neat that Tom didn't feel like he should fly it, because he's a man. I could tell that they had a mutual respect and love for each other and they were not only married, they were best friends! I was jealous that my marriage wasn't like that.

So Tom got into the back seat with the bag of munchies and Becky got into the pilot's seat and I in the co-pilots seat. I read the checklist for Becky and we got 71Mike started and taxied out to the runway. Again, I read the run up and take-off checklist and we pulled out onto the runway and took off. Becky is not a very big woman and hadn't ever flown a high performance retractable, so I had anticipated that I'd probably need to help her a little with some right rudder on take-off and climb out to offset the torque and P factor, which I did between laughing! I thought, it's dark, the stars are out, it's snowing big snowflakes and you can see the lights on the ground, a real spatial disorientation setup and I've got a woman flying the airplane that can't hardly reach the rudder pedals because her belly is hitting the control wheel!

Becky also had an instrument rating so l told her to not even look outside, just fly the instruments. I told them that I remember a flight in the Twin Comanche one night over northern Michigan when I was flying for Northland Homes with conditions just like we have tonight. I was on an IFR flight plan at about seven thousand feet. The stars were out, it was snowing lightly and you could see the lights on the ground. Every time I'd look outside I'd get a little vertigo so I quit looking outside until I absolutely needed to!

We got back to Eau Claire about 6:30 pm and after writing up a purchase order for the 180, N5200 and the floats I said good-bye to Tom and Becky, made a pit stop, and headed back to Duluth. I landed about forty, five minutes later and had the line crew put 71Mike in the hangar.

The next morning I spent thirty minutes cleaning up the peanut shells on the floor and seats of 71Mike and vacuuming it out! I didn't mind though because I had a feeling that I had met some people that I really liked and I'd be seeing more of them.

A few days later Tom called me and told me about a Cessna 180 on amphibs N5286D over in Pontiac, Michigan that he had seen in the Trade-A-Plane. I agreed with him that it would be a lot more convenient for them to have an amphibian airplane. So we cancelled the 180 on straight floats, deal and I got on a jet and flew over to Detroit, Michigan. The guy that owned the 180 amphib met me at the Detroit airport and we drove up to the Pontiac airport. I inspected the 180 amphib N5286Delta and negotiated s deal on it. I called Tom and Becky and told them about the airplane and they agreed to buy it. Then I called Gene and told him the Priors were going to buy 86Delta so he said he'd wired the money to pay for it.

While I was waiting for the money to arrive I called my sister In Grand Rapids, Michigan and told her I was in Pontiac and asked if she wanted to see her little brother? She did!

I preflighted 86Delta and loaded my bags aboard so I was ready to go as soon as the owner received the money. The money arrived within the hour so I called my sister and said I'd be in Grand Rapids in about an hour and to meet me at Northern Air.

This is the first time I've flown an amphib so it felt really different sitting up so high. I started up and called ground control and they cleared me out to 9 left, after I told them I'd be west bound. Also I had to steer it with the brakes, no nose wheel or tail wheel steering, just brakes! And you have to kind of spike the brakes to get it to turn even! It felt kind of clumsy, but by the time I got to the runway I had it figured out pretty good. I did a run up, dropped two notches of flaps, set the trim, checked the fuel selector, made sure again that the cowl flaps were open, checked the controls and called the tower and told them I was ready to go. He cleared me for takeoff with a left downwind departure and I pulled out onto the runway. I thought, hmmm, one thing nice about an amphib, compared to a tail dragger, at least your don't have to correct for P factor until you rotate! I held the brakes until I had about 1500 RPM and then released them. 86Delta started rolling straight down the runway and I kept applying power until I had full throttle. When the airspeed got up to the green arc I applied some back pressure and the nose came up and she ran along really nice on the main gear for awhile and pretty soon we were airborne! I flipped the gear up and when the gear was in the wells, I milked the flaps up and she was climbing out at about 600 feet per minute. I thought, hmmm, could be better, could be worse. I made a climbing left turnout and a downwind departure as I had told the tower I would and climbed up to 4,500 ft. I figured I'd stay south of Lansing's airspace and then go direct to Grand Rapids.

Now I'm thinking, hmmm, I got it off the runway without wrecking it, I wonder how you land one of these things? It's a little different sitting up so high, so I'll have to flare higher than I usually feel like flaring! Or I could just make a glassy water type landing instead of a full stall landing. I think I'll just make, a glassy water, or hmmm, would it be called a glassy runway type landing?

I stayed well south of Lansing's airspace and then made a turn to the northwest toward Grand Rapids. About thirty miles out, I called Grand Rapids approach. He gave me a squawk code and ident and said to expect runway 26 left and turned me to a 350 heading for a left base to 26 left. I noticed on my approach chart that 26 left is 10,000 feet long. I thought, good I'll probably need 10,000 feet to get this thing landed and stopped! About ten miles out approach handed me off to the tower. I called the tower and he said to enter on a left base for 26 left. I was on a wide left base when the tower cleared me to land. I lowered the landing gear and looked out to see if the front wheels were down and looked down at the floats to see the gear down markings were in the down position. Yup! They were all down! I rolled out on final and dropped two notches of flaps, then full flaps and flew down until the last 100 feet and set up for a "glassy runway" landing. Other than touching down a little sooner than I expected, it was a good landing! It taxied fairly well as long as you were, moving along pretty good. It was no problem making the turn off onto the taxiway and taxing in to Northern Aviation!

My sister and her husband Fred were waiting for me when I arrived. After a few hugs and handshakes we drove back to their house. We visited for awhile and then Fred suggested we go out for supper. I took a quick shower and put on some clean slacks and a shirt.

We drove downtown and stopped at a rather expensive looking supper club. Of course, to me anything other than a McDonalds is expensive looking! Fred said the food was really good there. We walked in and there was a maitre d' at the entrance. He looked at me and said it was formal seating and that I'd need to have a tie on to eat there. Fred always wore a suit and tie to work so he was OK. The maitre d' said they have some ties available and I could pick one out if I wanted to. I told him I had come here to eat, not to impress him or anyone, so we'll go someplace else. My sister turned about three shades of pink as we walked out. She always referred to me as her "hick little brother" after that!

I never did ask her if they ever went back to that place after I embarrassed her so much! I hadn't seen her so pink since the time they took the wife and me to a supper club that had a comedian on stage, a couple of years earlier. My sister had gone to the bathroom. When she came out of the bathroom the comedian asked her if she, "could hear us in there?" My sister said, "No." The comedian said, "well we could sure hear you out here!"

When we got back to their house I called the wife and told her where I was. I told her about walking out of a supper club because they wanted me to wear a tie. "That didn't surprise her," she said. I told her if everything goes ok I probably be spending the next night in Eau Claire. I thought about asking her to drive down to Eau Claire for an hour but didn't. Besides I knew, she wouldn't anyhow!

The next morning after a light breakfast Fred and my sister took me back out to the airport and we said our good byes. I preflighted 86Delta and started up and called ground and taxied out to the runway, did a run up, called the tower and took off and headed northwest toward Ludington on Lake

Michigan. It was a beautiful day, not even much of a head-wind. I still couldn't help but wondering, what do people do that don't fly?

I could see Lake Michigan from about 50 miles away! I noticed that the eastern shoreline is all sand as I crossed over it. I made a check of the oil temp and pressure, the cylinder temperature, all in the green arc. The fuel gauges are still above 3/4ths, and there's no oil on the windshield, I'm going! Who am I to get to do this I'm wondering? Why me God? I must, be the luckiest kid in the world!

The flight out over Lake Michigan is beautiful! I don't even have much of a pucker factor anymore. There's almost always a boat or ship of some kind in sight. I figured, I'm safer out here than in most traffic patterns. Besides I'm on floats and the lake is fairly calm! It can't get much better than this, I figure! Except I forgot to get a coke and a couple of candy bars before I took off!

Pretty soon I can see the far shore. I've got the VOR tuned to 115.5 at Green Bay and I'm on the 115degree radial so that will keep me north of the restricted airspace R-6903. 86Delta, is flying along really nice. And everything is work-ing, just like the owner said! I'm sure Tom and Becky will like her! About ten miles from the west shoreline I turned to a heading of 280 degrees so as to pass south of Green Bay's airspace and North of Appleton's airspace direct toward Stevens Point. I figure, hmmm, I must have about an hour and half to go? I dialed in 110.6 for the Stevens Point VOR and headed direct towards that. I also figure, hmmm, as long as I've got an airport off the left wing and another off the right wing it might be a good time to check fuel quantity, oil pres-sure and temps again. Everything's in the green, except me. I need to go to the bathroom! I knew I couldn't make Eau

Claire so decided to land at Stevens Point. Then I could call Tom and Becky and give them my ETA (Estimated Time of Arrival) at Eau Claire too! The wind at Stevens Point was favoring runway 30 and I didn't hear or see anyone else in the pattern so I just made a straight in "glassy runway" approach. That worked out good and this time the wheels touched the runway just about when I expected them to! And it was a smooth landing! I used the bathroom and called Tom and Becky and said I'd be there within the hour!

I was glad I had made another landing at Stevens Point and that I'd got to taxi 86Delta some more and get in another takeoff. After all, I needed to be an "expert" on 86Delta by the time I get to Eau Claire so I can check Tom and Becky out in it! You know what they say an "expert" is? Anybody more than 100 miles away from home with a briefcase! Yup, I guess that makes me a "expert!"

I dialed in the Eau Claire VOR on 112.9 and got a solid "to." It's always a good feeling to confirm that, I really am heading the right direction!

I remember flying 06Alpha up northwest of Duluth on day back in 1966 and flying the colored range that ran from Duluth to Winnipeg. One side of the airway was an "A" and the other side was a "N." In Morse code, a "A" is "dot dash" and a "N" is "dash dot". It was called a colored range because one side of the airway was green and the other side red. The green side was "A" and the red side was "N". So if you were flying along and hearing a "dot dash" you knew you were on the green side and a "dash dot" meant you were on the red side of the airway. And when you were right on course you'd hear a steady tone! Can you imagine the airline and mail pilots back then flying along picking up ice, maybe bouncing all around and just listening to their headsets and trying to fly a heading to stay on course! I sure like having a VOR or Localizer needle!

I gave Eau Claire Flight Service a call on 123.0 for a airport advisory about ten miles out. They were using runway 22 he said and there was no reported traffic. I just made a modified left base and rolled out on final about five miles out. I turned on a landing light and lowered the wheels on about a three mile final. Again I looked out to verify that the mechanical indicators also showed that the wheels were down. When I was ready to start down I reduced the manifold pressure to 18 inches and lowered two notches of flaps and trimmed in a little nose down trim. 86Delta is very stable and predictable, I thought. I'm getting to really like her! On a 1/4 mile final I went to full flaps and then made another "glassy runway" landing. This time I touched down exactly when I expected to and carried the nose gear for awhile and then let them down. Now I really, really like 86Delta! I had already learned that the, secret to taxing 86Delta is to taxi along briskly and then spike the brakes a little and she turns pretty good then!

Tom and Becky were waiting for me when I taxied in. They were excited to see 86Delta! After walking around looking it over Tom asked if he could fly it? I said, "Let's go!" So Tom got in the left seat, Becky in the back and I rode "shotgun." I read the pre-start checklist while Tom verified everything was where it was supposed to be. We still had a little more than 1/4 tanks so that was good. We weren't going very far anyway. Tom started up and we started taxing out. He commented too that it seems strange to be sitting up so high. (I didn't say, wait until you land it!) We taxied all the way back to the end of runway 22 and I had him doing some S turns along the way. He was doing good! He did a run up as I read the checklist. Then I briefed him about the takeoff and talked him through it. I could tell he was having fun. We took off and climbed straight out until we had 2,500 feet and the he turned right and headed north for a few miles to see how it cruised. Then I had him do a couple of stalls, steep turns etc and we headed back to the airport. I told him how I was landing it and he said, "that sounds good to me too!" So I acted as his verbal checklist and talked him through the landing. He made a perfect landing! I thought, hmm, I must be a better talker than I am a pilot! I asked Becky if she wanted to fly it but she said she knew I had put in along day already, so she'd wait. I was kind of tired and thought that was very considerate of her.

We found a tie down with some longer ropes and tied 86 Delta up for the night. And then Tom said they had some steaks ready to put on the grill and that I was staying at their house tonight! I was right! I knew I was going to like Tom and Becky from the start! I was a little jealous though, they had the kind of marriage that I wished I had.

We took the logbooks and aircraft manual and drove out to their house. It didn't take Tom long and he had the grill going while Becky prepared some mixed vegetables. While the steaks were on the grill Tom made us each a cocktail. He didn't even ask me if I drank! He just asked me what I liked! I thought, hmmm, do I look like a drunk or what?! We had a nice steak supper. They were both so appreciative of me going to get 86Delta for them. I got out the bill of sale and registration and I filled out those for them and Tom gave me a cashiers check. Now I liked them more! (I didn't tell them my house payment was due.) We sat up and talked and watched the ten o'clock news and went to bed. I didn't feel like calling home, so I didn't. I was wondering why I didn't have a nice marriage like Tom and Becky do?

The next morning we went back out to the airport and we did a thorough pre-flight using the checklist. Tom and Becky had studied the aircraft manual after I went to bed so they pretty much had 86Delta figured out. I thought, hmmm, maybe I should start reading the manual before I fly a different airplane. I wasn't sure if Becky was happy to see 86Delta or me, or both, or was she laughing at my burnt orange polyester slacks!

The author and Becky by 86Delta

I just watched as Tom went through the starting checklist and taxied out to the end of runway 22 again. He was doing a good job so I just sat there and sucked my thumb, so to speak. He pulled out onto the runway and started the take-off roll. When the airspeed got up to the green arc I applied some back pressure and showed him how it would run along on the main gear only and fly off, "when it was dam good and ready!"

We had a nice trip up to Duluth and Tom made another nice landing and didn't have any problem taxing in and parking. We went into the office and I introduced Gene to Tom and Becky. Gene was really happy to meet them and welcomed me home! He even took us over to the Officer's Club for lunch!

When we got back from lunch I watched as Tom and Becky preflighted 86Delta. Just before they were ready to get in I told them, "I hope this isn't the last time I see you." They said they hoped it wasn't either! Tom asked Becky if she wanted to fly 86Delta back to Eau Claire so 6 month pregnant Becky climbed up and got in the pilots seat! I thought that was just great!

I thought, hmmm, if I ever get married again she's going to have to be a pilot. I've told a few of my friends that and they all say I'd drive her nuts if she busted altitude by 50 feet or was off course a quarter mile! I don't think I would! Especially if I was horny I wouldn't! I'd just tell her, do whatever you want, just don't kill me!

Becky, Heather and 86Delta on the beach of Bark Lake, 90 miles north of Gore Bay, Canada

Chapter Fourteen

On April 23rd, 1973 I flew a Cessna 337, N1890Mike, complete with new King radios, over to Ashland to check Jake Walker out in it. Jake was the pilot for the Lake Superior District Power Company. Jake was also a friend of Russ's and Darrell Kline's so I had met him before. We read through the manual, paying particular attention to the fuel system and did a thorough preflight. Jake had been flying a 1969 Cessna 207 N1517U for the power company and was also managing the airport and instructing at Ashland, so he already had a lot of good experience. We got ready to start up and I told Jake we'll always start the front engine first in case anyone is near the rear engine, which we can't see, so it will give them time to move! After the run up Jake pulled out onto the runway and I told him to apply power to the rear engine first just to make sure it's still running and then the front engine. We took off and flew out to the southwest about ten miles for some air work. I had Jake do some standard turns, left and right, some slow flight, stalls, and some steep turns left and right. Jake was doing great! So I diverted his attention out the left window, "Do you see an airplane over there Jake," and reached up and shut the fuel off to the rear engine! It wasn't very long and that engine quit! Jake gave me that same look that Russ used to give me, like *you jerk*! It's a little harder to tell which engine has failed on a centerline thrust airplane because you don't have the yawing moment like you do on a conventional twin. The best way to determine which engine has failed is to look at the EGT gauge I told Jake. We spent just about an hour or a little more in the practice area and Jake was doing very good with 90Mike, so I handed him a hood and we repeated everything that we had already done, under the hood. It was time for a pit stop so I told Jake to take the hood off and let's go land at Ashland. Jake made a nice approach and landing with 90M. He said it flew just like the 207 just more power and faster.

Darrel Kline and Jim Musso were at the airport. Jim also worked for the power company. Jake asked them if they wanted to go with us to Duluth. Of course they jumped at the chance to fly in the brand new Cessna Skymaster!

So I told Jake to take us to Duluth for lunch! I had worked him pretty hard and long already so I thought it would be good for him to relax a little and just fly the airplane without wondering what I'm going to do next!

He made a nice takeoff and a climbing right turn, off runway 20 and climbed to four thousand five hundred feet and contacted Duluth approach. Approach gave us a heading and altitude and it wasn't long and the wheels were on the runway at Duluth. Jake had done very well. He wasn't having any problems with 90Mike! And to make things better, Gene took us all to lunch over at the Chalet!

After lunch I had Jake file an IFR flight plan from Duluth to Hibbing and back to Duluth. There wasn't much of any wind so when he contacted ground control I had him request runway 27 being it was closest. Ground gave him 27 along with his IFR clearance. Jake did a full run up, using the checklist of course, and called the tower and said he was ready to go. The tower cleared us for takeoff and when Jake lined up on the centerline I handed him the hood. Again I got, that same look that Russ used to give me, like, *you jerk!*

Now I'm wondering if it's something in the water over there at Ashland causing this! Jake made a good ITO and got the airplane all cleaned up and was making a climbing right turn direct to Hibbing and up to 6,000 ft when I throttled the front engine. I got that same look again! He immediately determined which engine had failed so I gave it back to him. Approach control vectored him for a straight in ILS 31 to Hibbing and then handed us off to Hibbing FSS. Jake reported over the outer marker and put the gear and flaps down. It was such a smooth day that once he had the airplane set up, it was like it was glued to the localizer and glideslope! I thought, hmmm this is too easy for him. So when he called the missed approach and started climbing out I covered up all the vacuum instruments! I heard, "Thanks a lot Hubbell!" He didn't dare take his eyes off the instruments long enough to give me that you jerk look though anyway! I told him that when he contacts Duluth approach to request vectors for the ILS 9 approach and he did. I kept him partial panel right down until he called out the DH of 200 ft and looked up and saw the runway. He had done well and I told him so.

We taxied into Havair and shut down. Jake and I went into my office and I signed his logbook off and told him he had done a very good job. Of course Jake already had several hundred hours of instrument time in the 207.

On April 24th I took the 310 N4133Quebec down to Monticello, Iowa and demo'd it. I struck out. No sale, no house payment!

On May 8th I demo'd and sold a 1955 Cessna 180 N7854A to Bill and Laura Radtke! Bill had been one of my private students a year earlier! I spent an hour with Bill going through the manual and giving the airplane a thorough preflight. Then we started up and taxied out for takeoff on 27.

Bill liked having all that power compared to the 150 he had learned to fly in! We talked about the effects of more horsepower torque and more P factor that a tail dragger has compared to a tricycle type airplane and why he'd need to apply more right rudder on takeoff than he was use to. I told him a tail dragger was just like a wife, if you don't treat her just right she'll make you look like a fool in a hurry! I also told him you never take your eyes off the far end of the runway when you're taking off or landing an airplane, especially a taildragger. I had him apply the power especially slow on the first takeoff to minimize the effect of torque and P factor. Bill did a good job. We leveled off at four thousand five hundred feet and let 54Alpha accelerate to cruise speed and I just let Bill get use to flying the airplane for about ten minutes. Then I had him do some standard rate turns left and right, some slow flight, power off stalls, climbs and descents, etc. We spent an hour and a half playing with 54 Alpha and then flew back to Duluth and I demonstrated how to make a three point landing, with Bill following through. I got lucky and kissed it on! I didn't get to fly with Bill again until the 23rd of May when we spent another hour doing more maneuvers and takeoffs and landings.

I was really busy flying the 337 N2565Sierra all around the state for the next two weeks to St Paul, Amery, Wisconsin, Lake Elms, Baudette, Grand Rapids, Minneapolis, etc. It was June 11th before I had time to fly with Bill again in the 180! On the 14th I flew the 337 N2565 Sierra up to Grand Rapids, back to Duluth and then down to Little Falls and demo'd it and back to Duluth, all in three hours! I was so busy I had to get one of the instructors in the flight department to finish checking Bill out in the 180.

On June 16th, I flew a 1971 Cessna 180 N9093Mike on floats up to Lake Vermillion and sold it to Lloyd Beaurline!

Lloyd had told me to pack a bag because I was going to be spending a few days at their lake place giving him his float rating. We flew 2.5 hours on the 16th, 4.0 hours on the 17th and 3 hours on the 18th and ended up landing in the, pond at Grand Rapids so Lloyd could take his floatplane checkride with Gordy Newstrom. Lloyd had taken to 93Mike like a duck to water so his checkride went very well. It was always fun to visit with Gordy for a while. Lloyd flew me back down to the Sky Harbor airport where I had left my car and then he went on back to Lake Vermillion and I drove home. I was happy to get back home and see my family! As usual though the kids and Ginger were glad to see me, the wife was vacuuming the living room floor and hardly looked up.

Jake standing by N1890M. Unfortunately, Jake came down with cancer and passed away March 29, 2004. I ll miss you, Jake.

Chapter Fifteen
Landing on a restricted Lake in Akron, Ohio!

On June 21st, 1973 I got on a jet and flew out to New York to bring back a new Cessna 180 N42372 on Edo 2960 floats. Gene had flown it out there a couple of weeks earlier to have EDO put the floats on it and asked me if I'd go get it. That's like asking a dog if he wants a steak or not! I can't figure out why Gene is letting me have all the fun though! I'm getting to really like selling and delivering airplanes! And to be flying so many airplanes that I've never flown before!

Jay Frey from EDO met me at the La Guardia airport and drove me out to Zahn's airport on Long Island where the EDO factory was. The first thing I noticed was that 372, was sitting on a three, wheeled dolly. I loaded in my bag and pre-flighted the airplane. I thought they were going to tow it someplace and put it in the water. The only problem was, there wasn't any water nearby! The dolly was to take off from on the runway, Jay explained. I thought hmmm, I ain't never done this before. And then I thought, hmmm, is this why Gene didn't want to come get it? But I'm always up to doing something different so I asked Jay how we were going to do this? He said, "We tow it out to the runway and line it up. And then we've got this long legged kid here. He'll hang on to the left rear float rudder bar and steer you down the run-way until he can't keep up anymore." "And, after he drops off," Jay said, "you're on your own so don't abort because you won't have any steering or brakes". Then he added, "The trick is to takeoff without the dolly going off the runway and wiping runway lights and markers out!" Sounded like fun to me! He said after I take off to fly over to the seaplane base on Sands Point and he'd bring the landing gear over in a truck and we'll put them in the airplane. Then I could top the fuel off for my trip home.

So they towed it out to the runway and sure enough, they had a long legged kid to hang on to the left rear float rudder bar. They put a set of chocks under the main wheels of the dolly so I could start up and do a run up. I started up and let 372 warm up a little and did a run up and signaled that I was ready to go and the kid was ready and the runway was clear so they pulled the chocks. I applied the power smoothly and fully before I figured the kid had dropped off and rolled right down the centerline. I had decided to keep it on the dolly until I knew it was ready to fly and then just pop it off the dolly. About a hundred feet in the air I started a left turn

Les Hubbel of Halvair, Inc., Cessna dealership at Duluth, lifts off float-equipped '73 Cessna 180 on specially designed take-off dolly at Edo factory, Lindenhurst, N.Y. The Edo-designed dolly features internal brakes which apply automatically when the aircraft lifts off to bring the dolly to a safe, quick and stable stop. It has been used by Edo during flight-test and delivery of a wide-range of float-equipped Cessnas, including the Model 150, Skyhawk, Skywagons 180 and 185, and Stationair.

toward the water so I could see where the dolly went. It stayed on the runway!

I found the seaplane base and landed and taxied up to a dock. Soon the truck from EDO arrived and we loaded the landing gear in the back seat, and then I had them top it off with fuel. And then the fog moved in, and stayed. They said it happens every day about this time. John O'Neal ran the seaplane base. There was also a guy named Chuck there. Chuck flew a 206 on floats and ran a scheduled flight to downtown New York and back several times a day. They also had a ping pong table inside and it wasn't long and I was playing ping pong with Chuck, John, Bill Dayl and a couple of other guys that showed up. I had hopes of the fog lifting so I could get a start heading home but they told me I could forget that. They said, "That's why we've got this ping pong table, for days when we can't fly." We played ping pong non-stop until it was time to leave for the night. John O'Neal dropped me off at a motel and said he'd pick me up at nine in the morning. I checked in and had supper and a beer and went back to my room and called the wife to let her know where I was at and that I'm fogged in. Then I talked with the kids for a while and called it a night.

John picked me up in the morning and we stopped at a little diner and had breakfast. It was still foggy. It was still foggy when we got out to the seaplane base. John said, "Sometimes the fog can hang in here for days". Hmmm, great I thought, I ain't had any sex for two days now and it don't look like I'm going to get home anytime soon!

Soon Chuck showed up and challenged me to a game of ping pong. Him and I were just about even. I'd beat him one game and he'd beat me the next. A couple of other guys came around and they were pretty good too! We had a hell of a lot of fun playing ping pong! You could tell these guys had been fogged in a lot and had played a lot of ping pong! Luckily I'd had a table in the motel basement and Ted and the other guys and I had played a lot. It had taken me a few games to take the rust off but now I was back up to speed. We played, ping pong all day, the fog never lifted.

The next morning it was still foggy. We played ping pong until lunch time. It was still foggy and raining now. After lunch the fog lifted about a hundred feet and the visibility came up to about a half mile in rain. I called New York approach control directly because I was about 12-13 miles northeast of La Guardia airport and under the TCA. I told the controller I had a floatplane down here at the Sands Point Seaplane base and I was tired of playing ping pong and needed to get back to Minnesota. (I didn't tell him I needed to get back because I was horny too though.) I told him the airplane was a brand new Cessna 180 with just a basic avionics package of one nav/com, ADF and a transponder but no encoder. I said it didn't have an encoder because it was going to Alaska when I got it back to Minnesota and it wouldn't get higher than 500 feet the rest of it's life. "But," I said, "If you can give me a heading, altitude, frequency, and a transponder code I could get out of here and be on my way back to Minnesota. He asked me, "how much time do you need before you can takeoff?" I said, "about ten minutes" and he filled out an IFR flight plan for me and gave me a clearance! I said, "Thanks a lot!" Then I said a quick thanks for the hospitality and the ping pong to Paul, Chuck and the other guys and started up 372 and taxied out. I did a run up on the go and took off to the northeast as per my clearance. I was in the fog for about 3-4 hundred feet and popped out on top and it was raining cats and dogs! I contacted New York approach and they turned me on course with a climb to six thousand feet and I was heading home! It rained all the way across New Jersey and half way across Pennsylvania! It was coming down so hard that I was glad I was on floats! I finally broke out into VFR conditions but decided to stay on my IFR flight plan until I found the seaplane base southwest of Akron, Ohio, another 200 miles ahead.

When center handed me off to Akron approach I checked in and asked if they could vector me out to the seaplane base. The controller asked, "What seaplane base?" I said, "My sectional chart shows a seaplane base about five miles southwest of the Akron airport." He said, "Just a minute and I'll ask the other controller." He was back in about twenty seconds and said, "Yes, I guess there is one out there and gave me vectors to it." I was of course following along with my finger on my chart and the vector was taking me to the seaplane base. So far so good I thought! Besides, I was tired and getting low on fuel! Approach vectored me right out to the area of the seaplane base but the seaplane base symbol covered the three little lakes below me. I circled around a couple of times but couldn't see any seaplanes or a windsock even. Finally I told approach to, "cancel my IFR and, I'll go land on one of these little lakes and ask someone where the seaplane base is." There were quite a few boats on all three of these little lakes so I picked the lake in the middle and found a safe place and landed on it.

It wasn't long and I saw a boat coming my way at a fairly high speed with a flashing blue light on it. I thought, boy that's pretty, if I ever get a boat I'm going to have one of those flashing blue lights on it too! I had shut down and was sitting sideways in the seat with my feet hanging outside when the boat pulled up along side. It said "Water Patrol" on the side of it and the two guys in it had park ranger uniforms on. They pulled up alongside the left float and one of them said,

"You can't land here, this is a restricted lake." I said, "Ya I did." He said, "Well you're in trouble, you should have talked to the control tower before you landed here!" I said, "I did, they radar vectored me out here." Then I showed them my chart, which showed a seaplane base symbol covering all three lakes. One of the rangers got on his radio and I assumed he was calling their office. He had his back to me so I couldn't hear what he was saying and pretty soon he hung up. Then they both asked me about where I had come from and where was I going. And they wanted to know what it was like to fly a seaplane, etc. One of them asked me if there was any chance that I would give his kids a seaplane ride once we found the seaplane base? I said, that I sure would but I needed to refuel first. About fifteen minutes later their office called them and must have confirmed that I had talked to the tower and was vectored out there and they said, I was free to go! I asked them if they would call their office back and see if they could find the seaplane base in the yellow pages and call them to find out just where it is. In another ten minutes their office called back and said there had been a seaplane base on the next lake north. It had been owned by a Mr. Vandevere but had closed a year ago. I asked them if they'd call Mr. Vandevere and ask him if he had a place I could park for the night and if he had any fuel. In another ten minutes they called back and said, "Yes he had a place I could tie up for the night, but no he didn't have any fuel." I've always had more guts than sense so I asked the rangers if they might do me another favor. They said, "What?" I said, "Would you call your office back and see if they will call a cab and send it out to Vandevere's for me?" They kind of looked at each other and grinned, and then one of the rangers said, "We'll do better than that, I'll come over and pick you up in our truck." I said, "Thanks a lot!"

By now there was about fifty boats circling around the airplane about 100 feet away. One of the rangers asked me how much room I needed to take off. I said, "If you just get all these boats to move over behind you near that little island, all I need is enough room to make a couple of circles and I'll be right on out of here." They said, "We've got to see that!" So they got on their loud speaker and told all the boats to "move over there by that island," pointing behind them to the north. I started up and headed southwest and then started a fairly tight turn to the left. 372 was light so it wasn't very long and I had the right float out of the water and I was circling on the left float with the left wingtip about a foot off the water. I made a turn and a half like that and pulled 372 off the water and made another 360 in that attitude and leveled out heading north and cleared the Island. I flew over and circled the next lake to the north looking for Mr. Vandevere's place on the northwest corner. Pretty soon I spotted a guy standing out on a dock waving a white towel and figured, that must be Mr. Vandevere! So I found a safe place amongst the boats and landed 372 and taxied up to his beach. I got out and introduced myself. He had a nice sand beach so I just tailed 372 around and tied her up to a tree. There wasn't any stormy weather forecast so I figured she would be OK there for the night. It wasn't long and the ranger arrived and the first thing he said was, "That takeoff was beautiful, I've never seen anyone takeoff in a circle like that before!" He gave me a ride to a motel about five miles away. I told him, "I couldn't find any fuel so I wouldn't be able to give your kids a ride. Mr. Vandevere had even called the Akron airport," I said, "but they couldn't come out because their trucks weren't licensed to be on the roads." When he dropped me off at the motel he said, "I'm sure glad you landed here, we haven't had this much excitement for years!" I said, "Thanks for all the help!"

I checked into the motel and then walked down the road a ways and had a hamburger and a beer at a bar and grill. By the time I got back to the room I was plenty tired. I'd had a long and interesting day. I called the wife and then talked to the kids for a while and was sleeping by nine.

The next morning I was still concerned about getting some fuel. I knew if worse came to worse I could always drop 5-10 gallons of car gas in each wing if I needed to. I always figured, they run better on car gas than nothing! I was looking at the sectional when my eyes focused on Cleveland. Ah, I thought, I landed at Cleveland Burke Lakefront airport last year with 46Quebec! It's right out in Lake Erie! I found the telephone number for the Cleveland tower and called them. I told them I was down at Akron with a floatplane and needed some fuel. I asked, "If I land in the lake and taxi up near the taxiway, is there someplace a fuel truck can get to me?" The tower operator was sure there would be, so I said I'd be there in about an hour or a little more. It was only about 40 miles from where I was at to Burke Lakefront airport. I figured, hmmm, twenty minutes flying time at the most.

I had breakfast at the motel and then called a cab and got packed up. The cab arrived shortly and fifteen minutes later I was back out at Mr. Vandevere's place. 372 was sitting pretty level on the beach so I turned the master switch on to check the fuel gauges, they were showing 1/4 tanks. 372 had long range fuel tanks with 42 gallons a side so I figured, hmmm 1/4 tanks should be about 10 gallons a side for a total of twenty. She was burning about 12 gallons an hour so I figured I had plenty of fuel to make Cleveland. But just to make sure the gauges weren't lying I borrowed a stick from Mr. Vandevere and, stuck the tanks. There was almost two inches of fuel so I was comfortable with that. I preflighted 372 and said thanks and good-bye to Mr. Vandevere and started up and taxied out for takeoff. I check that the fuel was on both, the trim set, checked the mags and cycled the prop on the takeoff run and as light as 372 was she just leaped into the air! I made a left climbing turn and headed northwest toward Cleveland and climbed up to four thousand five hundred feet. As soon as I leveled off I switched the fuel selector from both to the left tank. I figured, just in case my figuring wasn't right I wouldn't wait for both tanks to run dry at the same time. This way, if the left tank ran dry I'd have at least five-ten minutes to get to a lake or a river. Within ten minutes I was talking to Cleveland approach and told them I'd like to land in Lake Erie to the east just north of the runway. He said, "No problem," and soon handed me off to the tower. As soon as I had Lake Erie made I switched back to both tanks and landed just where I said I would and the tower handed me off to ground control. Ground said I could just taxi in past the east end of the runway and go into the marina there and a fuel truck was on the way. "Thanks a lot," I said! It was kind of crowded in the marina and I had to be careful of all the sailboat masts. I circled around and finally found a place next to a dock where the fuel truck driver could get a hose to me. About 70 gallons later 372 was topped off! I paid the driver and started up and called Cleveland ground and said I was taxiing for takeoff. I taxied out past the east, end of the runway and called the tower and told him I was ready to go and he said, "The whole lake is yours just avoid the takeoff and approach paths on both ends of the runway." Even I was smart enough to know that! The lake was virtually calm so when I was past the runway I brought the power up to 1700 rpm's and did a mag check and cycled the prop. I check the gauges, lowered two notches of flaps, pulled up the water rudders and poured the coals to 372 heading northwest and in a matter of seconds she was airborne. I liked 372! But I'm thinking, hmmm, why is Gene letting me have all the fun? I called back to the tower and thanked them for the help and turned to a heading of 300 degrees and climbed up to four thousand five hundred feet. I like to get high enough so I clear most airspace but low enough to keep the headwinds as low as possible and, I just like to look down and see what's below me! I guesstimated that 300 degrees would take me down the lake and I should pass north of Toledo and south of Detroit, over Kalamazoo, across Lake Michigan, over Racine and into the lake just west of the Madison airport. The sectional showed a seaplane base there on the southwest corner of the lake.

The weather was clear and not even much of a headwind! Plus, 372 had an ADF so I always had that tuned to a country station ahead! I thought, it doesn't get much better than this! And I think it's great that Gene is letting me do all of this! Of course, I'm not getting time to sell much, but Gene always puts a little more in my check to make up for it. Gene was good to me! But, why is he letting me have all the fun? I decided I wasn't going to ask him either because then he might start taking these trips if he finds out how much fun I'm having! I figured, it's just like the wife, sometimes it ain't good to ask any questions. It might open some doors that I'd just as soon keep closed!

It was peaceful out over Lake Erie and 372 is running perfectly, and she even trims out perfectly! I thought, It, don't get much better than this! Then I got to thinking about something else. I thought, hmmm, I never did ask those rangers if that next lake to the north was restricted too? Hmmm, I bet

I landed on one restricted lake, took off from that restricted lake and went over and landed on another restricted lake, spent the night and took off from that restricted lake this morning! I suppose those rangers knew that. They must have figured the safest thing to do, was to just let this kid spend the night and then hope he gets the hell out of town in the morning before he lands in the little pond downtown in the park, looking for some gas! I also thought, hmmm, it's a good thing that radar had vectored me out to those lakes or those rangers might not have been so nice. They might have made me take the wings off and trailer 372 to an unrestricted lake or river to take off from? I thought, maybe I shouldn't tell Gene about this trip, or at least this part of it.

I could see Toledo ahead off to the left and Detroit off to the right so I was right on course. My 300degree heading is working good! In another 30 minutes I was back over land. My occasional time checks over the ground are coming out a little over two miles a minute so I don't have much of a headwind either. That's unusual heading northwest, but I'll take it! Plus, at 4,500 feet I can still enjoy the view on the ground too! Every time I fly I can't help but thinking, what do people do, that don't fly? To be up here looking down at the land, the lakes, the little towns, big cities and looking around at the clouds, I just can't help wondering, who am I, farm boy Les Hubbell to be able to do this? I said, "thank you God, for letting me do this."

I'm right over Kalamazoo and can see Lake Michigan on the horizon. Pretty hard to get lost on a day like this I thought! It isn't very long and I'm on the shoreline. I've crossed Lake Michigan several times already in single engine airplanes so I'm not at all concerned about it now. Especially since the lake is fairly calm and I'm on floats!

I remember the first time I crossed it though. Dad and I were going to visit my sister and her family in Grand Rapids, MI in the 170 N8006Alpha. We sold 06Alpha in 1968 so it was probably in 1967, so that was about six years ago already. Where does the time go? We left Cloquet and I climbed up to 9,500 ft heading for Green Bay. It was a nice clear day and we had about a 20 mph tailwind. I had measured the distance across the lake and from Manitowoc across to Ludington and it was about 55-60 miles. I had asked other pilots about flying across Lake Michigan and didn't find anyone that had done it. They all said, they'd either go to Mackinaw and then fly south to Grand Rapids or else go around Chicago and fly north to Grand Rapids. I thought, hmmm, if I'm going to do that I might as well drive my car! Besides, I figured, if Lindy can fly across the Atlantic, I can fly across Lake Michigan! I had also computed that from 9,500 ft, there would only be about five minutes out in the middle of the lake that if 06Alpha decided to throw a rod through the side of the case, that we might get wet. But I also knew that if she decided to throw a rod through the case taking off out of a lot of airports, I might be landing in the trees or on someone's roof! Dad wasn't concerned about flying over the lake so I wasn't either. I figured, when we crossed the shoreline, if I had good oil pressure, no oil on the windshield, and a lot of fuel, we're going! I've got to admit I was a little apprehensive the first time. It was a little hazy over the lake so I couldn't see the other side and I didn't have an instrument rating yet either. I just kept the wings level by looking at my venturie driven artificial horizon and held a heading. I found it was better not to even look outside for a while because I'd start getting some spatial disorientation even! It wasn't long and Dad said he could see the other shore! I thought, good I've got a horizon again! I bet Lindy felt like that when he saw land too! I've thought about his flight many times. I couldn't have done what Lindy did. First of all, I couldn't have stayed awake that long! Lindy didn't have hardly any instruments to look at I guess! And he couldn't even look forward except for a little periscope! I couldn't do that! Second, I don't like to go that long without sex! I've got to admit, I felt a little better when I knew we had the other shore of Lake Michigan made! My pucker factor went from about a 6 back down to 0!

Today though, in this brand new Cessna 180 on floats out over Lake Michigan, with only twenty, five hours total time on it, just enough where if someone had forgotten to tighten the rod bolts, I'd known it by now, my pucker factor is 0". My horny factor is getting up around 8 though! But at least I'm heading in the right direction! One thing nice about being in a floatplane out over Lake Michigan I thought, if the engine quits at least you don't have to look around for a good place to land! I realize however that even though the lake looks calm from up here that with any wind at all there are probably 3-4 foot rollers down there. I wouldn't have any problem landing 372 but it wouldn't be long and she'd weathervane into the wind and I'd be drifting backwards. Soon the tails of the floats would submerge, followed by the elevators and she'd be over on her back! I would have opened the door before she sank and swam out holding onto the floats spreader bars and end up sitting up on the floats. At least she's not going to sink! Hmmm, maybe I should have a life preserver when I do this? Maybe I should have a portable ELT too? Oh well, like I've always figured, "if you ain't living on the edge, your taking up too damned much space anyway!" Plus, I've known for years that God loves me and is always protecting me. He probably gets a little ticked at my jokes and lack of planning ahead and flippant attitude once in a while though I'm sure!

It's nice out here over the lake today. I can see the skyscrapers of Chicago on my left and Milwaukee off to my right and Racine should be, right about in the middle, I figured. What do people do that don't fly? I've often thought, when I can't go flying almost every day they might as well plant me in the ground. To me there are two basic needs in life, sex and flying airplanes! Well I admit, food and shelter are kind of important too!

I can see Madison, Wisconsin up ahead. I'll stay south of town I figured so I don't have to bother talking to the tower. Also, just like with wheels, when I'm flying floats I maintain my altitude until I've got the water made. Once I've got the lake just off the prop spinner I lowered the nose of 372 a little and started down. I descended down to about 700 ft over the lake and circled it to the left looking for the seaplane base. I don't see one. I don't even see a wind sock. I've got the same feelings I just had in Akron! I dialed up Madison tower and asked them if there was a seaplane base over here? They didn't think so. I've got a current chart even and it shows a seaplane base, where is it? I circled some more. Now I'm just looking for a boat ramp that would be handy for a fuel truck from the airport to come over and fuel me. I found one on the north side not too far from the airport. I called Madison unicom and told them I was flying a seaplane and I was over this big lake to the west and about the boat ramp, etc. and could they come and pump about 45 gallons in this thing? The lady said, "Yes, they will!" I said, "Can you send over a coke too?" She said, "Yes." I said, "Can you send over a couple of candy bars too?" She said, "Yes!" I figured this was just like the wife, once you got her saying yes, get everything you can! Do you want a new dress, yes, do you want to go out for supper, yes, do you want to go dancing, yes, do you want to have a few drinks, yes, do you want to have sex? yes! (sometimes)

Pretty soon the fuel truck arrived and I got up on the refueling steps and he handed me the hose. I topped 372 off and checked the oil. The driver gave me the coke and candy bars. I paid him and then I got on the left float and walked back to the tails of the floats, taking the weight off the fronts of them. The driver gave a shove and 372, was floating again! What little wind there was, was out of the south so I just let 372 weathervane into the wind and started up. I did a quick control check, felt the fuel selector was on both, checked the cowl flaps were open, dropped two notches of flaps, the water rudders were already up, brought the rpm's up to 1700, checked oil pressure, did a mag check, cycled the prop and poured the coals to her! I loved flying 372! I headed south and made a circling takeoff to the right and broke water heading for LaCrosse, Wisconsin! Luckily I had looked at my chart and noticed the restricted airspace at Camp McCoy so I needed to head a little west of a straight line to avoid that. I had heard they get pissed and want to talk to you if you fly through those. I climbed back up to 4,500 ft and set up cruise power, closed the cowl flaps, trimmed 372 up and slid my seat back a couple of notches and opened my coke and ate the candy bars. I flew 372 just like I used to ride a horse, I just neck reined her with a little rudder now and then to pick a wing up. I had 250 miles to go, a little more than two hours I figured with the headwind. Over La Crosse I turned right and pointed 372 toward Duluth. I always check oil pressure and temperature whenever I'm near or over water with a floatplane, just in case. 372, is running perfectly, I love her! I'm not going to tell the wife that though. She thinks I'm strange enough now, without her knowing I love

372 too! Besides, if she finds out I love an airplane she might tell me to go get my sex from it! Like I said, some doors just don't need to be opened! I remember reading someplace, better to keep your mouth shut and let people think you're a fool, than to open it and remove all doubt. Hmmm, I think that works with the wife too!

I can see the skyline of Duluth from 50 miles away! I called Halvair on unicom and got a message to Gene that I'd be landing at Sky Harbor in about 25 minutes. Sky Harbor is both a seaplane base and a land base so Gene flew down in a 172 and picked me up. Gene was always so enthusiastic about my trips! I thought, hmmm, of course he's happy, he's home having sex while I'm working and not getting anything! It was after 5:00 by the time we got back up to the airport, so we closed up the office and stopped by the officers club to, debrief. We just had one drink though because I was anxious to get home to see my family. I had called the wife from Sky Harbor and told her I was back. She said she had a nice roast supper ready for me. I thought, hmmm, maybe she does like me. As usual, the kids and Ginger rushed out to greet me, the wife was setting the table. It was a nice supper and I told them all about the great trip I'd had. (I didn't tell them about landing on the restricted lake though.) After the kids went to bed, the wife and I watched TV a little and I mixed her a few drinks. (I always figured, candy's dandy, liquors quicker!) We had three drinks and watched the news and then went to bed. I'm thinking, this is going to be great, I'm home, we had a great supper, I had a nice evening with the kids, Ginger was glad I was home, and the wife has had three drinks! She turned out the lights, took her clothes off and got in bed. I started rubbing her back and nibbling her neck and she said, "I've got my period." So much for hurrying home! I thought, hmmm, a man should be able to have two wives, one fourteen days out of sync with the other one!

The next day Gene flew me back down to Sky Harbor so I could fly 372 up to Grand Rapids. 372 needed to be uncowled so they could change the oil and inspect the engine before she left for Alaska. Then he flew the 172 up there and brought me back to Duluth.

On June 26th I flew the 210 N29276 down to Minneapolis and picked up Ken Bellows and Jack Bunch from Sitka, Alaska and took them up to Grand Rapids. Ken and Jack had come down to pick up 372 and take her to Sitka. I was going to miss 372, we'd had a lot of fun!

A couple of years later Ken sent me this picture of 372 sitting on Harlequim Lake near Yakutat, Alaska.

Chapter Sixteen
The Most Interesting Deal of My Career!

I was having a great time in the airplane business and now we had gone into an energy crisis about May of 1973! Gene and I would go a month or more without selling anything! We'd celebrate if we sold a little "Champ" even! It was like the world had stopped! We had been selling like great guns and now it just stopped! We weren't sure if we'd ever sell another new or used Cessna! And I was just getting started! I hated to think I'd have to go get a job! I never thought about selling airplanes as a job. To me it was just one great adventure after another! I loved it and didn't want it to end. But just like with the wife, there's some things I don't have any control over I guess.

Our Aero Commander sales rep from Rochester, Minnesota called me one day about the, first of October 1973. He told me he had been out to Jamestown, North Dakota showing a Commander and had heard about a farmer out there at Melville, about ten miles south of Carrington, that was going to buy a new pressurized Cessna Skymaster. He gave me the man's name and phone number and I thanked him!

That evening I called the man. His name was Mr. Reimers. He answered the phone and I said, "Mr. Reimers, this is Les Hubbell over here at Duluth and I heard that you're going to buy a new Skymaster from me!" He said, "Why the hell would I buy a Skymaster from somebody in Duluth?" I said, "Because I've got four hungry kids to feed, that's why." He kind of chuckled and said, "Yes, I've been there too, but you're wasting your time. I've bought my last four airplanes down in Texas and I'll probably buy the next one down there too." I said, "Well, just to keep Texas honest, tell me what you want on this Skymaster and I'll figure up a price for you." So he told me how he wanted it equipped and I spent an hour working up a quote. I called him back and read off the equipment and quoted him the price. Mr. Reimers said, "Well, you're only ten thousand dollars to high." I said, "No sir, I sell too many airplanes to be ten thousand dollars to high." He said, "Well, I'm telling you, you are." And I said, "I'm telling you I ain't." "But," I said, "maybe I hit the wrong button on my calculator, so I'll refigure it, and if I'm wrong I'll call you back." And he said, "If you ain't, don't." I checked all the options and re-added every thing twice and still came up with the same price.

The next morning I called Angelo Marasco, our Cessna district sales manager down at the Palwaukee airport in Chicago. I said, "Angelo, I've got a tough nut to crack out in North Dakota" and I told him about my conversation with Mr. Reimers and the price I had quoted and asked what else can I do? Angelo checked his inventory sheet and told me about a factory executive airplane that had 90 hours total time on it that I could sell for $10,000 less than a brand new one! It had de-icing boots, a flight director, strobes, leather interior, everything! I couldn't wait to call Mr. Reimers than evening! About 7 pm I called him and told him about N86Charlie at $10,000 less than a brand new one! He said he'd be interested in seeing it. I asked him if he'd wire me a $1,000 dollar deposit and I'd go get the airplane and bring it to him. He said, "No, I'm not going to do that." I asked him if I went to Wichita and brought it out to him would he buy it? He said, "I can't guarantee you that either, but I'd look at it." I asked, "If you do like it, are you in financial position to buy it?" He gave me his banker's name and number and said I could call him and ask him if he can afford to buy it or not. I detected a little sarcasm in his voice though. The next morning I called the banker and told him that I was going to bring Mr Reimers a new Cessna Pressurized Skymaster to look at for about $100,000 dollars and if he likes it can he get financing? The banker said, "he won't need no financing" and hung up on me! I thought, hmmm, yes I think Mr. Reimers can buy a $100,000 Skymaster if he wants to.

I talked to Gene about this deal and asked him if I could go to Wichita and get 86Charlie and go demo it to Mr. Reimers? Gene figured we didn't have much of anything else happening so he talked to the Vice President of Halvair, Tom Halvorson about it and then they said I might as well go do it!

So I packed my bags and got on a jet to Wichita! A Cessna rep picked me up at the terminal and drove me over to where 86Charlie was parked. I signed some paper work and they gave me the keys and logbooks. I had never flown a pressurized Skymaster so I spent some time with the operator's manual and then filed IFR to Jamestown, North Dakota. The weather was near lousy. About a 500 ft ceiling at Wichita and the same in Jamestown with 1-2 miles visibility in fog. I took off out of Wichita and climbed up to 10,000 ft and leveled off. The tops were a lot higher that day so I was going to be in the clouds all the way to Jamestown. I got leveled off and set up for cruise and turned the autopilot on. Then I sat back and studied the manual. I figured, I can't see, nothing outside anyway so I might as well study. Besides, I just knew I better know this airplane inside and out if I'm going to have a chance of selling it to Mr. Reimers. I suspected this would be one of those times that I wouldn't be able to, "dazzle him with my brilliance or baffle him with my bullshit!" So I studied and looked at the instruments and gauges, studied and looked at the instruments and gauges, studied and looked at the instruments and gauges until about 50 miles from Jamestown and then started planning the approach into Jamestown. The Jamestown weather was about 500 overcast and 3 miles visibility so I was going to do the ILS runway 31 approach and then I needed a special VFR out of the control zone. That all worked out good. When I broke out on the ILS at about 500 feet I cancelled IFR and got a special VFR out of the control zone to the northwest. Mr. Reimers had told me to over fly the airport and to stay between the highway and, that big lake to the east and to fly northwest and then I'll see his grass strip about a mile east of Melville, North Dakota. I had no problem spotting his strip from five miles away. It was a nice grass strip and about 2,500ft long. I landed to the northwest and taxied right into Mr. Reimer's farmyard. He and another man were over by a corn dryer and I parked about 75 feet from them. By the time I got out of the airplane Mr. Reimers came over. I introduced myself and we walked around the airplane. He noticed the only two chips on the airplane! I reminded him that it had 90 hrs on it and we had to expect it would have a few chips and that's why it's ten thousand dollars less that a brand new one. I just new I was in for a dog, fight! He was busy and I'd had a long day so he let me use one of his pickup trucks to go to town and get something to eat and to find a motel. I left him the operator's manual to look over.

I found a nice motel with a restaurant, the Chieftain Motel in Carrington, and had supper and a couple of beers and called it a day, I was tired.

About 12:30 am I was awaken by thunderstorms! It was blowing and raining to beat hell and I've got a new airplane sitting outside and not tied down! I hurried and got dressed and drove back out to Mr. Reimer's farm. 86Charlie, was rocking back and forth a lot so I parked the truck right in front of her to protect her from the wind. I sat up and kept an eye on 86Charlie for about half an hour and she was sitting fairly still so I laid on the seat and went to sleep. I woke up a couple of hours later and the thunderstorms had passed and 86Charlie was still on her wheels, so I drove back to the Chieftain motel and went back to sleep until about 8 am. When I woke up, I was still tired. I had breakfast and drove out to the farm. Mr. Reimers invited me in for a cup of coffee and introduced me to his wife Carol. She was very nice. She told me they also had two children, Ann and Steve who were grown up and living out east.

Then Mr. Reimers and I discussed the operator's manual for a while and went out to fly 86Charlie. It was blowing about 25-30 mph out of the west. Of course, since I'd been out to Johnson's so many times, I know it's always blowing 25-30 mph in the Dakota's. I remember asking Johnson one day if it's always so windy out here? He said, "No, one day the wind all of a sudden quit, and everyone in the state fell over!"

Mr. Reimers and I did a thorough pre-flight on 86 Charlie and climbed in. He already owned a non-pressurized Skymaster so he was familiar with the systems except for the pressurization system. I had studied the manual and had flown pressurized 421's so I of course acted like I knew everything about it!

He used the checklist and had no problem starting the airplane. I showed him where the avionics master switch was and he turned it on and we had radios! I thought he'd taxi down to his grass strip but instead he taxied out his driveway to the highway. He stopped and looked left and right and then turned left and parked it in the middle of the highway, heading west into the wind. I said, "Boy it was nice of the county to put in a runway for you right off the end of your driveway." Mr. Reimers just kind of grinned. He did a run up sitting there and then we started the takeoff run. I confirmed with him that we were in fact going to stay on the highway until we passed under the power lines crossing the highway about 500 feet ahead. He looked at me like, of course we are you idiot. I just wanted to make sure. We took off and climbed up to 15,000 feet checking out the pressurization and the flight director. We had worked our way down to Jamestown so we set up for the ILS approach and just watched how the flight director followed the localizer and then coupled to the glideslope. It was like 86Charlie was glued to the ILS. I could tell Mr. Reimers liked that. He was impressed by how quiet it was compared to his Skymaster. We landed at Jamestown and went into the FBO for a break and then got back into 86Charlie and flew back and landed on his grass strip. Mr. Reimers was a good pilot. But then I've never seen a farmer that didn't have a good feeling for an airplane. They are so used to operating hydraulics that they just naturally have a good feel for airplane controls.

Mrs. Reimers invited me for supper so I went back to the motel and showered and cleaned up a little before supper. I figured if I didn't shower and clean up a little it would be like the time I made a forced landing in the woods in Alaska. Unfortunately there was no water near by to bath in. So for the first week I'd burn a big fire to keep the bears away. After the first week, the bears started fires to keep me away!

The Reimers had a large social room in the basement. It had a bar on one end and a kitchenette on the other end with a nice wood table that was about ten feet long and four feet wide.

They had invited some friends and relatives over also. I just happened to be behind the bar mixing myself a drink, (imagine that!) when the friends and relatives arrived. Mr. Reimers introduced me as the "longhaired aircraft salesman from Duluth." He said, "Mix them a drink while your back there Hubbell." I said, "I might as well, the tips will probably be the only money I make while I'm out here!"

We had a super good steak supper with all the trimmings and then pie for desert. I couldn't have eaten one more bite. They were all great people and I had a good time visiting with them. I went back to the motel and called the wife. The kids were already in bed sleeping.

The next morning Mr. Reimers and I sat in 86Charlie and discussed the pressurized system, flight director, and de-icing system some more. Then he started it up and we tax-ied back out onto the road and took off and went back down to Jamestown and flew another ILS and made a couple more landings.

It was harvest time and Mr. Reimers still had a farm to run and quite a few employees to overlook so we landed back on the farm about lunchtime. I noticed that when Mr. Reimers told one of the employees to do something it was, "yes sir," or "no sir" and they hopped to it! Mrs. Reimers had made a lunch for us and then Mr. Reimers and I went into his office to discuss price. We were about $5,000 dollars apart from what he wanted to buy it for and what I needed to sell it for. So we were haggling back and forth a little. I went out to the kitchen to get a cup of coffee and Mrs. Reimers came over to me and said, "Les, I hope you realize his bite is not as bad as his bark." I said, "I think I'm getting the idea" and thanked her. I thought, Mr. Reimers is sure lucky to have a wife like her. And I could tell that she was the, apple of Mr. Reimer's eyes, too. I wished my marriage, was like theirs.

I knew Mr. Reimers wanted 86Charlie so I held my ground. I hadn't built a whole lot into the price in the first place and by the time I deducted the airline ticket to Wichita, my motel room, meals, etc. and my time that it was not going to be a fat deal anyway. I think Mr. Reimers got tired of listening to me whine and finally agreed that the price was fair but wouldn't commit to buy the airplane yet.

That night they invited some more company over and Mr. Reimers introduced me again as "the longhaired aircraft salesman from Duluth." I was almost starting to feel like I was an oddity out here in North Dakota! But we had steaks and drinks again and every one was very nice to me.

The next morning the ceiling was low, about 500 feet and about 3 miles visibility. Mr. Reimers wanted to go back down to Jamestown and do a couple of approaches to get some more instrument time in the airplane and get more familiar with the flight director. So I filed IFR down to Jamestown and we got back in 86 Charlie and this time he taxied down to the southeast end of his grass strip for takeoff. He did his run up and asked me if I was ready to go. I said, "Turn her loose but stay VFR until I can talk to Jamestown radio and get a clearance." We took off and in the process I dropped my pencil. When I looked up we were in the clouds! I said, "What happened to staying VFR Mr. Reimers?" I helped him get it leveled off and made a left turn to the south to stay in the uncontrolled airspace. Finally, Jamestown radio answered me and I got a clearance to climb to 6,000 feet direct to the Jamestown VOR and to expect the ILS 31 approach. I had reached a point where I figured I wasn't getting very far being a nice guy any more so I was going to start giving Mr. Reimers back some of the guff he was giving me. He wanted to turn on the flight director and I said, "It's not working." He said, "Dang it, what the hell am I going to do now?" I said, "Hand fly it." We were climbing through 4,000 going to 6,000 when I noticed the Jamestown VOR go out of service. I didn't say anything for a minute or so and then I asked, "Where are you going Mr. Reimers?" "I'm going to Jamestown, dang it!" Everything was "dang it" with Mr. Reimers. I said, "How are you going to get there?" He said, "Dang it, I'm going to the VOR, that's how I'm going to get there! I said, "The Jamestown VOR went off the air two minutes ago," as I pointed to the red flag in the instrument. "Dang it, what are we going to do now?" I looked at my low chart and said, "Well, let's go to Aberdeen then." So I called center and reported the Jamestown VOR out of service and asked for direct to Aberdeen and got a clearance for that. I flipped through the Aberdeen approaches and saw the ILS 31 and thought, that's for me! When center asked what approach I wanted, I requested the ILS 31 approach and got a clearance for that via the 13 DME arc. I wondered if Mr. Reimers had ever done an approach via the DME arc before?

I had to help Mr. Reimers intercept the arc and then stay on it until we intercepted the localizer. We were in the clouds the whole time so it was great! I said, "Mr. Reimers, I think if I spent a few more days with you, I could make a pretty good instrument pilot out of you." He said, "Dang it, I think you could." I had him hand fly 86Charlie right on down the ILS until we broke out and had the lights. Then we taxied in and had a cup of coffee at Aberdeen Flying Service. I liked Mr. Reimers and I realized that, his bite's not as bad as his bark, just like Mrs. Reimers had told me. One of the best gifts a man can get in this life is a wife like Mrs. Reimers, I figured. She knew and respected her husband. I don't think I have that.

That evening it was steaks and drinks again! Just about like Northland Homes! I'd still only have maybe two drinks being we were flying in the morning. But I was sitting there thinking as we were eating, that I haven't sold this airplane yet and it's not going to be good to go back to Duluth with a bunch of expenses and no sale. So I've got to fish or cut bait here pretty soon. We were sitting at this big table. Mr. Reimers was on my left at the end of the table and Mrs. Reimers was across the table from me. Finally I said, "Mr. Reimers are you going to buy 86Charllie or not?" (I hadn't learned yet to never ask a question that you might not like the answer to.) Mr. Reimers said, "No Hub, (that was the first time he had called me Hub) I'm not. I've taken a liking to you but I'm not going to buy that airplane." I asked, "Why not?" He said, "Because it's got 10,000 dollars worth of equipment on it that I don't need." I said, "Like the flight director and boots?" He said, "Yes." I said, "Mr. Reimers, what I'm going to tell you right now is going to ruin any chance I ever had of selling you this airplane, but it's going to save your life." He said, "What's that?" I said, "You're a hell of a good farmer or you wouldn't be looking at buying a 100,000 dollar airplane, but sir, you're not a professional pilot. If you take that lady there," as I pointed across the table to Mrs. Reimers, "and think that you're going to fly back and forth to Texas as often as you do, without getting a load of ice, or have to shoot an approach down to minimums at a strange airport without that equipment, you're a damned fool." Boy it got quiet in there. I knew Mr. Reimers was the chairman of the house appropriations committee for North Dakota and I'm sure no one had ever talked to him like this before.

He said, "I'll tell you in the morning." I said, "Tell me right now. I spent the first night here sleeping in your pickup parked in front of 86Charlie and you've had me so nervous ever since that I haven't had a good nights sleep anyway, so tell me right now." He said, "Dang it, I think you've sold an airplane!"

Just then the phone rang. I couldn't have planned that better if I had tried! Mrs. Reimers answered it. She said to Mr. Reimers, "It's the Minneapolis

Mr. Reimers at the North Dakota
House of Representatives

grain exchange wanting to know if you're coming to the meeting tomorrow?" Mr. Reimers said, "Tell them no, the weather is too bad." I said, "It's not too bad for the airplane you just bought Mr. Reimers." He said, "Are you going with me?" I said, "Yes sir, I'll go with you." He said to Mrs. Reimers, "Tell them I'll be there!"

The next morning Mr. and Mrs. Reimers and I got into 86Charlie and took off for St Paul, Minnesota. The weather was still about a 500 ft ceiling and 3 miles visibility. I had filed us IFR at 7,000 feet. We climbed up and leveled off at 7,000 feet solid on instruments and Mr. Reimers turned the autopilot/flight director on. After about 30 minutes, Mrs. Reimers tapped me on the shoulder and told me they had never flown in ice before and asked me if I had noticed the ice building on the wing struts and wings and should we be concerned about it? I said, "Yes I had noticed it and if Mr. Reimers would push that de-ice switch over there we'll get rid of it." Mr. Reimers said, "Well, dang it, we might as well see if it works," and he pressed the switch. Pretty soon the boots expanded and the ice was gone. Mr. Reimers said to Mrs. Reimers, "See how nice that works," and she felt better. And then I said, "Now Mr. Reimers, if you push that pitot heat switch maybe we won't lose our airspeed indicator." I couldn't have timed that better either. Just after I said that, the airspeed went to O! He said, "Well dang it, we might as well see if that works too!" I knew it was going to be a while before we got the airspeed indicator back because those flush mounted heaters aren't as fast as pitot tubes, and I also new the tops were at 8,000 feet so I called center and requested 15,000 and got it. I thought it would be good for Mr. Reimers to know that he could fly above most of the ice with 86Charlie. Mr. Reimers was all smiles once he got his airspeed indicator back and was on top of the clouds. Mrs. Reimers was comfortable again too!

The St Paul weather was VFR so the rest of the flight was routine and Mr. Reimers greased 86Charlie onto runway 32 and we taxied in and parked near the base of the tower. They were going to be in St Paul for a couple of days so I took off and headed for Duluth. There were a couple of minor squawks on 86Charlie that our shop in Duluth could fix and I had a major squawk myself that the wife could help me fix!

It was nice to get back home to my family for a couple of days. I don't sleep very, good unless I'm in my own bed. Hmmm, I wonder why?

Also, it gave me a chance to meet with Gene and to explain to him what the trade in was and what I was allowing Mr. Reimers for his trade-in etc, etc. I still couldn't believe that he was letting me do all this running around without having a deposit first! But he was glad to learn that it looked like it was going to work out. Of course he and I both realized that the deal, isn't done, until it's done.

The shop had the minor squawks on 86Charlie fixed and I had my major squawk fixed so it was time to go back to work!

I had asked Mr. Reimers to give me a call at home in the evening to let me know when they would want to leave St Paul. He had called and said he'd like to leave St Paul at 10 in the morning so I was up early and out to the airport by 8. Even though the weather was VFR, I filed an IFR flight plan to St Paul via V13 with a 30minute stop in St Paul and then V2 to Jamestown. I had already learned that it's just easier, and safer to fly IFR into and out of a busy metropolitan area. I took off at 8:30 and climbed up to 10 thousand heading down victor 13. I liked 86Charlie! Of course she had a pretty good rate of climb with the turbochargers and as light as I was, with just me and full tanks! And with the pressurization she was relatively quiet too! It was a beautiful morning, not a cloud in the sky! I like early morning takeoffs! Come to think about it, I like night takeoffs too! My only fear in life is when I can't go flying almost every day, and make love every night! Now if I could just get the wife to feel that way, but she doesn't like flying that much, come to think about it, I'm not sure she likes to make love that much either! I don't think I'll ask her either! I think that's another question that I might not like the answer to!

It was only going to be about a two hour flight from St Paul to Jamestown and up to Mr. Reimers farm bucking a little headwind so I didn't bother topping 86Charlie off when I got to St Paul.

Mr. and Mrs. Reimers were waiting for me so we "loaded up and headed out," as we say out on the farm! I did the radio work for Mr. Reimers and when I called ground I told them we were IFR to Jamestown and requested runway 14. Soon I copied a clearance to Jamestown as filed with a left turn after takeoff direct to Gopher and V2 to Jamestown and climb to 10 thousand. It doesn't get much simpler than that I thought!

Mr. Reimers was becoming very comfortable with 86Charlie and was doing a good job with her. But then he probably had a couple thousand hours in Skymasters already so that helped. Mostly he just needed to learn how to handle the turbos without over boosting them on takeoff, especially the first takeoff when the oil isn't warmed up yet. And he needed to become more familiar with the autopilot/flight director. Everything else was pretty much like the Skymaster he already owned, just newer! Of course you don't get to the position in life that Mr. Reimers had achieved unless your pretty "dang" smart, got a lot of guts, worked hard and long, and maybe have a little dumb luck and it sure helps to have a wife like Mrs. Reimers too. He had done good! And he was enjoying flying 86Charlie.

After we passed the Fargo VOR, I had Mr. Reimers tune the ADF to the Valley City NDB 382 and instructed him to call center passing it and request a descent down to six thousand. I'm not sure if he noticed the needle turning first, or just looked down and saw Valley City, but he called center and requested six thousand and got it. I just figured it would be good practice for him. Just after Fargo I had asked Mr. Reimers how he determined when to let down? I said, "When your flying down low VFR it doesn't matter much." I said, "I just hold altitude until I've got my destination airport or lake whatever, just off the nose of the airplane and then I lower the nose and adjust the power for whatever speed and descent I need to maintain that sight picture. Works for me"! "But," I said, "now that you've got a pressurized airplane, you're probably going to be up in the 10-15 thousand altitudes a lot." I said, "When you're IFR, center will get you down, but if your flying VFR, then you need to determine when to start down." I said, "One thing you don't want to do with turbos is all of a sudden realize that your airport is ten miles ahead and your at ten thousand feet and close both throttles to get down while the turbos are red hot." I said, "That's a sure way to crack turbo housings and you can kiss $5,000 dollars each good-bye to replace them." I figured I'd put it in a language that Mr. Reimers could more easily relate to. I said, "How many bushels of corn would you have to sell to pay for that mistake Mr. Reimers?" He just looked at me and smiled. I liked Mr. Reimers. I knew he liked me too. I told him the formula I use for determining when to start down. "Being we are up at 10 thousand feet," I said, "all I'd do is subtract your airport elevation from your altitude, in this case that's 1,500 ft from 10,000 for 8,500, forget the 500 ft and multiply the 8 by 5 and we'll start down 40 miles out. That will generally give me a rate of descent of 750 ft a minute and I can vary that pretty easy with airspeed and power as needed. That works for me!" And it worked for Mr. Reimers that day too! And I reminded him again, to always warm the turbos up slow and cool them down slow too!

Over Jamestown we cancelled IFR and turned right to track the 315 radial outbound toward his grass strip thirty miles away. Of course, Mr. Reimers had no problem locating his strip. He had been here many times before. We landed back on his grass strip and he parked "86Charlie" right up near the corn dryer where I had parked it when I first got there. It had been a great trip, CAVU all the way from St Paul and not a bump even!

Mrs. Reimers made us a sandwich and some soup for lunch and then Mr. Reimers said, "Let's go for a ride, I need to go check something up at the grain elevator." It turned out he also owned a grain elevator about ten miles north of the farm. When we got there he introduced me to the guy running it as "the long haired aircraft salesman from Duluth." He said, "Be nice to him; he's going to be coming to work for me." That was the first I had heard about that! He finished talking to the guy and we got in the pickup and were driving back to the farm. About halfway back he said, "What do you think of that?" I said, "What do I think of what Mr. Reimers?" He said, "Going to work for me, dang it!" I said, "Mr. Reimers, I don't know corn from gravel." He said, "Well, dang it, you could learn!" I said, "Yes, I guess I could, but then I'd have to call you "sir" like all these other guys around here do Mr. Reimers, and I just ain't very good at that." He said, "Dang it, I wouldn't expect you to." "Besides," I said, "my wife is an only child and there's no way I could ask her to move the kids away from her parents over in Cloquet." I said, "I really appreciate the offer Mr. Reimers, but I know she won't want to move out of Duluth and I really couldn't expect her to."

It was kind of quiet for the rest of the drive back to the farm. And I'm thinking, well there goes this deal. But when we got back Mr. Reimers said, "Let's get the paper work done." So we went into his office and I penned out a purchase order and a bill of sale. He called his banker and had him make up a cashier's check and we drove into town and picked it up. I got to meet the banker that had hung up on me. He looked just about exactly as I had imagined he would! And, I had the feeling that the cashier's check had hardly put a dent in Mr. Reimers bank balance. I wonder if I'd ever reach that point in life? I doubted it.

When we got back to the farm it was late afternoon and I asked Mr. Reimers if I could use the pickup to go to the motel. He said, you can stay here tonight. I felt honored that they'd invite me to stay at their house. I knew then for sure that Mr. Reimers liked me. I was also feeling very sad that I couldn't work for him and be his pilot, because I liked him too.

Just like about every other night they had company over and we had another great steak dinner and a few drinks! Everyone was very nice to me! But then, they had never met a "longhaired aircraft salesman from Duluth" before! I couldn't help but imagining Mr. Reimers laughing on the telephone as he was inviting his friends to, "come over and see this longhaired aircraft salesman from Duluth!" I didn't think my hair was that long though. Hmmm, the wife never told me my hair was to long? Neither had anyone else?

The next morning after breakfast we pulled Mr. Reimers 1967 Skymaster N373Echo out of his hangar and put 86Charlie back in it.

Mr. Reimers and son Steve by N373Echo

I shook hands and said good-bye and thank you, "sir." He said, "take care of yourself." I was feeling very sad. I respected and liked Mr. Reimers very much. He was just like his wife had said, "his bite was nowhere near as bad as his bark." If I had been single or my family situation was different, I would have stayed and been Mr. Reimers pilot.

A week later Mr. and Mrs. Reimers flew over to Duluth and took the wife and me out for supper at the Highland supper club and tried to convince the wife that I should be his pilot. I was really honored that they thought that much of me, but I knew the wife wouldn't want to move out of the state. And I couldn't blame her. Her parents and all of her relatives were only about twenty-five miles away and they were a close knit family too.

The next summer Mrs. Reimers called me and said that Mr. Reimers was running for Governor of North Dakota and asked me if he won, would I come out and fly the State of North Dakota airplane for them? I told her that I would be proud to be their pilot if Mr. Reimers became Governor. That was the best compliment that I'd ever had in my life, that Mr. and Mrs. Reimers would want me to be their state pilot. I didn't give any thought about what I was going to do about the wife, but figured I'd deal with that if and when the time came.

Unfortunately though, Mr. Reimers lost the primary. I believe he would have been a great Governor of the State of North Dakota. I couldn't imagine why he had lost the primary.

Over the years anytime I was in North Dakota showing or selling an airplane and I was within, 150 miles or so of Carrington I'd call the Reimers. If Mr. Reimers answered the phone I'd always say, "Mr. Reimers, do you remember Les Hubbell?" Mr. Reimers would always say, "How the hell could I ever forget." Then we'd both laugh! I'd say, "I'm down here in Oake's or over here in Larimore" or wherever, "and how about I fly up there and take you and Mrs. Reimers out to lunch?" He'd always say, "you fly up here and we'll take you to lunch." It was always nice to visit with the Reimers.

And also, unfortunately, Mr. Reimers lost his race with life on September 3rd, 2003. He was 80 years old and had come down with pneumonia and a congestive heart problem. I was devastated when I was told that he had died and felt a huge lose. I had gained a great amount of respect and caring for both Mr. and Mrs. Reimers because of my dealings and flying 86 Charlie with him and our occasional telephone calls and visits over the years.

While I was attending his funeral in Carrington, North Dakota on September 8th, 2003 and reading his obituary, I learned why he had become so important to me. He was born June 15th, so was I, his mother's name was Clara, so was mine, he was raised on a farm, so was I, he married a Norwegian, so did I, he had learned to, and loved flying, so did I. And his bite, wasn't as bad as his bark, neither is mine. Other than him being 14 years older than me, we were twins.

I'll forever miss being able to call him and say, "Mr. Reimers, do you remember Les Hubbell? And hear him say. " How the hell could I ever forget."

Chapter Seventeen

About the last week of October 1973 Gene asked me if I'd demo a 337 for him down at Maple Lake, Minnesota, just west of Minneapolis about 30 miles. Gene figured I was a lot more current in 337's than he was, being I had just spent so much time flying 86Charlie and bringing that trade back to Duluth from Carrington. And of course, I said I would. He had been talking to Bill Mavencamp Sr. who operated the Maple Lake Airport. So the next day I flew the 337 down there. That was the first time I had met Bill Mavencamp Sr. and his son, Bill Jr. We test flew the 337 and Bill Sr. said he liked the airplane and wanted to know if he could fly it to Montana, to go mule deer hunting? That was a decision I couldn't make so I called Gene and asked him. Much to my surprise, Gene said yes! So Bill Sr. gave me a ride back up to Duluth. About a week later Bill Sr. was back from hunting and called me. He said he liked the airplane except for one thing, he didn't like the Cessna radios. He said, "if it had King radios I'd buy it." I said that's not a problem, I've got another one just about like it that's got King radios!

So the next day I flew the other 337, N373Echo back down to Maple Lake. It was a raw windy day and I had a little headache so I told Bill Mavencamp Sr. and Bill Jr. that they sure didn't need me to go fly with them. I said, "I'm going to take a couple of aspirins while you guys go check 373Echo out." I found some water and took a couple of aspirins and leaned against the south wall, out of the wind, of a little white building, and watched them takeoff.

Pretty soon another man arrived. He asked me what I was doing and I told him, I was demoing an airplane to Bill Mavencamp Sr. but I had a headache so didn't go with them. He introduced himself, he was "Dr, Williams" he said, "and he was a veterinarian from Eden Valley and he was looking for a 172." I said, "I've got a nice one!" I told him about a 1971 model we had. He said, it sounded just like what he was looking for and we agreed on a price. He wanted to know if I would deliver it to Paynesville, Minnesota? I said, "in fact next weekend I'm driving out to South Dakota to go pheasant hunting and will be passing right through Paynesville!" I said, " I could fly the 172 to Paynesville and the wife could drive to Paynesville and pick me up!" So I told him all about the 172 and how nice it was and he agreed to buy it, if it was like I told him it was, of course.

Within thirty minutes Bill Sr. and Bill Jr. were back and landed. They didn't find anything operationally wrong with 373Echo so they put it in the hangar and did compression checks and opened a few inspection plates to look it over for corrosion. And they removed the oil filters and checked them for metal and they were clean. They couldn't find any thing wrong with 373Echo, so Bill Sr. bought it!

Years later I'd hear Bill Sr. tell the story about when, " I had brought this Cessna 337 down from Duluth for him to inspect. And how he had flown it to Montana hunting etc, but now he had gotten his hunting trip in and was back home and not sure if he could really afford to buy it so he was look-ing for an excuse not to." So he had told me that, "he liked the airplane but he didn't like the Cessna radios, and if it had King radios he's buy it." I said, "that's no problem, I've got another one almost identical to it that has King radios!" He'd say, "what could I do, I had to buy the dam thing!"

So Friday I flew the 172 to Paynesville and showed it to Dr. Williams. He was very pleased with the condition, the avionics and how it flew, so he bought it! We did the paper work and he gave me a cashiers check. About the time we were putting it in a hangar, the wife and kids arrived. That sure made my month, to sell a 337 to Bill Mavencamp Sr. and then a 172 to Dr, Williams! And I needed it!

I came into the office one day and Gene was in an especially good mood! He had sold a new Cessna 210 and Tom Halvorson had just given him a copy of the letter that the

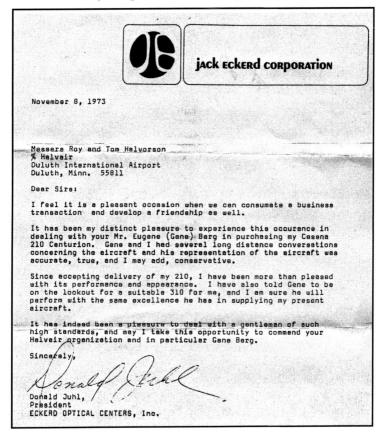

jack eckerd corporation

November 8, 1973

Messers Roy and Tom Halvorson
% Halvair
Duluth International Airport
Duluth, Minn. 55811

Dear Sirs:

I feel it is a pleasant occasion when we can consumate a business transaction and develop a friendship as well.

It has been my distinct pleasure to experience this occurence in dealing with your Mr. Eugene (Gene) Berg in purchasing my Cessna 210 Centurion. Gene and I had several long distance conversations concerning the aircraft and his representation of the aircraft was accurate, true, and I may add, conservative.

Since accepting delivery of my 210, I have been more than pleased with its performance and appearance. I have also told Gene to be on the lookout for a suitable 310 for me, and I am sure he will perform with the same excellence he has in supplying my present aircraft.

It has indeed been a pleasure to deal with a gentleman of such high standards, and may I take this opportunity to commend your Halvair organization and in particular Gene Berg.

Sincerely,

Donald Juhl,
President
ECKERD OPTICAL CENTERS, Inc.

customer had written to him and Roy, with a copy to Duane Wallace at Cessna. I congratulated Gene! And I bought him a drink at the officer's club later too to celebrate!

December of 1973 was very quiet in the airplane business because of the energy crisis. And I also figured, it's hard, to compete with Santa Clause too!

Just for something to do on January 16th, 1974 I took our new Cessna 180 N46069 and made a trip to Brainerd, Staples, Park Rapids, Detroit Lakes and out to Valley City, North Dakota showing it to people and spent the night there. The next morning I went to Cooperstown, Larimore, and Grafton, North Dakota showing it and was heading back home. The only problem was, I needed to use a bathroom pretty bad! Pretty soon I saw a grass strip coming up at Hallock, Minnesota. So I slowed up, dropped full flaps and landed and taxied as close to the "T" hangars as I could get. I got out and there were three guys standing there. I asked them where the bathroom was? One of the guys said, "Right over there behind that "T" hangar." I walked behind the "T" hangar and lowered my manifold pressure.

That kind of reminded me of the time my mother was complaining to my Dad about me writing my name in the snow out behind the barn when I'd take a leak. My Dad told her that was no problem and that, in fact when he was a kid he'd done the same thing. My mother said, "Yes but this is in, Suzzy's hand writing!"

When I came back from behind the "T" hangar, I went over and introduced myself to the three guys standing there and gave them my card. One of the guys was Maurice Sugdon, the other guy was Charlie Cedarholm, and believe it or not, the third guy was John Deere, just like the tractor! I never forgot that!

About the 20th of January 1974, Herb Evers from Cloquet called me and asked me how the airplane business was? I said, "Horse shit!" He said, "Good!" I said, "What the hell's good about that Herbie?" He said, "I want you to go into business with me down in Arizona." "What are you going to do down there?" "I'm looking at a hardware store in Coolidge Arizona," he said. I said, "Well, I've got to deliver an airplane to Texas, so I'll get on a jet and go over to Phoenix and rent a car and drive on down there and look at it."

A few days later I delivered the airplane to Texas and then got on a jet and went to Phoenix and rented a car and drove on down to Coolidge. It wasn't hard to find the hardware store. It was a big old corrugated metal building. I went in and introduced myself to the old guy behind the counter and told him Herb Evers had asked me to come down and look at his store. I walked around and looked at all the valves, tools, electrical stuff, etc. etc. and etc. I thought to myself, I'd sure hate to have to do inventory on all this stuff! And then I thought, I can't, just sell $3.50 worth of something. I've got to be selling $35,000 worth of something! I thanked the old guy and asked him where I'd find a motel for the night. He recommended the Francisco Grande out west of Casa Grande. So I drove on down to Casa Grande and out west about five miles to the Francisco Grande. It was a first class place out in the middle of the desert. I checked in and cleaned up a little and went down to the restaurant. It turned out the Francisco Grande was the winter training camp for the San Francisco Giants.

After dinner I thought it would be impolite if I didn't have a drink in the bar, so I did. And there across from me on the wall was a picture of Carl Hubbell. He had been a pitcher for the Giants some years back. It was good I thought to have a famous relative.

The next morning I drove back up to Phoenix and turned the rental car in and caught the next jet to Wichita and picked up a new Cessna 180 N46361 and brought that back to Duluth on the 6th of February.

I had been gone five days so my horny factor was up to a "9"! That's like, mayday, mayday, mayday, I need some help! I think the wife figured I just had her around for sex! That wasn't true! She kept a neat house too!

I called Herb and told him I didn't think I wanted to be in the hardware business and that I didn't think I wanted to live in Coolidge, Arizona either. He said he was thinking of living in Casa Grande and I said I kind of liked Casa Grande as I drove through there.

On the 11th of February I went down to Rochester and picked up a Cessna 206 and flew it out to Vermillion, South Dakota and demo'd it for Gene. I ended up spending the night and taking it back to Rochester the next day. No sale. (No sale, no house payment!)

Chapter Eighteen
Buying a Business and Houses

About the middle of February, Herb and I got back on a jet and flew down to Phoenix. We rented a car and enjoyed the drive down to Casa Grande and couldn't help commenting about the difference between driving to the airport in Minnesota this morning on icy roads and now driving through the desert in the afternoon!

When we arrived in Casa Grande we drove around for a while just getting a feel for the town. We liked, Casa Grande, it felt good. It was late afternoon by the time we finished touring the town so we drove out to the Francisco Grande and checked in. Naturally it had been a long stressful day so we figured we better stop in the bar for a little un-stressing therapy. And of course, I couldn't help pointing out to Herbie that there was a famous Hubbell picture on the wall behind the bar but I didn't see any famous Evers pictures around. I told him that if he bought the drinks though that I'd consider him famous in my mind at least. That didn't work. In fact, I ended up buying the drinks!

The next morning after breakfast we drove back over to Casa Grande and met with a realtor. They showed us the business's that, they knew were for sale, an apartment building, a couple of bars, a laundromat, and an automotive service garage. Herbie didn't want anything to do with fixing cars anymore, he'd done that. Finally they told us about an appliance and furniture store, CG Mart. (Casa Grande Mart.) That sounded kind of interesting so we drove over and took a look at that. It wasn't a real big store, but just about right for us we figured. It was about half "n" half furniture and appliances. We thought it would be just right. The girls could sell the furniture and we'd sell appliances!

We looked around town for another day and didn't see anything we liked better so the next morning we got together with the realtor and the two guys, Gene and John that owned CG Mart. After a few hours of talking and looking at their financials, etc., we cut a deal! Of course, this was the middle of February and we weren't going to move to Casa Grand until after the kids were out of school in June. So we made a deal and signed a purchase agreement and put a deposit on it with the closing being finalized when we arrived back in Casa Grande sometime in June.

Well now we had a business but no place to live so we started driving around town looking at houses. Herbie found one with a swimming pool so I dropped him off at the realtor's office to check it out. I wasn't interested in a pool for several reasons, so I kept driving around looking. I ended up northest of town a mile or so at a sub-division called Rancho Grande. It was out in the desert and had been developed by a guy from Minnesota, a Johnson I think. Johnson's are good I thought. The southern part of the development was older homes and they got newer as he built north I noticed. I drove up and down the streets looking and didn't see anything I was interested in until I was on the last street on the north, heading west. It was a strange feeling. I saw a for sale sign coming up, for sale by owner. From the first I saw this house I liked it. The first thing I liked about it was that it was all stone and brick because I hate painting, I thought. I got where I hated painting after painting the rooms in Sunnyside

Motel every winter. One thing that was strange to me look-ing at houses in Casa Grande was, that there are no garages, just carports. I thought, what the hell do they do when it gets 20 below zero! Of course, I realized that it doesn't happen down here! If it gets down to 30 degrees I'd be surprised, I thought.

I pulled into the carport and got out and rang the doorbell. Soon a lady opened the door. I introduced myself and explained what I was doing and she invited me in to look at the house. She said that her husband worked out at a mine south of town and he was getting transferred. They had bought the house a few years earlier when it was brand new, she said. I liked the house from the start. It wasn't fancy but it was functional, kind of like me, I thought. It had three good size bedrooms. One for the girls one for the boys, and one for me and the, wife. It was just right I figured.

All the back yards were walled in with block about six feet high. I thought, I like that. It will keep the snakes out! And I hate snakes! I asked the lady if she'd ever seen any snakes around and she said she hadn't. Of course I realized she's probably not going to tell me even if she had. "There is a horse corral just to the east of the development," she said, "and once in a while they might see a snake over there."

The back yard was big enough if we ever wanted to put in a pool, but I doubted if we'd ever do that. Besides, I didn't want every kid in the neighborhood in my backyard and run-ning through our house. Plus, I figured the kids would make more friends if they went to one of the public pools.

I liked the house. Naturally it was air conditioned too. And the price was right to me. It seemed like I could buy a bigger house in Casa Grande than I had in Duluth for less money! Of course that was because they don't have basements. They just pour a slab and build a house! I asked the lady to give me a first refusal for a day so that I could call home and talk to the wife about it. She said she would. I went out to the car and got my camera and took pictures of the house inside and out.

I was just about to get in the car when I noticed the neighbors next door sitting out under their carport. I walked over and introduced myself and he offered me a beer. So I accepted! Normally I might not have, but I didn't want to offend them in case they were my new neighbors. Their names were Bill and Marjorie Graves. They were from over in Gallup, New Mexico they said. Bill had just retired from the railroad. He had been a signal maintainer. I asked them how long they had lived there, etc. and about the house next door and everything seemed to add up. So I told them I was probably going to be their neighbor unless the wife threw a wrench in the works for some reason.

I drove back over to the realtor's office where I had dropped Herbie off. He had bought the house with the pool. We drove back out to the Francisco Grande. I called the wife and described the house I had looked at. I told her I had taken a roll of pictures and was sure she'd like it. She was all excited about it and said, "Buy it!" I thought hmmm, maybe I should show her pictures of houses in bed to warm her up?

So I called the lady and told her I was going to buy the house and I'd get a local lawyer to draw up a purchase agreement, again with a closing when we arrived back in Casa Grande. That was all agreeable with her and she said that would work perfect with their plans to move also. It must have been "meant to be," I figured.

I looked through the yellow pages and called a lawyer. His name was Lavell Harper and he said he'd be glad to help me with some paper work. So Herbie and I drove back into Casa Grande and I took him out to Rancho Grande for a curbside view of the house. He liked it too! I drove back into town and found Harper's office. When we walked in I knew I was going to like Harper too! He was leaned back in his office chair and had jeans, a shirt, no tie and cowboy boots on, with his feet up on the desk reading the paper! He said, "You Hubbell?" "I said, "I'm Hubbell if you're Harper." I had gotten a description of the property from the lady at the house and gave that to Harper and told him what the purchase terms were, etc. He said he'd have a contract ready for me in the morning.

Herbie and I had done enough for one day we figured so we went to a pizza place, that the guys that owned the store had told us about. They must have had a hundred different kinds of pizzas there! I always like a supreme and Herb got whatever he wanted for his half and we got a couple of beers! Before we took a drink, I proposed a toast to a successful day and we clanked bottles and relaxed. We ate pizza and toasted our successful day two more times and headed back to the Francisco Grande. Of course, once we got to the "Grande," as we now called it, we decided we should toast our successful day there too! As we sat at the bar, I again pointed out Carl Hubbell's picture and casually asked Herb if he had seen any famous, Evers pictures anyplace yet? He gave me a look like my students use to when I'd hand them the hood to make an ITO. It was that same look, that "you jerk" look. I said, "Well excuse me. I can't help it that I come from a famous family!"

When we got up to the room I called the lady that owned the house and asked her if she or her husband could come to Harpers office about ten in the morning. She could, she said.

The next morning I met the lady at Harper's office and we signed a purchase order and I gave her some earnest money and Herb and I were heading back to Phoenix by 11:00!

On the way back to the airport in Phoenix, Herbie and I couldn't help but say how nice it was going to be to get out of the ice and snow! And the 20 degree below zero weather that Minnesota was so infamous for!

It was nice to get back home after five days away. The kids were glad to see me, Ginger was glad to see me and for once the wife was glad to see me! But mostly because she wanted to see the pictures of the house! Everybody was happy and excited about the house. Everybody, that is except the oldest daughter. She was a senior in high school and didn't want to move. She wanted to stay in Duluth and be with her class when they graduated.

Chapter Nineteen

The airplane business was very slow. Now Gene and I would celebrate just because it was Monday, or Tuesday, or Friday or anything!

On May 17th, 1974 the wife and I drove up to Cook, Minnesota and then met up with Loyd and Mary Jane Beaurline and went out to their beautiful rock house on an Island in Lake Vermillion. I spent the next three days giving their sons, Korkki and Allan, float instructions in the Cessna 180 93Mike that Loyd had bought from me.

They had two black labs, Brutus and Mimi and they, like all labs, just loved to swim and retrieve a stick. The only difference was these two would bring the stick back and force it into my hand while I was standing on the dock and then they'd run up into the apartment above the boathouse and come out on the deck. Then they'd wait anxiously, their tail wagging like crazy, until I'd throw the stick into the water and they'd jump off the deck from about twelve feet above the water and swim out to get it! They thought that was great fun and would do that all day or until I got tired of throwing the stick!

On May 20th I signed Korkki and Allan off for their flight checks. I had called Gordy Newstom at Grand Rapids and gotten them scheduled a couple of days earlier. So I called Gordy again to check his schedule for the next morning about 10 am. He said to call him on unicom ten miles out and he'd meet us down on Lake Pokegama at the boat ramp on the south shore, just west of the bridge. He said that way he can take both of the boys with at the same time. So the next morning we flew down to Grand Rapids so they could take their check rides with Gordy. We sat on a picnic table while he did the oral exam. Gordy's orals were always entertaining. He'd always end up telling about some of his experiences flying floats so it was as much of a learning experience as it was an oral exam. They both passed with flying colors!

I've always remembered that trip as Korkki and Allan learned how to fly floats from me and we learned how to grill walleyes from Mary Jane and Loyd. Crunch up some Hi Ho or similar crackers in a paper bag, roll the walleye filets in melted butter and put them in the bag and shake it up, and put them on a hot barbecue grill for about six minutes a side. Delicious! Try it!

We had put our house on the market as soon as I got back from Casa Grande and the first people that looked at it bought it! Of course we made the deal so we could live there until the kids were out of school and a few days later to get loaded up.

About May 23rd I flew a 1967 Cessna 172 down to Caledonia, Minnesota to demo it to Len Kragness and the Caledonia Flying Club. Caledonia was the last airport down in the southeast corner of the state. It was a really, really windy day. In fact, I was going to have a direct crosswind of about 25mph when I landed! When I had circled the airport I noticed about 6-8 guys huddled out of the wind next to a hangar facing the runway. I was getting all bounced around coming down final and when I flared out I had the left wingtip about a foot off the runway to keep from being blown across it. I lucked out and made a decent landing and taxied to the end of 31 and up to the ramp. When I taxied up to where all the guys were waiting and got out, I found out that they had been taking bets on whether I'd wreck the airplane or not on the landing! I met Len Kragness who I had been talking to about the 172. They put it in the hangar and opened it all up and looked it over for corrosion, they did a compression check and opened up the oil filter and inspected that. Pretty soon Len said, "they'll go to town and get me a check!" I asked them if they wanted to fly it first but they didn't think they would be as, lucky, as I was on the landing. So, we went to town and had lunch and then they got a cashier's check from their bank. I did all he paper work and got it signed. They didn't feel like flying me back to Duluth in that wind! So they told me to fly it back to Duluth and they'd come and get it in a few days when the wind died down. I said, "OK." I figured, No guts No glory!

I saw an ad in the paper that one of the truck rental companies was going out of business. I called Herbie and suggested we buy one of the, 16 foot trucks for use at the store and I'd fill it with our stuff for the move to Arizona. Herbie thought that was a great idea so we bought one. It would be perfect for the business with the pull out ramp we thought

Herb and I, drove down to Minneapolis the last part of May and took a three day course in refrigeration at a Frigidaire service center. Neither one of us had much of an idea how a refrigerator worked. We still weren't too sure after the school either!

We spent the first two weeks of June getting things boxed up and out in the garage.

I had made arrangements to leave the 16 ft truck we had bought parked down where we had bought it because I had no room to park it at home. About the first of June I went down and drove the truck over to Herb and Howard Sunnarborg's garage, Lakeland Oil and Tire Company, in Cloquet. We figured it would be good to change the oil, grease it and check it over for the trip. Herbie thought it looked like a pretty good truck. Then I drove it back to Duluth and parked it where I had bought it again.

A couple of days after school was out I went down and drove the truck home. I backed it up to the garage and we spent the next few hours filling it up. I don't think there was a square foot of space left in that truck when we got it packed! We had sold our house with the appliances and some of the furniture, and whatever we had left we had ran ads in the paper and sold. The Arizona house was going to need appliances and furniture but we figured, as long as we owned a furniture store, we'll just buy new appliances and furniture from ourselves! Besides, that way we could get everything we owned into the 16 ft truck and save the expense of renting and driving another truck to Casa Grande.

After we had the truck loaded we took the kids and drove over to Cloquet to say good-bye to friends and relatives. The next day we headed south. Tim, Keith and I were in the truck and the wife, Rhonda, LeeAnn and Ginger were in the station wagon. I had made arrangements to meet up with Herb and Joyce and their kids at the truck stop south of Cloquet that Herb and Howard had owned. Herb had rented the biggest Hertz truck he could get for the trip. We headed down Interstate 35 until Des Moines, Iowa and then west on I80 and I76 to Denver and south on I25.

We'd get an early start in the morning while it was still cool and then stop at a motel in the mid-afternoon so the kids would have time to play and swim in the pool, etc. And we would have time to have supper and go for a walk to get some exercise after sitting all day too. We had decided to make this a fun trip and if it took an extra day or two that would be better than just busting our ass's to get there. And we were lucky we never had a mechanical problem with either truck! Not even, a tire problem. Of course Herb and I would always check the tires and check oil every time we filled up with gas. I suspected God was still looking after us! Or else I must be the luckiest kid in the world!

When we got into New Mexico we stopped at the rest stop at Raton Pass to have lunch. While the girls were getting lunch set out on a picnic table, my two boys and Herb and Joyce's son Randy climbed up a high, steep sand hill. When they got up to the top they hollered down that there was a snake up there and to come and see it! So I climbed the hill. It was all sand. You'd make three steps forward and slide one step backwards! Finally I got to the top and sure enough there was a snake. It was a rattler snake and was coiled up and rattling like crazy. I had never seen one before. So I thought we'd do the people of New Mexico a favor and kill it, so we got some rocks and killed it. We were proud of ourselves for killing that snake! I figured we had probably saved at least a dozen lives by getting rid of that rattlesnake.

We stayed on I25 until I10 in New Mexico and hung a right and went past Tucson and got off at the Casa Grande exit. We'd had a great trip!

The people we had bought the house from had moved and left the keys with Harper so I stopped in at his office and gave him a check and got the keys. It was really easy moving our belongings in. I just backed up to the carport, pulled the ramp out, opened the truck door and everyone pitched in and we had everything moved inside within an hour and a half! It was easy when everything was on one floor! We didn't have beds for a couple of days but we didn't care. We were home and it was exciting!

It wasn't but a few days later when I told Bill and Marjorie about the rattlesnake that I learned we shouldn't have killed it because of all the mice and rats, etc. that they eat. Well, so much for doing a good deed I figured!

The next day I went to get some insurance on the house. The guy told me I'd need flood insurance because the subdivision was on a flood plain. I said, "Something must be wrong with my ears because I think I heard you say I'd need flood insurance on a house that's out in the desert." He said, "That's right, about every hundred years there's a flood." I couldn't believe that I had to buy flood insurance on a house out in the desert!

After a couple of days Herbie and I went and met with the guys at CG Mart and finalized that deal. So now we had houses and a business!

We liked Casa Grande but it was hot out though! It would be 95-100 degrees most days. Some days it could get up to 110-115 degrees. They say it's a dry heat, but it's still hot! The evenings would cool down into the 70's so that wasn't bad.

Chapter Twenty

The Appliance and Furniture Business

It didn't take us very long and we were comfortable in the appliance and furniture business. Herb and I spent a few days studying the appliances so we'd know what we were talking about. We had Gibson, Frigidaire, Maytag, Indesto, Whirlpool and a couple more brands. The girls did the same thing with the furniture department.

We had run an ad in the local paper saying we were from Minnesota and had bought the CG Mart. It was surprising the number of people that were from Minnesota that came in to meet us! And also the local people. The people in Casa Grande were very friendly. I remember one of my first customers, Rosa Hernandez. Rosa Hernadez came in and bought a Frigidaire washing machine from me. The next day she brought her sister in and she bought a dryer. Soon she brought in another family member who bought a washing machine. I liked these people! The Mexicans were very polite people, the cotton farmers were real nice to deal with and so were the Indians.

In fact, when we first looked at the store they had a Maytag wringer washer on the show floor. I asked, "How many years have you had that?" Gene said, "You'll sell one or two of those every month." "Who the hell is still buying wringer washers? I didn't know they even made them anymore!" I said. He said, "The Indians do because they don't have running water out on the reservation." I said, "I'll be damned." And he was right, just about every month or so we'd sell a wringer washer.

One thing though, we had people calling saying that they had bought a Frigidaire refrigerator a year or more ago and the icemaker had never been hooked up or didn't work and would we take care of them? We said, of course we would. So Herbie and I took an icemaker out of one of the refrigerator's on the floor and took it apart and found out how it worked and we'd take turns going out on service calls. We probably spent the first two months installing and fixing icemakers along with selling appliances and delivering and hooking them up!

One day a lady called and said she had a Maytag washing machine and that every time it would go into the spin cycle it dances all over her laundry room floor. She asked if I could come over and fix it? I asked her name and she told me. I asked, "Ma'am did you buy it at CG Mart?" She said no she hadn't, she had bought it up at Phoenix. I said, "I'm sorry ma'am, I am so busy trying to catch up with what this store has sold and should have been fixed before we got here that I just don't have time to look at your machine." She said, "Please, Mr. Hubbell, I've taken this washer back up to Phoenix three times and they tell me it's OK but when I get it home it still shakes and dances around the floor." She said, "I don't care what it costs to fix it, I just need it fixed. Will you come over and look at it, please?" Well it had been a long time since any woman had said "please" to me, so I told her I was going to be driving by her place pretty soon anyway and I'd stop and take a look at it. But I said, "It's $18.00 for a service call whether I'm there for 5 minutes or an hour." She said, "I don't care, just "please" come fix it." I'm thinking, I'm going to like this appliance business. Women beg me to do something. I've never had that happen before either! So I stopped by her house and there was her Maytag washer and dryer in the porch. I turned washer on and selected the spin cycle and sure enough it danced all over the floor! So I lifted the lid and there was the shipping ring, still installed! I took the shipping ring out and hung it on a nail on the wall and closed the lid again and it just sat there and spun as smooth and quiet as a fine watch. She asked, "What was that you took out of the machine Mr. Hubbell?" I said, "That's the shipping ring. You put that in when you transport the machine." What had happened was, when she'd pick the machine up in Phoenix nobody told her to take the shipping ring out when she got it back home. And when she took it back to Phoenix they would take the ring out and check the spin cycle and it would be OK. So they'd put the shipping ring back in and send her back home with it, but nobody thought to tell her to take it out and hang it on a nail when she got home! I said, "That will be $18.00.' She was glad to pay me even!

I had to get used to one thing while living in Arizona though. Every week Herb or I would have to drive the truck up to Phoenix to pick up furniture and appliances. I drove up a couple of times and picked up some appliances first and then I'd go to the warehouse to pick up some furniture. This time, as I was backing up, all the overhead doors closed. I thought what the hell is this? I'm here to pick up $5,000 dollars of furniture and they close the doors! I went into the office and asked the lady if my check had bounced the last time or what? She kind of laughed and said, "No, it's siesta time." I said, "What do you mean, siesta time?" She said, "The Mexican's all take a nap from 12:00 to 1 o'clock and that's their custom." Now I knew why they're so happy all the time. I'd probably be a lot happier too if I took an hour nap everyday! So after that I got an earlier start so I could be loaded up and on the way back to Casa Grande before siesta time!

I had sold a guy over near Eloy a portable dishwasher a week earlier and he had called and said it was leaking on the floor. So after I, "fixed" the ladies washing machine I headed over there.

When I had delivered it he had showed me his collection of guns and knives. He had a whole room full of them. Some mounted on the walls and some standing on the floor. He must have had 100 rifles and pistols and at least fifty knives I figured. And he had boxes and boxes of ammunition on the floor next to the walls. I was impressed! All I had was a 20gauge shotgun, a 30-30 Winchester and a Ruger 22 automatic pistol.

It didn't take long to get to Eloy from Casa Grande and when I got there he let me in. I pushed the dishwasher over by the sink and hooked it up and started the wash cycle. I was lying on the floor with my flashlight on looking under the machine to see where the water, was leaking from. Pretty soon the hair just stood up on the back of my neck. I rolled over and looked up and there was a woman just glaring down at me. She was really dark around her eyes. She said, "Are you going to hurt me?" I said, "No ma'am, I'm just going to fix your dishwasher and I'll be out of here." She said, "I think you're going to hurt me." I said, "No ma'am, I'm not going to hurt you." Then she said to the man who had bought the washer, "I think we should call the police." He said, "No we don't have to call the police." She said, "Well, when I feel like my life is being threatened, I think we should call the police." He said, "Mr. Hubbell is not going to hurt you. He's just going to fix the dishwasher so it doesn't leak water on the floor anymore." She glared down at me again and asked, "is that was true? I said, "Yes ma'am, I'm just going to fix your dishwasher. That's all I'm going to do."

I could see it was in fact leaking and took the back cover off to see where, it was leaking from. It turned out to be the gasket on the water pump. I didn't have a gasket with so I told the man I had to go into Eloy and check someone's ice-maker and I'd get some gasket material from the hardware store and come back and make one for it. He followed me out to the truck. I said, "I'm sorry if I scared your wife." He said, "She's not my wife and not to worry about it." He said, "She has some problems, but most of the time she is OK." I asked him, "Aren't you worried about having all those guns and knives around?" He said, "No, I keep that room locked and she wouldn't know what bullets to put in what gun any-way." I'm thinking she'd know what knife to put between my ribs though!

I was really kind of hesitant about going back there but my dedication to getting the job done was greater than my fear, so I bought some gasket material and drove back to the house. When I rang the doorbell the lady answered the door. She was all dressed up now and had her hair fixed and was very pleasant. I remembered the guy called her Sharon, so I said, "Hi Sharon." She said, "Mr. Hubbell, it's good to see you again" and she opened the door and let me in. It only took me five minutes to take the pump plate off and remove the gasket so I could use it to draw a replacement one on the gasket material. I had asked Sharon for a newspaper to put on the countertop, which she got for me. So I sat on one side of the counter and she was on the other side and we talked as I traced and cut out a gasket. It turned out she had been a school, teacher and she could talk about anything I could talk about. Of course, I don't consider myself any rocket scientist either! She was actually very intelligent and quite attractive now. I replaced the gasket and checked it for leaks and said good-bye to Sharon. I ended up feeling very sorry for her because of her problem.

Chapter Twenty One
Flying the Birddog, a 210 and Gliders

On July 10th 1974 I joined the local CAP and started flying their "birddog" with Walt Lehman who was a brother to one of the guy's we had bought CG Mart from. I flew with Walt on the 10th, the 20th and the 22nd and then he signed me off to fly N5579Charlie! You couldn't take anyone flying with you except another CAP member, but at least I had something to fly! Of course the "birddog" is just a Cessna 170 so I had a lot of hours in those already having owned N8006A with Byron and Lloyd Backus back in Cloquet.

On July 27th I drove out to Maricopa and started glider lessons at the Estrella Glider Port. It was, owned by Les Horvac and his wife. I got assigned to this cute little instructor, Judy Whitacker. I don't think she weighed 90 lbs. We got along really good! We flew a SGS 2-33A on the 27th for .2 hrs and I didn't get a chance to fly again until August 11th when we flew for 1.2 hours. We towed up to 1500ft agl (above ground level) and released, and I found enough thermals to make it up to 7,500ft msl! (above sea level) I learned to look for areas of rising air, like clouds, plowed fields, hawks, smokestacks and ridges, etc. If you see a hawk circling around at least you know there's some rising air over there. I liked flying gliders too! It was nice and quiet, peaceful I thought. And you didn't have to worry about the engine quitting either! I didn't fly with Judy again until August 24th and then we did three tows up to 1500 ft agl and released. We couldn't find any thermals going up so we just released and entered the downwind and landed. After the third landing and a total of 2.1hrs of dual, she signed me off to solo! So I got another tow and went back up to 1500 feet agl and released. By this time though the afternoon sun was heating up the black fields and I found some thermals and was able to stay up for 30 minutes! I loved it! You had to solo 10 times before you could take your check ride so I soled again twice on the 25th, 3 times on September 1st, three more times on the 2nd, and twice on the 7th. I didn't get to fly gliders again until the 15th when I made my 11th solo.

I had met a guy by the name of Roy Lee through my neighbors Bill and Marjorie Graves. Roy had a jewelry store downtown and made turquoise jewelry. He said he had a friend out west of town near Maricopa that had a Cessna 210 he could use and asked me if I'd fly him up to Santa Fe, New Mexico so he could buy some turquoise. That sounded like fun to me! So I called the guy with the 210 and told him what ratings and approximately how much 210 time I had and he said I could fly his 210! Roy and I drove out there on the 16th and I met the guy. I showed him my license and logbook and asked him if he wanted to fly with me first. He said, "You've got a lot more time in 210's and more ratings than I do so it would be a waste of time to fly with you." The guy had a grass strip in amongst some walnut trees so he said to try and get back before dark so I could be sure to find the strip otherwise if it got dark, to just land at the Casa Grande airport. I said OK.

So Roy and I flew up to Santa Fe in the 210. It was a 1967 model N711PV. The scenery was beautiful! I had this feeling again, like, who am I to be able to do this? I rode into town with Roy and walked around while he was buying turquoise. I had never been into Santa Fe before. It was a neat town. All the sidewalks were board walks and all the buildings were like from the late 1800's early 1900's. At least the part of town we were in was. Roy bought his turquoise and we headed back to Maricopa in the 210. When we took off from Santa Fe, I headed southwest staying west of Albuquerque and leveled off about 600 ft above the ground. The scenery was absolutely beautiful! After I got southwest of Albuquerque I dropped down to about 300 feet and slowed the 210 down to about a 125 miles per hour and did some terrain flying. I was just winding around the buttes to the left and right. I had never flown in country like this before. Around every corner was another magnificent scene! We went by St Johns and I had to look up to see the VOR on top of the butte. Roy was enjoying this as much as I was. I told him to keep an eye out for high wires though because you never know where you might find them. I was just generally heading southwest toward Casa Grande. When we got to Show Low I pulled up and got some altitude, about 600 feet over the ground, and then we just kind of followed hwy 60 back to Florence Junction and back out toward Maricopa. It was dusk by the time we got back but I didn't have any trouble finding the strip and landing. We pushed the 210 back into the "T" hangar and stopped at the house and thanked the guy for using it. We didn't tell him about our terrain flying though!

I had to force myself to stay out of gliders and airplanes for a couple of weeks and pull my weight in the store! I figured Herbie was about ready to cut me off the payroll pretty soon! I made up for it by doing service work and deliveries in the evenings though while he was home enjoying his pool.

One day an elderly couple from Minnesota came into the store to meet us and they were looking for a hide a bed. They had bought a lot that had, had a mobile home and a garage on it. The mobile home wasn't there any longer and they were fixing up the garage to live in they said. I showed them a hide a bed we had for $495 dollars. That was more than they could afford they said. I asked them if they had a stove and they said no, they didn't. I asked if they had 220volt electric service and they did. I said, "We just took in an apartment size electric stove that was like new that I could sell that for a hundred bucks." They looked at it and liked it and bought it. I said, "Do you have a washer and dryer?" They didn't. I said, "I've also got a used Frigidaire washer and dryer that are really nice too that I could sell you for about half the price of new ones!" They bought those two for $300 bucks! I asked, "Do you have a refrigerator?" They didn't. So I showed them a 17 cubic ft Frigidaire for $479.00 dollars, but that was more than they could afford. I said, "Well, we've got these Indesto refrigerators. You have to defrost them but they are only $199. So they bought one of those too! Then I said, "I'll tell you what, being your from Minnesota and are buying all these other things from me, I'll sell you that $495 hide a bed for $300. She was keeping a total on her notebook and added it up. It came to $899.00 dollars and she said that was good because they only had $1,000.00 to work with! I felt good that I was able to sell them what they needed and keep them within their budget!

I asked them how far out of town did they live and how soon did they want it delivered. They were only about five miles out of town and they needed it as soon as possible. So I said, "If you want to sit down for about 20 minutes, we'll load it on the truck and I'll follow you out to your place and hook everything up for you." One of the girls got them some iced tea out of the refrigerator and they sat at our employee table and relaxed while Herb and I loaded the truck. By the time we finished, Tim was out of school, so he and I followed them out to their lot in the desert and hooked everything up. I noticed that the garage wasn't even insulated and they didn't have an air conditioner either. I couldn't imagine how hot it must be in there in the afternoon heat. They had a couple of box fans to move some air though. I figured they were pretty near 75-80 years old. I felt sorry for them. I thought, I hope when I'm 75 I'm not living in a garage out in the middle of a desert. I wondered if they had a million bucks in the bank and just wanted to live this way, or are they really destitute? I thought, hmmm, my idea of roughing it is watching black and white TV at Holiday Inn! Where is their family I wondered? Herb or I would stop by and see how they were doing anytime we were out in the area after that.

One day we put an "out to lunch" sign on the door of the store and the four of us drove out to the Francisco Grande for lunch. When we got there I headed to the men's room while Herb and the girls went into the restaurant. When I came out of the men's room I saw this big guy standing over by the door. He looked familiar so I walked over there. I said, "Are you John Wayne?" He stuck his big hand out and said, "Sure am partner," and shook my hand. I said, "Nice to meet you." And then he asked me where I was from, etc. When I got in the restaurant the wife asked me what had taken me so long? I said that I was talking to my friend John. She said, "John, who?" I said, "John Wayne." She said, "Oh, you were not." I said, "Go look around the corner." So the three of them went over and looked and came back and Herbie said, "I'll be damned, it is John Wayne." It turned out that John Wayne and another man had a cattle feeding lot about ten miles further west.

Roy Lee called me again to see if I'd fly him back up to Santa Fe to get some more turquoise. I thought, hmmm he must have liked that terrain flying as much as I did! So I said I'd fit it in someplace. He called me back an hour later and said the guy with the 210 had let another guy use it just a few days ago. But he said the guy had came back at night and lined up on the wrong lights and landed it in the walnut grove and totaled the airplane. He had walked away from it though with just bruises and scratches. And I'm sure a very hurt ego too, I figured.

I didn't fly gliders again until September 30th! I went back out to Estrella and flew with Judy again for .3 hrs. There wasn't any lift anyplace, she said, so we just got a tow and released at 1,500 ft agl and came back in and landed. Then she told me I was ready to take my check ride. And she said that with all my time I might as well take a commercial check ride, so she signed me off for that.

Rosa and Jose Hernadez invited the wife and I over for tacos and beer one night. I drank about 4 beers and ate about four tacos. I was putting a quite a bit of guacamole on my tacos and thinking, what is everyone saying about guacamole? This stuff ain't hot or nothing. But after the fourth taco I started to feel sick. Very sick! Jose was just sitting there smiling! I barely made it into the bathroom! I was sicker than a dog, so to speak! In fact I was sick for three days! Just the thought of beer and tacos sent me to the bathroom again! I think it was three months before I got over that! And that damn Jose, just sat there and smiled!

A couple came into the store one morning. They were just moving into town. He was an engineer out at one of the mines he said. His name was Sam and hers was Brenda. They had just bought a house in town and needed furniture and appliances. They bought everything they needed from us! And they were, super nice to deal with too! We delivered everything out to their house and helped them put things where they wanted and hooked up all the appliances and the icemaker. Then the wife and I invited them and Herb and Joyce out to our house for drinks and steaks on the grill that evening. We had a good time! The only problem was the wife had too much to drink and didn't feel like making love that night! I made a mental note to limit her to three drinks after that!

On October 6th I took my commercial glider check ride. The examiner was giving three check rides that day so the three of us were doing the oral at the same time. He was of course asking questions of us and then was quizzing us about airspace, etc. But he had control zones and traffic areas backwards, so I corrected him. He was embarrassed and looked at me and asked, "what are you a flight instructor or something?" I said, "Yes, I'm a kind of a rusty flight instructor now but I know the difference between a control zone and a traffic area and I only corrected you so these other guys wouldn't be confused." I knew I had shit in my mess kit, as we used to say in the Air Force!

He cut the oral short after that and we went out to fly. He said I'd be first. I made arrangements for the tow plane to get in position and the ground kids got the towrope hooked up. I noticed the examiner over talking to the tow pilot. Finally he got in and buckled up and closed the door and I flicked the rudder a few times signaling the tow plane pilot I was ready to go. When you're being towed, you maintain position by keeping the tow plane's wheels on the horizon. A lady had just made an off airport landing in the desert so I was looking down at her and wondering how bad the glider got damaged when the examiner started chewing my ass for being out of position. I popped back into position and when we reached 1500 ft I was going to release but the examiner said to not release yet. About then the tow plane rolled into about a 60degree bank to the right. By the time I realized what he was doing the tow rope was going slack, I rolled left to tighten it back up but it still got a pretty good jolt, and then the tow plane rolled about 60 degrees to the left. I hit some right rudder and skidded enough to keep the towrope taut and then the examiner said to release. I released and immediately entered the downwind because there wasn't any lift to be had. I made a nice landing and we got out. The examiner said, "What happened to the spot landing?" I said, "You didn't ask for one and if you don't ask for it you don't get it." I thought, hmm, it's nice to take a check ride when my job doesn't depend on it! He said, "If you want your glider license you need to do a spot landing." I said, "Are you paying for the tow or me?" He said, "If you want your rating, you are!" And I said, "What the hell was the deal up there with the 60 degree banks? If you're doing that on a check ride it should be in the syllabus!" I said, "I think you're pissed because I corrected you during the oral, is that right?" He didn't say anything, just got back in the glider. The ground kids got us hooked up to the tow plane again and I flicked the rudder that I was ready. This time I kept the tow planes wheels on the horizon, like a good little glider pilot. When we reached 1500 feet I released. The tow plane went into a bank to the right and I banked left back into the downwind. The examiner said, "I've got it, you just talk me into a landing." He was doing OK and on short final he asked how he was doing. I said, "You're doing OK, but at this rate your going to land twenty feet short of the line." He brought the spoilers in and still landed about ten feet before the line. He got out. I could tell he was still a little pissed. He wasn't used to people like me. He said, "You and I have a personality problem, but I think you're a damned good pilot, so I'm going to give you your glider license." So we went into his office and he typed up my glider rating and gave it to me. Then he shook my hand and congratulated me and said, "I'd like to fly with you someday in a powered aircraft." I said, "I'll call you."

One day a lady came into the store looking for a counsel TV. She was beautiful, about 40 years old I figured. She bought a counsel TV from me with the understanding that I would deliver it and I'd have to install an antenna in the attic. I agreed to do that and wrote it up on the purchase order.

The next day I got Tim to help me deliver it to her apartment. We hauled the TV in and set it down where she wanted it. Then I unloaded my toolbox, drill, step ladder and the antenna, etc. Herb needed Tim back at the store to help him so I told Tim I'd call when I was done here and he went back to the store.

The lady had a bathrobe on. When I went back in I noticed that now she had more cleavage showing than before. I assumed my farm boy attitude and pretended I hadn't noticed and went about finding a place to snake a cable down from the attic, etc.

After about 45 minutes she offered me some coffee and cookies. I sat on the couch and she sat in a recliner chair. Now her bathrobe was opened more and she had her legs crossed exposing her thigh. I'm thinking, hmmm, am I being teased here?

I had to go up in the attic to find a place to mount the antenna and hook the cable up. I figured out what I needed to do and hollered down for the lady to hand me the antenna. Soon I saw the antenna being handed up to me through the "cubby hole" and went over to get it. When I looked down her bathrobe was almost wide open and I was looking at a gorgeous pair of tits! About 36C's I figured. It was all I could do to pretend that I hadn't noticed!

I got the antenna installed in the attic and hooked the cable up to it. Then I came back down and turned the TV on to see how the picture looked. The picture looked pretty good, the lady was looking pretty good too!

This was the first time in my life that I was being teased like this. But I had never cheated on the wife and wasn't ready to yet. And then I had the sense to realize that if I did, she could claim rape and it would be her word against mine. And I could just see the headlines in the paper, new CG Mart owner rapes customer! And there would go the store and my marriage. I finished the job, thanked her and called for Tim to come get me.

A couple of days later she called me and said she thought the TV needed some adjusting. I drove over there and sure enough she met me at the door in her bathrobe again. I knelt down in front of the TV and she leaned over with her bathrobe partially opened again. Now I knew for sure she was teasing me. I assumed my "dumb farm boy" attitude again and pretended I didn't notice. But I was realizing for the first time in my life, that I could get a little excited about the thought of another woman. I had never experienced this before. I was totally in love with the wife and had never thought about another woman.

I fiddled with the TV adjustments a little while and she went over and sat in her arm chair to see how the picture looked from there. She had her legs crossed but again showing a lot of thigh. I adjusted the TV the best I could, under the circumstances!

Then she went and got us some coffee and cookies again and sat with her robe loosely opened. I maintained my dumb farm boy attitude and drank my coffee and ate my cookies, thanked her and left.

She was sure pretty and I'm sure she would have been a lot of fun to make love with, but I wasn't ready yet to cheat on the wife.

A few days later she called me to come and adjust her TV again. This time I think the wife was getting a little suspicious! And I wasn't sure I'd have the strength to be a farm boy again so I took Tim with me.

Sure enough, this time she kept her robe tightly closed. I adjusted her TV again and never heard from her after that. I enjoyed the memories for a little while though. I had never been hit on like that before. I've got to admit though I had enjoyed it!

It was October 20th before I got back out to Maricopa to fly a glider again. It was another day with very little lift around. Everyone was just getting towed to 1500 and coming back in. I told the tow pilot I wanted to go up to 2,500 feet before I released. What little wind there was favored runway 27. So we took off and he climbed straight out until we had 1500 feet and then he turned left 90 degrees to avoid any traffic entering the right pattern for 27. Pretty soon he turned back to the east and we climbed up to 2,500 feet above ground and I released. The tow plane rolled right and I rolled left and then rolled back to the east and continued straight ahead for a few minutes looking for some lift.

There was a little more wind out of the northwest than I had figured on so pretty soon I had drifted southeast farther than I should have. By now I haven't found any lift either and I'm down to 2,000 feet. I'm looking back at the glider port and thinking, this ain't going to be good. I pointed that little 2-33A, N7766S right at the glider port. The only problem was I was sinking about 200 feet a minute and the runway is getting higher on the windshield. I was at my best L/D (lift to drag) and knew I didn't have enough altitude to make a normal right hand traffic pattern for 27. In fact, I had gotten myself in a situation where I figured I'd be lucky to even make the runway from where I was! I got one little bump of lift that lifted me up about a 100 feet. That, and the fact that I made a left base, actually a modified 45 degree left base, instead of a normal right base, is the only reason I landed back on the runway instead of in the desert!

When I got out of the glider I could hear my name being called over the loudspeakers, "Hubbell to the office! Hubbell to the office!" So I walked over to the office and Les Horvac greets me with, "What kind of pattern was that Hubbell?" I said, "That's the kind of pattern you make when you don't want to land the man's nice little glider in the cactus." Horvac said, "I appreciate that Hubbelll, but from now on keep yourself in position to make a normal pattern like everyone else." "Right Horvac," I said.

On November 3rd I started giving my son Timothy dual toward his private pilot's license. Walt Lehman, Gene's brother, was a fireman and also ran the FBO out at the airport and had a Cessna 150, N22613 for rent. Tim and I flew that for 1.6 hrs in the morning while it was cool and then another 1.5 hrs that evening. We flew again on the 8th, twice on the 10th, again on the 13th, 14th, and on his 16th birthday, November 15th 1974, I soled him with 8.5 hrs of dual. Of course, he had been flying on my lap since he was about three years old. He could practically fly instruments by the time her was five because he couldn't see over the panel.

I was as proud as I could be to solo Tim on his 16th Birthday. I had told the wife I was going to do that and for her to come out to the airport and watch. She and Marjorie came out but she didn't want to stand by me, "in case Tim crashed," she said. I said," he's not going to crash or I wouldn't be soloing him". But she wanted to go about a half a mile away, "in case he crashed," she said. So her and Marjorie drove to the far side off the airport, about a half a mile away. I was really disappointed. I wanted her to share that moment with me. It took a lot of the fun out of it just knowing that she lacked trust in my teaching Tim to fly. I wondered, what is it about this woman that I love? Just sex? But now, I've learned that, I can get excited by the thought of another woman. Hmmm?

Tim made three nice takeoffs and landings and taxied in. It was somewhat anti-climatic for me to congratulate him without his mother being there. I made a mental note to not have sex with her for at least eight hours to punish her.

One evening I drove out to Estrella thinking I'd get in a quick glider flight but the weather was changing for the worst. I could see some thunder bumpers building off to the west and southwest. I was standing out of the wind next to a hangar on the south side of the glider port. All of a sudden here comes a glider from the south right over top the hangar and lands to the north on the taxiway and crossed the runway, stopping near the wind sock. I thought, what the hell is this guy doing? I watched as the guy got out of the glider, and it was Les Horvac! I walked over toward the office so he'd have to pass by me.

As he approached me I said, "Horvac, what the hell kind of pattern was that?" He said, "I was hoping you wouldn't be here!" And then added, "But that's the kind of pattern you make when there are thunderstorms approaching." I said, "Well from now on Horvac, keep yourself in position to make a normal pattern like everyone else around here." He knew he had been had, so he just kind of grinned and walked by. I laughed!

We found out one thing, when you live in Arizona you get a lot of company in the winter! And we enjoyed it!

I gave Don Hudson and his brother Bob glider rides on December 29, 1974. On January 1st 1975, I gave my sons Keith and Tim their first glider rides. January 5th I gave the father-in-law his first glider ride. After that I gave the wife her first glider ride too!

I figured I better spend more time in the store before Herb fires me! Although, I was still doing a lot of the service and delivery work in the late afternoon. It was cooler then too!

On Thursday morning a lady called me from over in Coolidge to tell me her dryer wasn't working and she had company coming from back home for a week and really needed her dryer fixed. "Could I "please" come over and fix it this afternoon?" she asked. I liked that "please" word. It was nice to hear it. I don't think it was in the wife's vocabulary.

I had another service call over in that area so I told her I would stop and fix it. She warned me that she has a vicious German Shepherd chained out on the carport and the dryer is in the shed off the carport, so she will make sure to put the Shepherd in the house or I won't be able to get to the dryer. I told her I'd sure appreciate that!

So I drove over there and to my surprise the Shepherd was still on a chain on the carport and there was no car there so I knew she had forgotten to put the dog inside. I turned around and backed the truck up to within ten feet of him and got out. The Shepherd was straining against the chain, barking and growling at me. We had a Shepherd out on the farm. I knew he wasn't as mean as he sounded. But I'm not just going to reach out and pet him either! I just ignored him and rolled up the back door of the truck and got a screwdriver and flashlight out of my toolbox. When I turned around he was still straining on the chain and growling at me with his teeth exposed. I walked briskly up to him, stopping about two inches from his jaws and shouted, "lay down!" To my surprise, he laid down! I knelt down, still out of reach of his teeth and talked to him. I said, "You're not a mean dog are you? You're just pretending to be mean dog. You can't fool me. I know you're not a mean dog, you're a nice dog." I said, "I'm not here to hurt you or steal anything. I just need to fix the dryer for your master." Pretty soon I reached out and started scratching him behind the ears, then I started petting him. Pretty soon he rolled over on his back so I could scratch his belly. So I scratched his belly. Then I stepped right over him and walked to the shed where the dryer was and he followed me. It didn't take me long to determine that the electrical heating element was burnt out. So I pulled the dryer out onto the carport and took the cabinet off. Then I took the electric heating element off and walked over to the truck and got a new one. The dog followed me back and forth. I sat on the concrete while I was replacing the element and the dog was licking my face and ears. I think he was happy that he didn't have to act like a mean dog anymore! And he was having a really good time licking my ears and face! I was wondering if I had forgotten to wash some food off my face the way he was licking me! I thought, hmmm, that feels good, I wonder if I can get the wife to do that?

When I finished putting the element in and the cabinet back on, I put it in the shed and plugged the electrical cord back in. I set it on the dry cycle and it was putting out heat so I shut it off and closed the door. The dog followed me back to the truck and I petted him some more. I had some munchies left in the truck so I gave him a treat and petted him some more and drove away.

I went and did another service call on an icemaker over in Florence and was back at the store about 4:30. I wasn't there ten minutes and the phone rang. Joyce said it was for me, so I picked up a phone and answered. It was the lady with the dog. She said, "I'm sorry Mr. Hubbell, I forgot to put the dog in before I left, can you come right back over here and fix this dryer please?" I said, "Nope I won't." She said, "I'll pay you double your normal charge if you will because I really need the dryer this week. Please say you'll come back." I said, "Nope, I'm not coming back." She said, "I realize it's late and you've probably had a long day, but I really need this dryer fixed. I'll pay you a extra $50." I said, "Nope, I'm not coming back." She said, "Why not?" I said, "Because I already was there and fixed it." She said, "You were not, there's no way you could get by that dog." I said, "That's the most gentle dog I've ever seen, he licked my face and ears the whole time I was fixing your dryer." (I didn't tell her I was going to ask the wife if she would lick my face and ears though.) She said, "I don't believe you." I said, "I'll hang on the line while you go out and check the dryer." A couple of minutes later she came back on the line and said, "It's working. I wouldn't believe it if I hadn't checked it." She asked me what I had done to get by the dog and I told her. She said, "I wish I could have seen that!" I thought, hmmm, I wonder if she'd lick my ears and face too? I better not ask her, I'll ask the wife first. At least she already thinks I'm strange.

Actually the appliance and furniture business was pretty good over the Christmas and New Years Holidays. Men would buy their wives new dishwashers, microwaves, refrigerators, etc. I kind of liked the appliance and furniture business. The only problem I was having was that I always felt like I had a cold. My allergies were acting up like crazy. I went to a dermatologist up in Phoenix to be checked and he said I was allergic to just about everything in the state. I said, "I thought Arizona was the place to come to if you had allergies." He said, "It use to be until all you mid-westerners moved down here and brought all your plants." I had hay fever real bad back in Minnesota but that was just in the fall. That was one of the reasons I had moved to Arizona!

On February 9th, 10th, and 13th 1975, I did a CAP check flight in a C305 "birddog" N 5289Golf with Walt Lehman.

On the 22nd I gave John Cartier his first glider ride. On March 13th I gave Herb and Vonnie Bromme and their son Mark and daughter Lisa their first glider rides. On the 30th

Les and Steve landing

I gave Ted Micke and his sons Steve and Brian their first glider rides.

Chapter Twenty Two

One morning the phone rang at the store and I answered it. It was a local builder. He told me he was building a 109 unit, apartment building and that he had bought 109 Frigidaire refrigerators. He said, "54 of them had gotten laid on their backs when they were lifted by a forklift to the upper level. And now they don't work." I said, "No wonder, the compressors are full of oil from being laid on their backs." (I bit my tongue and didn't add, "you idiots") He wanted to know when I could come over and fix them because he had people ready to move in. I asked, "Where did you buy 109 Frigidaire refrigerators from?" He said, "From Mr. Smith, the Frigidaire commercial salesman." Mr. Smith was also our Frigidaire sales rep. I said, "I'm sorry, I don't have time to replace 54 compressors. You'll have to call Mr. Smith and have him find someone else to fix them." He said, "I've already talked to Mr. Smith and he said you have to fix them." I said, "Let me tell you something about me, I don't have to do nothing that I don't want to do. You bought them from Mr. Smith, call Mr. Smith to get them fixed. If you had bought them from this store, I would have made sure they didn't get laid on their backs when they were lifted up to the second floor and I don't have time to correct your mistakes. This is Mr. Smith's problem, not mine. Call Mr. Smith," and I said, "good-bye." I was pissed that our sales rep had come to town and sold 109 Frigidaire refrigerators!

It wasn't 15 minutes later and Mr. Smith called me. He said, "Les, I just got a call from the guy with the 54 refrigerators and he said you refused to fix them. Is that true?" I said, "You damned right that's true, you sold them; you fix them. I'm still busy fixing things that should have been fixed before we bought this store, and I don't have time to replace 54 compressors. And I sure the hell ain't going to buy 54 compressors and wait six months to get reimbursed from Frigidaire for them, plus my labor." He said, "We will ship the compressors no charge and I'll see that you get paid for your labor as soon as you're done." I said, "I still don't have the time to do it. You'll have to get someone else." He said, "According to your contract you have to fix them." I said, "I'll tell you what I told him, I don't have to do a damned thing that I don't want to do. If I had sold them, they wouldn't have gotten laid on their backs. You came into town and sold me some Frigidaires and then you went over there and sold that builder 109 Frigidaire refrigerators. I'll fix what I sell, you fix what you sell, it's that simple," I said. He said, "Either you fix them Les, or we'll cancel your contract with us." I said, "Tell you what, if this is the way you guy's do business you just tear that contract up and send a driver over here with a cashier's check and a semi truck and I'll load up every Frigidaire we have and he can haul them back to California." I said, "And that's final. Good-bye Mr. Smith," and I hung up the phone. (I hate myself when I'm like that.)

When Herb arrived I told him about the 109 refrigerators and my conversation with the builder and our sales rep, Mr. Smith. He agreed that it was their problem and not ours.

Not long after my conversation with Mr. Smith I got a call from some people that had bought a Frigidaire refrigerator from the store several years ago they said, but now it's not working and can I come and fix it? I got their address. They were just on the south side of town. I drove over there and looked at the refrigerator. After looking it over for a while I could see that the "A" coil was all frosted up which means that the defrost heater isn't working. The defrost heater is down under the "A" coil, which is under the freezer compartment. I had never replaced one before, but then there have been a lot of things I hadn't done before, I figured. So I got a cardboard box from the people and unloaded everything from the freezer compartment into it and closed the top. Then I removed all the trim pieces from inside the freezer compartment. When I got all that stuff out of the way I was able to remove the bottom of the compartment exposing the "A" coil. I lifted it up enough to get to the heater and removed it. I didn't have one on the truck so I had to drive back over to the store to get one. Luckily we had one in stock. I drove back over to the house and it only took a few minutes to install it. Then I took a hair dryer on high heat and defrosted the "A" coil. In about another twenty minutes I had put the freezer compartment back together. It was a Mexican family that had bought the refrigerator. As I was putting the freezer back together they sat down for dinner. He said, "Señior Les, will you join us for tacos." I said, "Sure, just give me a couple more minutes to put this back together." I liked the Mexican people. They were all so gracious and polite. I've never heard one of them complain about anything either. And they always seem to be so happy. I thought, hmmm, maybe I can learn something from them.

As I was putting the freezer compartment back together the man said, "Señior Les, it must take a lot of years to learn how to do what you do." I said, "Yes it sure does, you don't just learn it overnight." I didn't tell them that this was the first one I've ever done!

I got back to the store about 1:30. I was sitting in the office about 4:30 when I happened to notice three suits coming through the front door. It was Mr. Smith and two other guys. They came into the office. I called Herbie into the office also. Mr. Smith said, "We need to talk, Les." I said, "You need to talk, not me." "Tell me, how come we're the Frigidaire dealer here in Casa Grande and you come to town and sell 109 refrigerators right in our backyard? What the hell are you doing coming over here and selling 109 Frigidaire refrigerators, and then think I'm going to fix 54 of them for you?" They pulled out some paper work and showed me the contract that Herb and I had signed. I said, "Yes, but show me, where it say's I have to fix what my own sales rep sells." Well, they didn't have a paragraph that specifically showed that, they said. "But, you have to fix them." I said, "I told you on the phone, I don't have to do nothing that I don't want to do." (I didn't even tell them to ask the wife, if they didn't believe me!)

I said, "By the way, how did you guy's get over here so fast?" "Oh, we came on the company jet," they said. I said, "Well, you should have brought the company semi-truck because I'm still not fixing those refrigerators. I told you I'm up to my ears still fixing icemakers and things that were sold out of this store that should have been fixed before we got here and I don't have time to fix what you sell too."

Well, I guess by know they were convinced that I wasn't going to replace all those compressors and they'd have to get someone from Phoenix to come fix them. Before they left I had gotten an agreement out of them that from now on, if you come to town and sell something that you might want us to do warranty service work on, send us a check for $20.00 per unit and then we'll service it. And then they called a cab and went back to the airport and got in their jet and went back to California. I never heard another word from them.

Herb wanted to have a meeting with the girls and discuss what had happened and what I had told the contractor and the Frigidaire people, etc. So the wife and Joyce came into the office and Herbie told them what the meeting had been about, etc. He asked the wife, if she thought I had been to hard on them? I was stunned when I heard her say, "Well, he can be a son of a bitch sometimes, but he gets the job done." I said, "What do you mean by that? We've been married 19 years, I've never cheated on you and everything I do is with you and the kids. I work hard to support my family, I've never even hollered at you, I always buy the house you want, I give you my check, I treat your parents with respect, and you think I'm a son of a bitch sometimes?" She tried to recant her statement, but the damage had been done. I'm wondering, just what is it I love about this woman? And now I'm not even going to let her lick my ears and face and have as much fun as that dog had either! I thought, hmmm, I wonder if that lady still needs her TV adjusted?

Chapter Twenty Three

I flew commercial up to Duluth about the middle of May1975 and went up to Canada fishing with Gene and a few other guys. We flew a Cherokee six up to Sioux Lookout and spent the night at Carl Reinke's Hidden Bay Lodge and then flew up to Blackstone Lake the next morning in a 1964 C185 on floats that I had sold Carl a couple of years earlier. As usual the fishing was fantastic.

Gene had asked me how I liked Arizona and I said I liked the appliance and furniture business but my allergies were acting up like crazy and it was just too hot for me. I asked how the airplane business was going and he said, "Good, come on back." I said, "I might just do that."

When I got back to Casa Grande I told the wife Gene wanted me to come back to Minnesota. I asked her what she thought about that? She liked Arizona but missed seeing her parents and relatives so she was in favor of going back. At supper we asked the kids what they thought and they were all in favor of going back to Minnesota. I think even Ginger wanted to go back!

So I called Gene to make sure he was serious. He said, I've sold enough new Cessna's to win a trip to Hawaii for two and if you'll come back, you can have the tickets! I guess he was serious! And the wife liked the idea of going to Hawaii!

I discussed the possibility of us going back to Minnesota with Herb and Joyce and asked them if that would create any hardships for them. They and their family didn't mind the heat, they said, and they liked the appliance and furniture business and Casa Grande. So we sold our share of the business to Herb and Joyce and listed the house with a realtor.

We spent the next couple of days packing things up and then I went and rented the biggest Hertz truck they had. It was just as easy to move out as it had been to move in being everything was on the ground floor! This time though we had appliances to load so we loaded them first and stacked boxes on top of them. Next came the bedroom dressers and again we stacked boxes on them right up to the roof. With everyone helping we had that truck all loaded and ready to go in just a few hours. We had so much room in the truck we didn't even have to put anything in the station wagon! After a final check of the house, we walked next door and said good-bye to Bill and Marjorie Graves and asked them if they'd keep an eye on the house until it got sold. Of course they would, they said. Bill said he'd miss having a beer with me once in a while.

We stopped by the store and said good-bye the Herb and Joyce again and wished them success in the business.

Just for the change of scenery, we decided to head north on I10 to Phoenix and then I17 to Flagstaff and East on I40 toward Albuquerque, New Mexico. The first day we made it to near Grants, New Mexico and found a neat little motel with a diner for the night. We had a nice supper and then the kids played on the swings while the wife and I went for a little walk. Something is wrong within me though. I'm not feeling the same about the wife. That statement she made, "he can be a son of a bitch sometimes," is haunting me. Also, the fact that she didn't want to be with me when I, soloed Tim, "in case he crashed." Then I got reminded about, "my mother thinks you're bored because you fell asleep on the family room floor." Other than that though she's a good woman. She keeps a good house and takes good care of the kids. She doesn't waste money and she's never turned me down for sex. But I sense something is wrong, something is missing?

One thing nice though, we were at about 6,500 feet so it was cool! We were all glad to be out of the heat! But the altitude also made us a little short of breath walking!

We all slept really good though and were up bright and early! The diner was open so we had breakfast and loaded up and headed out by 7 am! In about an hour we were near Albuquerque and heading north on I25. Once again both vehicles were running perfectly. I had refueled and then checked the oil and radiators on both the truck and station wagon and neither one needed anything!

It was about noon when we got to Raton Pass so we decided to stop there for a little exercise and lunch again. Plus the boys wanted to climb the sand hills again! They didn't find any snakes this time and even if they had, we had learned not to kill them.

We stopped at a service station in Trinidad for fuel and then I called Ed and Roberta Sutton in Littleton, Colorado to see if they wanted company for the night. They did! I told Ed we'd be near Littleton about 5 pm and he said he'd meet us at a nearby truck stop and lead us to their house. Ed was there when we got there and after a short greeting we followed him up to the house. Roberta is always so glad to see us! She had made a very nice supper, which we all enjoyed! We visited while our kids played with their kids, Grant and Maren out in the yard.

The next morning after breakfast we said good-bye and thanks for everything to Roberta, Ed, Grant and Maren. Usually the boys got into the truck with me and the girls went with their mother in the station wagon. But this time LeeAnn wanted ride in the truck so Tim rode with the wife in the station wagon. Then Ed lead us back out to the Freeway and we headed north on I25.

We made it just north of Des Moines, Iowa that day and pulled into another motel with a restaurant nearby. It had been another long day, so we had supper and took a walk and turned in early. The kids were getting excited about seeing their grandparents the next day if everything went right. We called the wife's parents and told them where we were and I said if everything went right we should be getting into Cloquet about 3-4 pm the next day. We were going to be staying with them until we found a house in Duluth.

The next morning everyone was up and ready for breakfast by 7 am and we were back on I35 by 8:00. It was good to be back in familiar territory. And I was thankful that we hadn't had any mechanical or tire problems on either vehicle. We arrived safe and sound back at the wife's parents place just about as scheduled, around 4 pm.

It felt good to be home. But, it had also been a great experience for the whole family to live in Arizona for a year. And the appliance and furniture business had been interesting and fun too. And I had a lot of fun learning to fly gliders and then giving rides to our visiting friends from Minnesota.

Chapter Twenty Four

Back Home

We spent a few days unwinding at the wife's parents. They were really happy to have us back home. Then the wife and I drove over to Duluth to see if we could find a house. Somehow we ended up in the Kenwood area and driving out the Jean Duluth road. I turned left and up a hill on Morningside Avenue. It was a nice neighborhood. We had gone a few blocks and pretty soon saw a sign, for sale by owner. It was a two, story house with a walkout basement and an attached garage. Nice looking house we thought. I pulled in the driveway and we got out and I pressed the doorbell.

A lady came to the door. I immediately got a mental rating that she was an "8M". I'm not sure just when I had developed this talent but somehow I had a few years back. I have the unique ability to just look at any woman and in a blink, I get a mental readout on the 1-10 scale, like 8M. That means she's an 8 out of 10 and she is a moaner. An "S" is a screamer and a "P" is a painter. Naturally a moaner, moans when she's making love, a screamer screams, and a painter, she looks up and says, this ceiling needs painting. I didn't dare demonstrate this gift to any of my friends though by telling them what their wives are for fear of them saying, "how the hell do you know that!" It was many years later before I openly started demonstrating this talent to anyone.

The house was nice with four bedrooms upstairs. The master bedroom even had a 3quarter bath. I liked that. It had a nice kitchen, living room and dining room and bathroom on the main floor. Downstairs it had a den with a fireplace, a utility and laundry room, an unfinished room, another bathroom and a lot of storage space. We went out and walked around the yard. It had a lot of slope to it being the house was built on the side of a hill. I thought, hmmm, at least the basement will never be flooded! We liked the house. It just felt right to the wife and me. I asked the lady for a couple of days to bring the kids over, etc. and she said, OK. We thanked her and left. We drove further down the street and whenever we saw people out in their yard I'd stop and go over and ask them about the neighborhood, etc. Everyone we talked to liked the area. The kids would have to ride a bus to school. I guessed that would be OK with them. We drove around for a couple more hours but didn't see anything we liked better, so drove back down Morningside Avenue again for another look at the house. We still liked it. The next day we brought the kids over and showed them the house, the neighborhood and the school. They all liked it too!

But I was still haunted about these feelings I had about the wife. I gave some thought to getting a smaller, cheaper house in case we ended up getting divorced. But then I thought, I'll keep trying. I didn't want to hurt my kids with a divorce.

Being I hadn't sold my house in Arizona, yet I wasn't in position to just buy another yet, so I went downtown to the Northwestern Bank and talked to Bill Radke. Bill was a super nice guy. I told him I had owned Sunnyside Motel and Mobile Home Park, etc. and was going to be selling airplanes with Gene Berg up at Halvair Aviation. Bill was familiar with Halvair and Gene he said. I filled out a financial statement for him and he said to call him tomorrow. The next after-noon I called Bill and he said he'd be glad to finance the house for me. So I called the lady and told her that! They had already bought a house wherever it was her husband had been transferred to so it was only going to be a day or two and they could be moved. It took Bill a couple of days to get all the paperwork done and the lady met us at Bill's office and an hour later we owned another house! I wasn't real sure if I could afford two houses, but somehow I figured it would work out. But, like I always figured, if you ain't living on the edge you're taking up to damned much space anyway! Besides, I know God loves me and will help me. I also know that when I meet him he is going to want to discuss some of the jokes I've told. And he'll probably want to know just where I got this gift to be able to rate a woman and tell if she is a moaner, screamer or a painter. (Hmmm, I sure hope he has a sense of humor!)

We also were going to need another car so I went looking and came across a pretty little red 1972 Mustang. It was like brand new! I had sold my 67 Mustang when we moved to Casa Grande so I knew I'd like another Mustang. So I bought it!

It only took the lady a couple of days to move out of the house and she called and said she'd leave the keys in the mailbox. So early the next morning I drove the truck and the wife drove the station wagon and we drove up to Morningside Avenue to get moved into our new house! It was a lot more work moving into a, two story house than it had been into the house in Casa Grande with everything on one floor! We had to haul all the bedroom furniture and clothes up the stairs and the washer, dryer and hide-a-bed down the stairs. But after a few hours, a lot of water and a few beers we got the job done!

I took another day to mow the grass and get settled in and then went to work on June 18th, 1975. Gene was really glad to have me back. We spent the morning discussing the inventory he had and then he took me to lunch at the Officer's Club on the base. After lunch Gene and I flew down to Lake Elmo in a 210 and I flew a new Cessna 180 that Gene had bought from Ward Holiday back to Duluth. On the morning of the 19th I flew a Cessna 172 N64249 for an hour just to be current in one again.

On the 26th I flew a new Cessna 185 N1229F down to Superior and made four, wheel landings and takeoffs to get recurrent in it. One of the instructors, who just happened to be a very attractive female, had asked if she could go with me. I said, of course and automatically got a mentally read-out that she was a "8M". She didn't have any "tail wheel" time so this was her first ride in one. It was my lucky day and I greased all four landings to a full stop and the four takeoffs were straight down the center of the runway. The instructor said, "that she hopped someday she could fly a taildragger as good as I do." I took that as a compliment and mentally raised her from an "8" to a "8.5", she was still a moaner though.

I remember being up at Baudette for their pancake breakfast and Aviation Days a month or so later. There were several Cessna dealers from around the state with various airplanes on display.

I flew "29Fox" up there and displayed it with some Cessna pennants on it and handed out brochures for most of the day.

My dealer friend, Vern Evanson, from Iowa Aviation in Des Moines, was also there with a new Cessna 340. Vern and I had about the same warped sense of humor I thought. Our telephone calls usually started out with the latest sick joke either one of us had heard.

It was always good to see Vern. We had lunch together and he showed his 340 while I was showing the 185. When it became time to leave I said good-bye to Vern and we both got in our airplanes and started up. I taxied out just ahead of Vern. I did my run up and I could hear him behind me running the 340 up. I called that I was taking off on runway 30 and Vern said I'm right behind you. So I taxied out onto the runway and taxied down a ways so as to make room for Vern and to not sandblast his new 340. The wind had increased during the day to about 20 knots from the southwest and I'm taking off to the west, northwest so I've got a pretty good crosswind component from the left. The only trouble was I didn't think too much about that at the time, I'm just going to show Vern and everyone else just how short this 185 can get off the ground. So I dropped two notches of flaps and fire-walled, that 185 and pushed the tail up, all within 50 feet. I had kind of forgotten all about torque, "P" factor, the crosswind and losing tail wheel steering by doing that. I had a foot full of right rudder and 29Fox, was still heading for the left side of the runway. This had to be another time that God must have been looking down at me, probably shaking his head in wonderment, because I lifted 29Fox off the runway just in time to miss a runway marker. Then I heard Vern say on unicom, "Hubbell, you dumb shit!" I made a mental note to not do that again, and gave my takeoff a "2", being I hadn't damaged 29Fox. I'd come close though!

The realtor called from Casa Grande and said he had a buyer for the house. He wanted to know if he got a deposit, could he let them move into the house and they'd have the rest of the down payment within 30 days. He didn't have anything else going so I agreed to that.

On the 30th of July I flew a 210 for .6hr to get recurrent in a single engine retractable again. I liked 210's. Come to think about it, I like almost every airplane.

August 1st I flew another 185, N122F out to Jamestown and closed out a Skymaster deal. The rest of August was kind of slow. On the 20th I flew down to Hector in the 210 N1681X and picked up Gene after he delivered an aircraft down there. Gene and I were working good together. He helped me when I needed it and I'd help him when he needed help.

On the wife's birthday, August 12th, 1975, I was driving downtown trying to figure out what to get her for a present. She had a lot of clothes and about everything else she needed or ever wanted so I was thinking I'd just take her to the Highland supper club. I happened to be driving by Ryland Ford in west Duluth when I looked over and there was a pretty little orange Ford Pinto station wagon in the show room window. The wife's favorite color was orange! I thought, hmmm, that's what I'll get her for a birthday present! So I went in and made a deal on the little orange station wagon and had them deliver it up to the house right after lunch. I told them it was going to be a surprise birthday present for the wife and I wanted it to be in the garage before she got home from work about 4:30. They delivered it and I put some flowers in a vase and a card on it for her. The kids and I were watching as she drove up and hit her garage door opener. She got out and was really excited to see that little orange Pinto station wagon! We all piled in and went for a drive out the Jean Duluth road a few miles and back. (And no, I didn't know that the gas tank could explode if it got hit from the rear!)

I hadn't heard anything from the realtor in Casa Grande so I called him to see what was going on. He said the people really like the house but they are having a little trouble raising the rest of the down payment, but he felt they would have it soon. I asked him if he was still showing to other people but he said he hadn't, being these people had signed a purchase order.

On September 2nd I flew up to Eveleth and met with Jim Olson. Jim owned Virginia Homes. I had met him when I was flying for Northland Homes and his crews had moved a few homes that he had sold into Sunnyside when I owned it. We specked out a new Cessna 1975 182 for him. I suggested he personalize it with a custom "N" number. He thought about it for a while and said, how about "3VH" for Virginia Homes and that's what I ordered. I liked Jim. He was fair to deal with. He didn't try to cut me off at the ankles. I had learned already that other sales people are the easiest to do business with. They're so tired of people chiseling them that all they want is a fair deal. They realize that the other guy has expenses too. I'm that way when I buy something too, not that I'm going to just lay down and get screwed, but give me a fair price and I'll buy it.

On the morning of the 4th I flew down to Cable, Wisconsin and demo'd a 210 N1798X to Newman Foley. After lunch I flew N7646Quebec up to Grand Rapids. I missed flying 46Quebec so it was a real treat to fly her to Grand Rapids! They needed her for a charter for the Blandin Paper Company. I brought the 185 N1221Fox back to Duluth

On the 5th I got on a jet out of Duluth and went to Wichita, Kansas and picked up a new 172 N64062 and brought that home with a stop in De Smet, South Dakota to have lunch with Johnson and Peggy.

On the 6th Gene and I flew 21Fox back up to Grand Rapids for the MATA (Minnesota Aviation Trade Association) meeting.

Gene let me use a 172 N9915G to go to Grand Rapids, Michigan for one of my niece's, Debbie's, wedding! I and the wife and another couple loaded up our baggage and we flew over to Grand Rapids, Michigan for the wedding on September 11, 1975. As usual I crossed Lake Michigan from Manitowoc across to Ludington. Again I figured, "if you ain't living on the edge, you're taking up to damned much space!" Besides, the oil pressure was good, there was no oil on the windshield and we had a lot of fuel! Besides that, I was hoping the wife might learn to, "get as much as you can while you can, in case it's your last day!" That's always my greatest fear, that, I'm going to die before I had some sex for the day! I sometimes dream that I'm getting killed in a car accident and I'm asking God if I could go home for an hour first to have some sex before I come to heaven?

The weather was CAVU so the trip across the lake was beautiful. There were always ships around if I had to make a forced landing. The only thing you need to remember is to land about a mile in front of an ore boat because it takes them about that long to get it stopped. You might want to remember to land parallel to the swells too. But we had another uneventful crossing and a great time at my sister's house and my niece's wedding. On the trip home I decided to take a different route. So I just flew northwest until I was on the east shore of Lake Michigan and then followed that north until about Glen Arbor. Then I turned northwest and cut across the lake passing just south of South Manitou Island and then across to Washington Island and on to Iron Mountain for fuel and lunch. The weather was good VFR but

I was bucking a 15knot headwind so it was kind of slow going, but at least it was smooth and it was beautiful!

It had been a good trip. Except for the fact that whenever I'd pull carburetor heat the wife would about bail out. I must have explained to her 50 times why the engine changes pitch a little when I applied carb heat and every time, it would be, "is everything OK?" I was getting to where I'd just ignore her. She had already shown me that she didn't have any confidence in me anyway when I soloed Tim. Then, I wondered if that lady in Casa Grande still needed her TV adjusted?

I took a 210 N1798X over to Wisconsin Rapids, and demo'd it to Larry Grange on September 17th. Larry liked the airplane and I spent a couple of hours checking him out in it. Then we flew up and landed at Madison, Wisconsin to put it in his hangar and I was going to fly his Cessna 180 that I had seen earlier and was taking in trade, back to Duluth. As he pulled up in front of his "T" hangar I said, "Are you planning on putting this in there?" He said, "Yes." I said, "It ain't going to fit." The horizontal stabilizer of his 180 barely fit with only six inches on either side and the 210's stabilizer is about two feet wider than a 180's. He said, "I can't buy this if it won't fit in the hangar." I asked, "Can you trade hangars with anyone?" He said, "No, they're all the same size and there wasn't any room to build a new hangar anyplace." Well, he was truly disappointed and so was I, because I had two house payments due!

On September 19th I got on a North Central Convair and flew down to Madison to pick up a C180 N52067 that Gene had bought and brought it back to Duluth. The next day I got a special VFR out of Duluth and headed west with 067going to Larimore, North Dakota, about 20 miles west of Grand Forks. The weather in Duluth was about a 600 ft ceiling and

2 miles visibility. I understood it was going to get better as I went west but someone must have had the page upside down because it got worse! But, not to worry I figured, there's a railroad track heading that way so I intercepted it just west of Duluth. I always figured, they don't build towers in the middle of railroad tracks! I always put a landing light on and hoped there wasn't some other idiot coming the other way! It always amazed me what I would fly through when my house payment was due and now I've got two of them! I broke out of the fog about 20 miles west of Duluth and had an uneventful flight out to Larimore. I landed there and met Denny Kello. Denny and I flew it for about 20 minutes and landed back at Larimore for his mechanic to look it over. It was a very nice 180 and after about an hour of compression checks and opening the oil filter and a bunch of panels, the mechanic gave it his blessings and Denny gave me a check and flew me back to Grand Rapids.

I picked up a 310 N8917Z and flew that back to Duluth because the flight department needed it for a charter the next day. It was after supper when I got home. As usual the kids and Ginger were glad to see me. The wife was cleaning up the kitchen and hardly acknowledged that I was home. I was wondering why I even bothered buying her a nice house, on "snob hill," as our friends called it. I was starting to realize that I was married to the wrong woman. I wasn't getting what I wanted out of this marriage.

On September 27th I flew a Lake amphibian for the first time. We were brokering it for someone. Gene asked me if I had ever flown one and I said, no. He said, "Well go out and make a few landings until your comfortable." So I read the manual and preflighted it and got in and started it up and taxied out to runway 27. I did a run up, called the tower, got a takeoff clearance and pulled out onto the runway. I let it accelerate until the airspeed was near the green arc and nudged in a little back, pressure and pretty soon we were airborne! I got a right turn out from 27 and headed northwest toward Fish Lake. I did a couple of stalls, some slow flight, etc. and then landed on Fish Lake. The water was rough with about a foot chop. I must have had the left wing a hair lower than the right wing because when I touched down I ended up in a pretty sharp turn to the left because of the drag of the left sponson. That surprised me a little! So I took off and came around and landed again. This time it went to the right! I wasn't too sure if I was going to like this LA4 or not! I thought, if it ain't a 185 skipping across the water it's a LA4 dodging left or right! The third landing was OK so I called it quits while I was ahead and flew it back to the airport and made a decent landing. (Decent landing: any one that you can walk away from.)

On October 8th I took a C172 N1408V down to Albert Lea and demo'd it to Ron Buccanan. The 9th I went and made three more landings with the LA4 back up on Fish Lake. This time the water was fairly calm so I was able to just kiss it on the water. Now I liked it better!

Chapter Twenty Five

The Worst I've Ever Felt About Myself

One nice beautiful October day I decided to take a day off and take Ginger out partridge hunting. I called Gene to see if he could get along without me for the day. He said, "You've been working a lot of long days and you deserve to go, so you and Ginger have fun." Gene was great to work with. The kids were in school, the wife had gone to work, so it was just me and Ginger. All I had to say to Ginger was, "wanna go for a ride" and she'd beat me to the door. So I put my shotgun and some shells in the trunk and Ginger sat on the right front seat on a rug and we headed west on hwy 2 towards Brookston, where we hunted deer. I stopped along the way and bought a license and filled up with gas. It was a beautiful fall day, and Ginger was all excited, that she was going hunting. I had never taken her hunting before, just hiking once in a while, so I was anxious to see if she was a good hunter or not. Of course, most labs are born hunters. And Ginger was a golden lab. And of course like all dogs she just loved to have her head out the window and her ears flopping in the breeze! I never thought about getting a fan so she could do that at home in the winter. Hmmm, I wonder what she would do? Would she sit in front of a fan with her ears flopping in the breeze? Hmmm, I'll have to try that someday.

We finally got out to the hunting area and got out of the car. Ginger was all excited. I'd never seen her this excited. I thought, hmmm, maybe I should take the wife hunting? I put a few shells in the 20 gauge and we headed down the trail. Ginger was hunting just great. She was running back and forth across the trail and going into the woods about twenty-thirty feet on both sides of the road. I thought, how does she know how to hunt so good? And she was having fun! She was about like a kid in a candy store, I figured. We got about a quarter of a mile down the trail before she kicked a partridge up. It flew across the trail and I took a shot at it, and missed. When I turned around Ginger was running back down the trail toward the car. So I turned around and started walking back toward the car too. When I got to the car I saw that she had scratched the hell out of the drivers side door getting through the open window and into the back seat. And then I did the worst thing I've ever done in my life. I was furious that she had scratched the hell out of the door on my pretty little red Mustang, and I reached in and hit her in the rump, with the butt of my shotgun. And then I instantly felt like shit! I realized that she had gotten scared as hell when that shotgun fired and she couldn't help herself. I opened the door and knelt down and put my arms around her. She was shaking with fear. I said, "I'm sorry Ginger, I'm so sorry honey, please forgive me," and I had tears running down my face. And then Ginger looked at me as if she was saying, "I forgive you stupid" and she started licking my face. I hugged her more and apologized some more. I have never felt worse about myself in my life. I was too ashamed of myself to tell anyone what I had done when I got home. I just made sure Ginger had a good supper and petted her and hugged her some more. The next evening when I came home from work, Ginger met me at the door, her tail was wagging and she was obviously glad to see me, as usual. I've often thought, I wish I had a wife with a disposition like Ginger has. I know damn well if I ever kicked the wife in the butt before I went to work in the morning, she'd meet me at the door with a butcher knife in her hand when I got home! I must have apologized to Ginger 50 times for that over the years. I took her hiking after that but never again hunting. Earl King had his shop fix the door for me for a 100 bucks and it was like new again. But, I was too ashamed to tell any-one what a terrible thing I had done. I decided, I'm never going to tell anyone.

Several times when the kids and wife had left the house in the morning, and later I'd get in my car and leave, only to get a block or so down the road and remember something else I needed and I'd turn around. As I approached the house I'd hit the garage door opener and come through the kitchen door at a full run almost and Ginger would come creeping out of the living room. Her brown eyes would be looking up at me with a very guilty look. I'd scold her a little and say, "Ginger, you know you don't belong in the living room," and she'd creep back over to her rug. Somehow though I just knew that when I was a block down the road again, she was laying on the couch with the TV remote, flipping through the channels.

When Ginger died in 1982 Tim and I built a coffin and we painted it gold with a brown cross and put her name and dates on it. And then we laid her in it on her rug and put a half dozen of her favorite, chocolate chip cookies next to her and screwed the cover on.. Tim drove her from St Cloud up to Carl's place out west of Cloquet and buried her. I've had a couple of friends ask me why I had gone to so much trouble and expense for a dog. I said, "She wasn't just a dog, she was part of the family." I had taught Ginger several tricks and she had performed many times for the neighborhood kids on "snob hill." She was family.

Chapter Twenty Six

Gene had sold a Skymaster N5430S to Ray Grover and asked me if I'd check Ray out in it. So I flew with Ray on October 12, 13th and 15th and then again on November 10 on the way down to Maple Lake so he could take his check ride with Bill Mavencamp Sr.. He passed.

On October 17th Gene let me take a Cessna 180 N9965N to Erwin, SD, pheasant hunting for a few days. I loaded up the whole family including Ginger and we flew out and landed on the highway in front of Johnson's house and taxied right up into his yard. Johnson still hadn't modified his power pole but at least with a tail dragger I could get out in the field and go around it. I had given up on the idea of Johnson ever modifying that pole anyhow. I figured it was low on his list of things to do.

As usual the hospitality of the whole Johnson family was great as well as the food! And the hunting was always good too! I could never believe how many pheasant we'd kick out of Evert's tree line around his house at the end of the day.

When we left there on Sunday afternoon, Johnson went out on the highway and drove north about a half a mile and stood traffic guard. Peggy drove south on top of the hill. I did my run up on the end of his driveway, made sure everyone was buckled in, checked right for any traffic and pulled out and took off. I'd always circle back and wiggle the wings at Johnson's before we headed northeast.

The weather was, "clear and unlimited" with a little tail-wind, so we were landing back in Duluth in a little less than two hours. Every time I fly I wonder, what do people do that don't fly? Just to be able to take off and fly a straight line for 300 miles and enjoy looking down from a thousand feet at things on the ground, the farms, lakes, cities, woods, and the cars crawling along the highways, has always amazed me. My only fear in life is when I can't go flying every week. Actually, I guess that's not my only fear, the other fear I have is not making love every night! My perfect day would be to make love at 6 am in the morning, fly 46Quebec for an hour, sneak home for a "nooner," fly a 185 in the afternoon, and stop at the Chalet for a beer on the way home. And then have a nice supper, visit with the kids and make love again before the ten o'clock news. I probably would never have time to go home for a nooner though. Hmmm, I wonder if I could get the wife to drive over to the airport?

The day after I got back from pheasant hunting I demo'd the Lake amphib to Creighton Tripp.

I demo'd, sold, and checked out Denny Overland and Dick Hamilton in a Skymaster N86080 down in Albert Lea on October 22nd.

On November 19th, 1975 Gene and I flew down to St Louis in a 310 N8917Z for the annual Cessna meeting. It was fun. I got to meet a lot of dealers that I had talked to on the phone. I, remembered Duane Wallace from Cessna saying that they were going to sell 9,000 new Cessna's this year and would be selling 12,000 a year in the next few years. We flew back to Duluth on the 21st.

On November 26th I demo'd and sold a Cessna 180, N9965N, to Dr. Brown up in Bemidji, Minnesota.

November 28, 1975 Jimmy Olson from Virginia and I got on a North Central Convair to Minneapolis and then on to Wichita so Jimmy could pick up his new Skylane N3VH. I was picking up a new C185 N2258Romeo for inventory. Gene had called ahead to make sure both airplanes were at the delivery center and ready to go when we got there, and they were. That always saved some critical time so we could make the trip in one day. Jimmy was really excited to see N3VH! I was happy for him too. He had worked hard for a lot of years and it was nice to see him reap the rewards of all that hard work and time. Both the 182 and 185 were "no radio" airplanes and I had showed Jimmy the straight line route that we would be flying on his map while we were en-route to Wichita. The weather around Wichita was good but there was a cold front laying east and west along the north-ern border of Kansas that might be a weather problem I said. We bought a couple of cans of pop and some candy bars for the trip. Then we inspected both airplanes, they were OK so I signed the delivery acceptance sheets for them. We pre-flighted and then I told Jimmy to follow behind me in my 7:30 o'clock position so that I could see him now and then. "The 185 will be a little faster that the 182" I said, "so I'll adjust my power setting to give me a 150mph airspeed so you can keep up."

So we departed Wichita and headed northeast. Jimmy was staying right were I had asked him to. Everything was work-ing out good until we got about 10 miles north of Emporia, Kansas. Then I saw the meanest looking roll cloud I had ever seen. It stretched as far west and east as I could see. Even from a couple of miles away from it I was feeling the 185 get-ting slapped around. I didn't like the looks of this thing at all! I made a left 180 and looked back to make sure Jimmy was following me, he was. We went back to Emporia and I landed with Jimmy right behind me. We taxied up to the building and shut down. There was nobody around. We used the bathroom and then discussed plan "B". "I was thinking of flying east, staying north of Kansas City and picking up I35 and following that to Duluth," I told Jimmy. He said that sounded good to him too. The only problem was that while we were standing there talking about it, the front was rapidly approaching us. All of a sudden the wind picked up over twenty five or thirty knots and things were going to hell in a hand basket in a hurry! I told Jimmy to get into 3VH and start it up and keep it pointing into the wind and stand on the brakes and apply however much power he needed to keep it from being blown backwards and hold the nose down little. I did the same thing in the 185. I stood on the brakes and applied enough power also and with that wind and power I had the tail off the ground to put the wings at a negative angle of attack and it was like it was glued to the earth! I looked over and saw Jimmy and 3VHotel being buffeted around pretty good and the 185 was rocking back and forth. It was also raining so hard that for a while I thought I was under water. It came down in buckets! We sat like that for what seemed like an hour but it was probably only 10-15 minutes and then all of a sudden it quit raining and the wind died back down as quickly as it had started. We shut back down and got out of the airplanes.

I got a map out and was showing Jimmy where we were and where we wanted to go and all of a sudden, I noticed Kansas City. I told Jimmy, "I've got a brother over here in Fairfax that I haven't seen for over a year" and "If it's OK with you I'll call him and see if he's home and if he is, we'll just fly over there and visit him for the night". Jimmy said that would be OK with him. I said he's an airline pilot so he might be gone on a trip. With the help of an information operator, I found my brother's telephone number and called him up. He said he was between trips so come on over and that Fairfax airport was the closest to him. I found a number for the Fairfax tower and called them up. I told the controller we had two no radio airplanes, a Cessna 182 N3VH and a Cessna 185 N2258R over here at Emporia and wanted to land over there at Fairfax to visit my brother. He said, "No problem. Just circle those two smokestacks with the red and white stripes on them about 3 miles northwest of the airport. When I see you I'll give you a flashing green light and when I can clear you to land I'll give you a steady green light." Then he said to enter a right base for 18. I asked where the FBO was and he said it was on the west side of the runway so we agreed that I'd be making a right turn off and then taxi to the FBO. I showed Jimmy where we were going and pointed out the smokestacks northwest of the Fairfax airport. Then I told Jimmy that when we get a steady green light to follow me on a right base and then land on runway 18 and we'd make a right turn off and taxi to the FBO. I made a point of telling Jimmy that a couple of times, "Now Jimmy, we're landing here at Fairfax airport on the west side of the river, not down over here at downtown Kansas City on the east side of the river. Have you got that?" He said he did. I said, "Let's make another formation takeoff again and just stay on my tail." Before we left Wichita I had told Jimmy, "I'll take the left side of the runway and you stay behind me on the right side, got that?" He said," OK." We started up and taxied out, and after a quick run up I taxied to the left side and Jimmy took the right side. I made a partial power takeoff with the 185 so Jimmy could keep up with me. We took off to the northwest and I made a left turn back over the airport and rolled out heading for Fairfax. I looked back a couple of times and Jimmy was right in my 7:30 o'clock position. Right where I had told him to stay. It wasn't very long and I had the smokestacks northwest of the Fairfax airport in sight. I circled them to the left as I had told Fairfax tower I'd do and Jimmy was right on my tail. Good job Jimmy, I'm thinking! After the second 360 around the smokestacks I saw the steady green light from the tower so I broke off and entered a right base for runway 18. I turned final and all of a sudden, there goes Jimmy about a hundred feet over me heading for downtown Kansas City airport!

I landed and taxied in to the FBO and got out and found a phone and called the tower. I asked, "Did 3 Victor Hotel go land at downtown?" He said, "Yes he did, but I called over there and warned them and said to turn him around and send him back over here." I said, "Thanks a lot, I appreciate that!" About a half hour later Jimmy came back over and landed at Fairfax. He was kind of embarrassed but I told him, "if that's the worst mistake you ever make you'll be lucky."

I called my brother and shortly he was there to pick us up and he drove us back to his house. Nice place I thought. Maybe I should be an airline pilot?

His wife gave Jimmy and I a nice greeting and my brother mixed us a drink. We drank that one and then he made me another one and said to me, "Come on I'll show you the yard." So we went out and walked around his yard and then he told me he was going through a divorce and needed some money really bad. I said I could loan him ten thousand dollars if that would help him. He said he needed a lot more than that. I said I didn't have a lot more than that lying around, but if ten will help you, I can do that.

We went back inside and visited some more and then my brother said, "Let's go out for supper." I said, "I'll buy even!"

So Jimmy and I freshened up a little and my brother drove a couple of miles to a supper club. It was a nice place and the meal was great. Jimmy and I had another drink while my brother had a couple more. Things were going along pretty good until all of a sudden my brother accuses me of only stopping when I need free room and board and then for disrupting the family, because I had stuck up for a younger sister that my mother had been physically abusing. I had been the only one of nine kids that had tried to solve that problem.

Jimmy told him I hadn't said anything about free room and board, I had only said, "I hadn't seen my brother for over a year." I told my brother, "I have company credit cards and can stay anyplace I want and have steak every night if I want to, so just take us back to the house and we'll call a cab and be out of here." I paid the bill and we drove back to the house, but then it was the, arm around the shoulder and please, don't go etc. so I ended up spending the night, but I sure didn't sleep any The next morning he made coffee and pancakes and sausage and we ate breakfast.

Then he drove us back to the Fairfax airport. It was a marginal VFR day with a thousand foot ceiling with light snow and three miles visibility. We got out of his truck and I had walked about 30 feet away when I heard my brother holler, "I hope you bust your ass on the way home." I felt like I had been shot in the back. I didn't even turn around. I was stunned. I couldn't believe what I had just heard. And I believed he meant it. I'm thinking, how can a professional pilot wish another pilot, a brother no less, dead in an airplane? It brought tears to my eyes. I preflighted the 185. Jimmy came over to see if I was OK and said, "maybe I shouldn't be flying for a while." I said, "I'll be OK, let's just get the hell out of here."

I told Jimmy we were going to fly northeast and intercept I35 and head north. So we started up and taxied out and made another formation takeoff and went over and picked the freeway up. My mind wasn't on flying at all. I was just flying from habit. My mind was asking how could he say that? I had just offered to loan him ten thousand dollars even. I had loaned him money when he was going to college and living in my mobile home park too. And he's already lost one brother who died a violent death. How can he wish me, another brother and also a fellow pilot, a violent death in an airplane? My mind was full of questions and maxed out. I really shouldn't be flying I thought, but I wanted to get away from there and go home. I thought, maybe he'll call me tonight or tomorrow and apologize?

We hadn't refueled since leaving Wichita so I decided to land at Owatonna, just south of Minneapolis for some fuel. There had been a sleet storm through the area the night before so the runway was glare ice with about a 15 knot direct cross wind. The windsock was sticking straight out. I wheel landed the 185 down onto the icy runway and when I got the tail down it was sliding sideways. I was holding just enough power to keep from being blown off the downwind side of the runway. Finally I got slowed up enough to make a right turn and taxi up to the fuel pumps. I looked back and Jimmy was sliding down the runway sideways too and made the same turn off. We filled both airplanes up and took off and climbed up to 5,500 feet and passed just about right over the Minneapolis airport heading for Duluth. We landed back in Duluth about 3 pm. Jimmy drove his car back to Virginia because we were going to be installing radios in 3VH over at our radio shop in Grand Rapids. I told Gene about the trip and my brother wishing me dead and sliding sideways down the runway at Owatonna, etc. He thought we should de-brief over at the Officer's Club. He couldn't believe what had happened to me either.

When I got home the kids and Ginger ran out into the garage and were glad to see me. The wife was making supper and hardly acknowledged that I was home. After the kids had gone to bed I told her about being wished dead, but she didn't have any comment one way or the other. I'm getting a very sickening feeling that I'm married to the wrong woman too. Come to think about it, I've never heard a kind, supportive, complimentary, or appreciative word from her, ever.

I thought sure my brother would call me that evening and apologize, but I never heard from him. I was sure he'd call the next day, but he didn't. It started to dawn on to me more and more that he meant it. I'd never had anyone wish me dead before. It's a sickening feeling. Especially since I had never done anything to him and always was there to help him whenever he asked. Sure we used to fight as kids, but that was a long time ago?

Chapter Twenty Seven

On December 1st I flew 3VH up to our Grand Rapids operation to have radio's installed in it. The 2nd I flew the 185 N2258R out to Michigan, ND, about 25 miles west of Grand Forks, and demo'd and sold it to Don Orwick.

On December 5th, 6th, and 7th I flew our Cardinal RG N2090Quebec for a total of 2.7 hrs to renew my instructor rating.

On December 19th I flew a P337 we had, N92Charlie down to Des Moines, Iowa and demo'd it. No sale, no house payment!

Then I took a few days off for Christmas! It wasn't a good Christmas for me though. I was still haunted by the feeling that my brother wanted me dead. I was having a hard time with that. I get chills up my spine whenever I think about it.

We drove over to Cloquet and spent a couple of days at the wife's parents. The boys and I had a lot of fun riding Carl's snowmobiles on the trails on the 40 acres out behind the house. The weather was perfect, about 20 above and no wind with about two feet of snow on the ground. Once in a while Carl would come out and go snowmobiling with the boys too.

As usual, about twenty relatives arrived for Christmas day dinner. The mother in law had made pies and put a turkey in the oven over night and a couple of the aunts brought pork and beef roast. There was always enough food to feed an army and enough booze and beer to stock a bar. One thing though, I never saw anyone even a little "tipsy". I would never drink much either. After about three drinks I'd always go into the bathroom and look in the mirror, and if I started looking "blurry" to myself, I knew it was time to quit. I do that when I go out at night too. When the waitress ask me if I want another drink, I ask her, " if I looked blurry to her yet?" And if she say's no, I can have another drink. But I always tell her, "when I start looking blurry to you, cut me off." Some of those waitress's sure give me some strange looks. I don't know why, I'm just trying to error on the safe side!

New Years day was a just like Christmas day at the in laws except for the presents. All the aunts and uncles would come for dinner and as usual there would be plenty of food and drinks. I still missed being able to visit with "Uncle Lawrence" though.

I pretty much took the first week of January off and caught up on my family time. Some of the evenings were so cold that I didn't want the boy's out delivering their paper routes, so I'd drive them around instead of them walking their route.

Soon it was time to start thinking about the Hawaii trip that Gene had won for selling so many new Cessna's. After talking about it we decided that we were having a lot of fun flying around the country, going to Canada fishing, to Cessna meetings, etc. while the wives were at home taking care of the kids and cleaning the house. The Berg's had friends in Hawaii so we decided to let the "girls" take a trip for a change. When I thought about it, I realized the wife had never been away from the kids except for a couple of days in the hospital to have another baby. It would be good for her to get away for a week, I figured. So when the day came we drove the "girls" to the airport and watched them board the airplane and being all excited to be going to Hawaii. The only thing I didn't figure on was how lonesome I was going to be without her. I was miserable! I had never felt this way when I was out delivering an airplane to Florida or going to New York to bring 372 home. Why was I feeling this way now? I didn't know. All I knew was that I was miserably lonesome without her at home. I don't think the wife was in her hotel room in Hawaii 15 minutes and I called her and told her how miserable I was and to get on a jet and come home. She said, "I can't do that, I'm with your boss's wife." I said, "I don't care if you're with the president's wife, come home." Then she said, "You're just afraid I'm having an affair." I said, "I never thought that. Why, are you?" Of course she denied it. I couldn't figure out why she'd say that, it had never crossed my mind. I never worried about that when I was traveling and she sure didn't have to worry about me either. I thought, hmmm, why would she say that? I called a couple more times the next day and finally decided I was being unreasonable. I tried to keep myself busy with the kids, making them breakfast and seeing them off to school and being home when they got back, etc. I was still miserable though. And I was still wondering why would she even say that? She was a secretary at an architectural firm downtown. I thought, hmmm, could one of the guy's from there be on Hawaii? I've never been the suspicious or inse-cure jealous type either. She would call home once in a while and say she was going to stop and have a drink with the girls, or they were having an office party and I always told her to have fun. I would call her every once in a while to tell her that Gene and I were going to stop for a drink too, so I never thought anything about it. Besides, she had my complete trust. And besides that, I've always believed you only get to go through this life once so you better have as much fun as you can the first time. It would have hurt me if she had said, "Hubbell you're a bore, I want to go live with this other guy." I would have said, "Hey I'll miss you, but I'll get over it." I always figured, if you really love someone, you love them enough to let them go. I was still wondering why she would say that though? Little by little though things are starting to stack up in my mind. First I heard, "my mother thinks you're bored because you took a nap on the family room floor." Then she'd rather be with the neighbor lady than by me when I soloed our son Tim on his 16th birthday in Casa Grande. Then I heard her say, "he can be a son of a bitch sometimes, but he gets the job done. " And now, "you're afraid I'm having an affair over here." Hmmm, no I'm not afraid, but I deserve to know if you are. I realized that she's a pretty woman and naturally other guy's will be interested in her. If she wasn't, I wouldn't have been interested in her. Hell, I've always considered myself just an average "mutt" and I get hit on once in a while too! Hmmm, I wonder if that lady in Casa Grande still needs her TV adjusted?

I'm mostly happy with her, she's a good mother, she keeps a good house, she's never turned me down for sex, I give her my check and she pays the bills and buy's the groceries. I beg her once in a while for coffee money and we've never had financial problems. The only thing I hadn't figured out yet is, why is my dog always happier to see me than the wife is when I get home? Hmmm, does my dog know something I don't know?

When she got back from Hawaii I thought about asking Gene to bring her home as long as he was going to be driving down to Minneapolis to get his wife, Kathy. I also thought about sleeping in the den and putting a note on the door to not wake me because I had to work for the "boss" in the morning. The only problem was, I haven't had sex for a week! I figured, hmmm, I need sex first, we can talk later. So I drove down and picked her up and made it halfway home before I stopped at a motel in Hinkley. That took care of my animal instinctive needs for a day or two anyway. I waited a few days before I brought up the "affair" subject one evening. I made sure she had a couple of drinks first. (I hate myself when I do that!) I always figured a couple drinks, is about like truth serum. She said she didn't know why she had said that. So I said, "If your not happy in this marriage just let me know because I'll cut you loose so you can go be happy with someone else." I didn't want to do that, I loved her very much but I didn't want a marriage without trust either.

A week or so later I was out in North Dakota demo'ing a Cessna 310 to a guy. When I checked weather for the return trip back to Duluth I found out the weather had gone downhill, bad. Duluth had a 200foot ceiling and a mile visibility. I thought about staying overnight in North Dakota but I also wanted to be home with my family. Besides I was horny again, or still. So I filed instruments and headed home. I was on top at 7 thousand FDAH. (Fat dumb and happy.) The tops were reported about 4 thousand over Duluth so I just figured, what else is new? I was also thinking, I've never actually told the wife that I'd like a hug and a kiss when I get home. I thought, no wonder stupid, she doesn't know what I would like! I'll just ask her when I get home! I picked up the usual 2 inches of ice and couldn't see out the windshield when I landed, but at least I was home. I called to tell her I'd be home in 30 minutes. When I came from the garage into the kitchen I stood for a few seconds wiping my feet on the rug. The wife was over at the stove stirring something. I asked, "Can I have a hug and a kiss when I come home?" She answered, "I'm not that way, I might burn the gravy." I turned around and went back out and got in my car and left. I thought, and I landed with two inches of ice and an iced over windshield to come home to a wife that's afraid she might burn the f--king gravy! I thought, I've got to start doing some serious thinking about this marriage. There's something seriously wrong when a woman would rather stir the f--king gravy than to welcome her husband home! I drove around a while thinking about what I had just heard. Then I went down and checked into the Hotel Duluth. I needed to be alone to think. I also needed a couple of drinks to numb my mind. I was in a state of shock I think. I still couldn't believe what I had heard. I wanted away from this totally unappreciative, unloving, woman I figured. I called Gene the next morning and told him what had happened and where I was and that I needed a couple of days off to do some thinking. I also asked him to not tell his wife or mine where I was, he agreed. I didn't even go out of the hotel. I was thinking divorce. I figured I had wasted my young love and energy on this woman and if she doesn't appreciate me by now, she's never going too! Too many things are adding up, my mother thinks your bored, the solo, he can be a son of a bitch, the affair and now, I'm not that way, I might burn the gravy. She doesn't even know who brings the f--king gravy home! If it wasn't for the kids I would file for divorce right now, I figured. I needed to do some serious thinking about this marriage.

On the third day she found out where I was and called me. I told her I needed to be alone for a while. I went to work the next day but I went back to the hotel afterwards. The next day she called and wanted to come see me. I said I'd meet her in the lounge but only to talk, don't even touch me, I said. She was there waiting for me and I sat down across from her. I told her how I felt and how much it had hurt to find out she was more concerned about burning the gravy than welcoming me home after I'd flown through the fog and ice to get home to my family. She was crying almost hysterically and apologizing, So, I let her come to my room and make love with me. What else could I do, I figured. Besides, it had been four days and I was horny again. So I checked out of the hotel and went home. I said good night to the kids. I was too tired emotionally to even make love again. We just fell asleep in each other's arms.

Everything was going along pretty good for a few weeks until one evening I came home again after a couple of days out demo'ing another airplane. I hadn't slept, very good the night before and it had been a long day by the time I got home and I was very, very tired. When I came through the door the wife was setting the table. I told her that I was very tired and I was going to lay on the couch and take a nap until supper was ready. I had never done that before. I had no longer gotten to sleep and she was shaking me to tell me I had a phone call. I got up and took the call. It was a guy interested in a 172. When I hung up I said, I told you I was very tired, why the hell didn't you just take a message instead of waking me up! She said, "you told me you never wanted to miss a call." I got in my car and left again, back down to the Hotel Duluth. I needed more time to think. Now I'm not only thinking this woman doesn't love me, I think she hates my f--king guts too! I told the switchboard operator I didn't want any calls from anyone. I just needed some time alone to think some more. I told the front desk I didn't want them to give my room number to anyone, especially the wife! I even parked my car in the garage so she couldn't find it. I called Gene and told him what had happened and that I needed a couple of more days off. Gene was very understanding.

I suppose Gene's wife told the wife where I was at and a few days later she was at my door, crying again. Well, I'm just a softy so I let her in, besides I was horny again too. I hate myself when I'm so weak! After making love a few times we went down to the lounge to talk. We had a couple of drinks and agreed we needed to talk and get some marriage counseling.

So I did a little research on local marriage counselors and we selected a husband wife team that were highly recommended. The first time we went to them they sat on a couch, one on each end of it and we sat in chairs across from them. She was doing all the talking, he was sitting there sleeping! I had never been to a marriage counselor before so I didn't know if this was normal behavior or what? He would even snore a little now and then. But after 45 minutes I couldn't take that anymore. I said, "Do you want to wake up a minute," loud enough so he woke up. He asked what was the matter? I said, "You're charging me a 100 dollars an hour for this? I think at least you could stay awake and act like you're interested in our problem." He straightened up and appeared to be listening after that. We went to them about three more times when he accused me of being paranoid one session. I stood up and said, "I want you to take a good look at my back." He said, "Why?" I said, "Because this is going to be the last time you're going to see it, you damned quack." And I turned around and we left. When we got home I told the wife that she could have gained a thousand points with me if she had told that quack that I wasn't paranoid. I said, "You've lived with me twenty years and you've never heard me say that I thought someone was out to get me or anything like it." I said, "You wouldn't even defend your own husband to that f--king quack." I'm really thinking divorce more now but hate to do that to my kids. I'm becoming more and more convinced that I'm married to the most unloving, unappreciative woman on earth! And I think I want out. And after that all I would hear is, "you're the one that's paranoid, you're the one that's sick"

Chapter Twenty Eight

On February 15th1976 I got a call from Wally Freeman down in Atkin, Minnesota about a 1961 Cessna 180 with wheels and floats that we had a brokerage agreement on. I asked him if he was related to the Freeman department store family, he said he was. I figured, hmmm, I guess he can probably afford this 180 then. So a couple of days later I flew the 180 N8665X down to the Aitkin airport. It was windy and cold out, maybe about "0". Wally arrived looking like an Eskimo in an insulated fur collared parka and insulated coverall's and insulated boots. I only had on dress slacks and a light jacket. The owner had forgotten to put the log books in the airplane when he had brought it down to Duluth, so after looking the plane over, we decided we'd fly up to Bemidji and get the log books. Wally was a big guy, especially with all those clothes on. We were about five miles northwest of Aitkin, out over the swamp land, when Wally looked at me and said, "What the hell would you do if the engine quit and we had to make a forced landing out here in the swamp, dressed like you are?" I said, "I suppose I'd die." He just shook his head in disbelief. The heater was working good though, so I wasn't worried. And like I always figured, "if you ain't living on the edge your taking up to damned much space anyway!"

We made it to Bemidji and got the logbooks and flew back to Aitkin. Wally had the mechanic look it over and we made a deal with a fresh annual on it. So I shut up and wrote up! I had learned that from Gene too. He'd said a lot of sales people lose the deal because they don't know when to shut up and write up! They just keep talking until the buyer gets bored and goes home. I wasn't that way though! If a buyer gave me just one buying signal, I was writing! Wally gave me a check and I flew back to Duluth. Gene was always so happy for me when I'd sell something! I liked working with Gene. It was fun. The next morning I flew the 180 up to Grand Rapids so they could do the annual and brought a 172 N5470M back for the flight department.

The next morning February 22nd 1976 I flew the 210, N1681X up to Two Harbors and picked John Norlen up and we flew down to St Cloud to look at a 180 on amphibian floats. John didn't like it and said for me to keep looking.

On March 18th I flew a 172 N12491 down to Crystal and demo'd it to Ray Johnson.

The next day I flew with Jon Wells from Duluth up to Eveleth to see Jimmy Olson's 182, N3VH. Jimmy had been hired by Midway Airlines and then Reno Airlines and had decided he no longer needed 3VH being he could get passes for him and his family now. It wasn't long and he became an MD80 Captain for Reno Airlines. Sadly, it wasn't long also and Jimmy came down with cancer. He had lost his first wife to cancer and now he has it. Jimmy died October 9th, 1996. I will always remember my friend Jimmy Olson as one of the very nicest guy's I have ever known and done business with.

I will also forever feel very sorry for his son Brian, first losing his mother and then his dad to cancer. Brian is flying for a charter company in Minneapolis.

On the 19th I flew a Cessna 180 N9748G up to Winnipeg, Canada and demo'd it to Pace Aviation. I stayed overnight but I didn't bother calling home anymore. I flew back to Duluth the next morning. I spent the day at the office looking for my next deal. Gene was really great, but he was concerned about me flying all kinds of airplanes through all kinds of weather with this divorce on my mind. He said if I didn't feel like flying and he wasn't busy he'd do my demo's for me. I thought that was nice of him. And I tried to make more of an effort to leave my divorce problems at home and not bring them to the airport. But that was sometimes hard to do. I still couldn't believe that my high school sweetheart wasn't the woman I thought she was.

On the 23rd Gene flew me down to St Cloud to pick up a Cessna 180N 7612K and bring it back to Grand Rapids to have the floats put on it.

On the 29th I flew our Cessna 180 N7541K up to Grand Rapids and then flew another 180 N9748G up to Bemidji and demo'd it to George Williams. George liked it so he had Mark Shultz at Bemidji Aviation do a pre-buy inspection on it. Mark gave it a clean bill of health and George bought it.

May 7th1976, I flew the Cessna 180, N8665X, on floats down to Round Lake north of Aitkin. It was called Round Lake because it was just about "perfectly round". In fact, I had never seen a lake so round! I spent a couple of days checking Wally Freeman out in 65Xray on floats. Wally and his wife Elaine were the most hospitable people you could ever hope to meet. They had a very nice house on the lake. Wally was showing me around, everything was solid oak and very nice. I assumed my best farm boy attitude and said, "Wow Wally, I bet you've got 35-40 thousand in this place!" (Knowing damned well it was worth at least $100,000) Wally gave me that same, you idiot look, like he had given me when we were flying across the swamp land and I only had slacks and a light jacket on. I liked Wally and Elaine, they were a couple of the he most unpretentious people you could ever hope to meet.

So were Loyd and Mary Jane Beaurline up in Cook, I remembered. Both Wally and Elaine and Loyd and Mary Jane were the kind of people that when you looked at them you wouldn't think they'd have a dime, but you'd be wrong. When you look at me you wouldn't think I'd have a dime either, you'd be right, (I got that line from Johnson some years back!) especially after all this divorce stuff! (I thought though, if I'm ever worth any money I'm going to be non-pretentious too!) I think most all our friends and my family always thought I was rich. A few times I had heard that, we lived on "snob hill". And of course, I'd had airplanes, nice cars and houses. But nobody ever factored in that when we owned Sunnyside we both worked seven days a week, 10-12 hours a day. And now when I'm selling airplanes they didn't see me working 6 or 7 days a week and flying through all kinds of weather to get the job done. And the wife was working as a secretary too. That's one thing we had agreed on, until all the kids were in school she'd be a stay at home mom. After the youngest was in the second or third grade and the older ones were able to take care of them until their mother got home, she'd stay home. After that I figured it would be good for her to get out of the house and have her own friends.

Wally had a pool table in his walkout basement so we also spent a lot of time playing pool after flying. We were about even, he'd win one I'd win the next one.

There were several float compartments leaking pretty bad, so on May 9th, I flew 65Xray back up to Grand Rapids for Gene Voigt and his crew to repair the leaks. I flew their 172, N9603H back down to Duluth.

I hadn't seen or talked to Gene for a few days so we went over to the Officer's Club to catch up with what we were both doing. I didn't even bother calling the wife to tell her I was back in town. After a two drink debriefing I drove home. As usual the kids and Ginger ran out to meet me. The wife was setting the table. I didn't really even care anymore. I was losing the love that I had for her. The kids were always anxious to hear where I had been and what I had been doing. I loved my kids and it was tearing me up inside knowing that I was probably going to divorce their mother. I just wasn't excited to come home to her anymore. I felt like I had already wasted too many years with her. I had thought about just living in the den but I had heard and read that, that isn't good for kids either. I didn't really know what to do. All I knew though was that if this woman didn't appreciate me by now, she never was going to. And I was tired of hearing her say in our discussions that, "you're the one that's sick. The counselor says you're the one that's sick." And I'd say, "And you believed that quack rather than knowing the man you've been married to for twenty years." I can't believe I've loved this woman for twenty years and now I want away from her. Too many things are adding up, my mother thinks your bored, he can be a son of a bitch, you're afraid I'm having a affair, I'm not that way I might burn the gravy, waking me up so I wouldn't miss a phone call. I'm wishing I had gone home and packed my bags after, my mother thinks you're bored! I couldn't help but wonder what would be next? And I'm losing my desire to have sex with her. And I figured, when I get to where I don't want to have any sex with her, I'll get it someplace else.

But I wonder if any other woman would want to have sex with me? I've never considered myself to be very much to look at and seriously doubted if any other woman would want to have sex with me. After all, the wife was the only woman I had ever had sex with. Was I in love with the wife, or was I in love with the sex? Hmmm, I think I was in love with both? Wasn't I, I asked myself. I know my heart used to skip a couple of beats when I'd come home and her car was in the garage when I hit the door opener. I know I wasn't just in love with her for the sex. But I know now that my love for her is going down the tubes, so to speak. How come Johnson was so lucky to marry a woman like Peggy? All he did was change an engine on a gooney bird up in Martinsburg, West Virginia, and meets a pretty waitress in a cafe and they fall in love and get married and live happily ever after. And Peggy dotes over Johnson like crazy. She's always calling him handsome and running her hands through his hair and pampering him. If he just goes out and feeds the horses for twenty minutes, she tells him she missed him. Johnson must be the luckiest kid in the world! Hmmm, I think, with his luck, I'm going to fly out to De Smet and pick him up and fly to Las Vegas. Then I'm going to put $1,000 on a crap table and have Johnson roll the dice. I'd just leave it all on the table and let Johnson keep rolling the dice! I bet I'd be filthy rich in an hour!

I could be gone for two weeks I think and the wife wouldn't even know it, unless I didn't give her my check. I love my kids but I know I want away from this unloving, unappreciative woman and it's tearing me up inside. I never dreamed I would want to divorce my high school sweetheart. I wished things were different, but I don't want to waste much more time with this woman. It was a thankless job, I figured. I don't even want to have sex with her anymore. Well, maybe just every 4 days only.

Besides, with all this unhappiness with the wife, I was also concerned because the house in Arizona wasn't getting sold. I had called the realtor and asked what was going on down there and he said the bank keeps raising how much money down they want and the guy living in the house couldn't come up with it. That didn't sound right to me and two house payments are starting to bother me too.

Chapter Twenty Nine

On May 13th1976 I flew the 172 N9915Q back up to Grand Rapids and then delivered the 180 N9748G to George Williams in Bemidji.

Gene had gotten a brokerage agreement on a Cessna 180 N9161C on amphibian floats that was based in Bemidji, so when I got done with delivering the 180 to George Williams, I called the guy who owned the amphib and flew that back to Grand Rapids. I called John Norlan and told him about this amphib and he said he'd be interested in looking at it, so I departed Grand Rapids and flew it up to Two Harbors. The runway at Two Harbors was northeast southwest and kind of narrow. And the buildings were up off the northeast end. There was a little wind, maybe 3-4 knots out of the west so I decided to land northeast with a little tailwind/crosswind rather than land to the southwest and try to get 61Charlie turned around on the narrow runway. You really have to stomp on the brakes to get 61Charlie to turn around. So I figured it would be a lot easier to land with a little tail/crosswind and taxi right off the far end to the buildings than it would be to land into the wind and make a 180 degree turn on that narrow runway. So I made my approach to the northeast holding the left wing down a little and some right rudder to compensate for the left crosswind. I touched down on the upwind wheel first, put the right wheel down, and then the nose wheels. A perfect landing, I thought. John and one of his employees were waiting for me at the airport office. I got out and shook hands with John and his employee. We all walked around looking at 61Charlie. John liked the looks of this one. He had owned a Cessna 180 on amphibs before so I asked him if he wanted to fly it. He said no, he'd take right seat. So we loaded up and I taxied out and took off to the southwest and made a left turn towards Lake Superior. John flew it until we got to Lake Superior and then I took over and flew on down and made a landing on the lake. John wanted to see how it handled on the water so he taxied it for a few minutes, making left and right turns and was satisfied the way it handled. I made a takeoff from Lake Superior and flew it back up to Two Harbors. Once again I decided to land to the northeast with the little bit of a tailwind/crosswind rather than turning it around on that narrow runway. John knew from his last 180 amphib that they were hard to make a tight turn with. Once again I made my approach with a little left wing low to compensate for the crosswind. My mind was only half on flying the airplane though, the other half was still on the late night, not so good conversation I'd had with the wife. The approach was perfect right down to touching the left gear down. When it touched down at first I thought I had a flat tire and I automatically added a little right rudder and power to compensate for it. But when I let the right side down I said, "Aw shit!" I hadn't put the gear down! I asked John, "Why didn't you tell me to put the damn gear down?!" He said, "I didn't think about it either." I was never so embarrassed in my life, a 5000 hr pilot with instructor and multi ATP ratings and I forget the f--king landing gear!

John was in the logging supply business so we went to his place of business and got four tractor jacks and some 2x4's and came back out and jacked 61Charlie up and I lowered the gear, being they were electric. I flew it back to Duluth and then I did the next stupid thing, I called the FAA in Minneapolis to report it! Tiegan answered the phone. I told him what I had done. He asked, "Where is the airplane now?" I said, "It's out here on the ramp." He wanted to know how I had gotten the gear down so I told him. Then he said, "And then you flew it back to Duluth?" I said, "Yes, it's out here on the ramp." He said, "Did you do any structural damage?" I said, "Define structural damage?" He said, "Did you wear the keel strips down into the skin?" I said, "I don't think so." He said, "I want Jerry Bergman, the mechanic, to go out there and look at that airplane and call me back and if you did, I'm going to hang your ass!" So I got Jerry and we went out and laid down on the ramp and looked at it. Jerry said, "Close Hub, but not quite." So he called Tiegan back and told him that.

Once again, Gene was very understanding. He told me, "Les, you're a great pilot and a great aircraft salesman, but you need to get your divorce over with." I told him if it hadn't been for the kids, I'd done it by now. He knew that too.

That evening I told the wife what had happened. I got no comment one way or the other from her. Not even a, "hey I'm sorry for my part." I want away from this woman, I thought.

I took a few days off to lick my wounds and think. One day I took Ginger and drove back over to the hunting area out west near Brookston and we went for a walk in the woods. Ginger was having fun working both sides of the road. She kicked up a couple of partridges and I'd say, "Good girl Ginger!" She was having fun. I sat down against a tree for a while and Ginger licked my face. I figured she was telling me that she still loved me even if I was, a horse shit pilot. I was thinking, I wish I had a wife that was as loving and understanding as my dog.

On May 19th I flew 61Charlie up to Grand Rapids to have new keel strips put on it. I wouldn't let Halvair pay for them either. I figured it was my mistake, I'll pay for it. And I did, it cost me $800.00.

About May 25th I got a call from Len Kragness down in Caledonia, Minnesota and, "he wanted to buy a new Cessna 180 from me," he said. I said, "I'm not too sure that I want to sell a new Cessna 180 to someone that was betting I'd roll a 172 up in a ball landing in a cross wind in Caledonia." "But, I said, I'm a forgiving person so I'll sell you a new 180," and we laughed. We talked about equipment and color and I suggested a personalized "N" number. We kicked around a few numbers and then Len suggested 123LK. I said, "That sounds good to me. Send me a check for $3,000 and I'll get it ordered." He said he would so I picked up the phone and placed the order. And then I said," thank you God," and breathed a sense of relief because I had two house payments coming due again.

May 28th I took a 172 N73187 up to Two Harbors and demo'd and sold it to Dan O'Day. At least I didn't land it upside down or something!

On June 11th I renewed my biannual with Cal Lucas in our Cardinal RG, N2090Quebec. On June 28th Gene flew me up to Grand Rapids so I could bring our Cessna 180, N7541Kilo, back to Duluth. I liked 41Kilo, it was white and yellow and brand new!

The next day I flew Dan Byrnes up to Two Harbors to see John Norlens' Champ.

June 15th, 1976 was my 39th birthday. I told the wife the day before to not bother with a cake or anything, because,

"I've got to work for the boss." I was getting "pissy" and wanted out of this marriage. If it wasn't for the kids, I'd be gone, I told myself. I didn't even want to have sex with her anymore either.

Harold Chandler from the Alexandria airport had called me a few days earlier and told me about a guy down in Morris, Minnesota that wanted a new Cessna 206 with a float kit on it. He said, "I see you guys have one advertised in the Minneapolis paper." I said, "Yes we do," and he gave me the man's name and telephone number. Harold had bought a couple of Warriors from me for his flight school. He was also a very nice person to deal with.

I called the number and told the man that Harold Chandler had said to call him. He said, "Good, what have you got?" I described the 206 to him and read all the options off the spec sheet and told him the list price and what I could sell it to him for and that it was a "no radio" airplane. We ordered our inventory airplanes with no radios in case the buyer preferred King or Narco brand radios instead of the Cessna brand. And some people wanted a full IFR package while others just wanted a basic VFR package. The man thought that it sounded just about what he was looking for and asked if I would fly it down for him to look at it? I asked, "How's tomorrow for you?" He said, "About 10 am would work good," and I said, "that will work for me too, so I'll see you at the Morris airport at 10 o'clock tomorrow morning." So the next morning I landed at the Morris airport a few minutes before 10 am and the man and his brother were waiting for me. After the man looked the airplane over he asked if he could fly it. I said, "Let's go!" So he got in the left seat, his brother in the back seat, and I got in the co-pilot seat. It was a beautiful day. We took off and went up about 600 feet and leveled off. He set up cruise power, closed the cowl flaps and waited to see what speed it would cruise at. Then he did a couple of steep turns and a stall and we came back in and he made a nice landing. His brother left and we stopped at a restaurant and he bought me lunch.

After lunch we went to his office, to design a radio package. When he opened the door to his office and we walked in, I looked around. It was a room about 14x14 square and full of baseball memorabilia, pictures and trophies. I looked at the man and said, "Boy you're really into baseball aren't you?" He said, "Don't you know who I am?" I said, "Your Jerry Koosman." He said, "Don't you know what I do?" I said, "No I don't." He said, "I'm a pitcher for the New York Mets." Then he picked up a picture and asked if I knew who that was? I said I didn't know. He said, "That's Babe Ruth." Then he picked up another picture and asked me if I knew who that was? I didn't know. He said, "that's Whitie Ford." Pretty soon he said, "You don't know much about baseball do you?" I said, "Jerry, I don't want to hurt your feelings, but I've never watched a baseball or football game in my life. The only sports I've ever watched on TV was if Cloquet was in the High School basketball tournaments. Other than that, I'd rather be out hunting or fishing or mowing my grass." We designed a radio package and he wrote me a check for a sizable deposit so I'd take it to our radio shop in Grand Rapids and have the radios installed. I penned out a purchase order and Jerry gave me a ride, back out to the airport. Before I left Jerry said, "Can we be friends?" I said, "I hope so." He said, "I'd like to go fishing with someone sometime that doesn't talk baseball, baseball, baseball." I said, "If you don't talk airplanes, airplanes, airplanes, we'll go fishing."

To Les
Thanks For Putting
Me In The Pilots Seat!
Best Always
Jerry Koosman

July 10th I got back on a commercial jet and went to Wichita to pick up 123LK for Len Kragness. Len came up on the 12th and we flew 123LK down to Minneapolis up to Hibbing and then left it at Grand Rapids to have some radios installed.

The morning of July 14th I flew for 8 tenths of an hour with Romona Larson doing basic maneuvers in N2090Q getting ready for my check ride with the FAA. I liked flying with Romona, she was pretty and a lot easier on the eyes than the male instructors!

That afternoon Harold Olson from the Minneapolis GADO (General Aviation District Office) came up to talk to me because of my screw up with the 180 amphib up at Two Harbors. He looked at my license and my medical and then paged through my logbook to make sure I was legal and current. We talked about the flight and my divorce proceedings, etc. and then went out to fly the Cardinal RG, N2090Q. Mr. Olson followed me around as I did the preflight, asking a few questions as we went. Then we got in and he watched as I went through the checklist and started up. He instructed me to fly out to our practice area about ten miles southwest of Duluth and we'd do some maneuvers. So I started up and called ground and taxied out to the midfield intersection for runway 27. I did a run up while Mr. Olson watched. I called the tower and got a takeoff clearance with a southwest departure. I asked Mr. Olson if he was ready to go and he replied that he was. I reconfirmed that the doors were locked and taxied onto the runway and made a normal takeoff with a left turnout and climbed up to 2,500 feet. I leveled off and got 90Quebec set up for cruise. I got halfway to the practice area and Mr. Olson said, "Let's turn around and go back and make a few landings." So I called Duluth approach and told them we were returning to the airport. It wasn't long and approach sent me over to the tower. I told the tower controller I'd like to make a, stop and go, on runway 27 and then stay in the pattern for a few more landings. The tower cleared me for a stop and go on runway 27. I entered a left downwind for 27, lowered the gear, and checked "down and green". I'm thinking to myself, don't forget the gear on this check ride stupid! I extended the first notch of flaps, turned base, second notch of flaps, turned final, full flaps, reconfirmed the gear was down and locked, pushed the prop and mixture in, pointed the nose just short of the numbers. I touched down on the main gear just above stall speed, right on the numbers and came to a stop well before the diagonal taxiway going in toward the tower. I retracted the flaps and opened the cowl flaps and asked Mr. Olson what kind of takeoff he'd like. He looked at me and said, "Let's just taxi in." But now I'm wondering if he's happy or did I blow the whole check ride somehow? So I taxied back to Halvair and shut down, using the checklist of course, and we got out. We were walking back across the ramp to Halvair and Mr. Olson isn't saying anything. So I asked him, "What do you think Mr. Olson?" He said, "There isn't a damn thing wrong with your flying, just get your divorce over with." I asked if he wanted to enter anything in my logbook and he said, "No, you don't want anything in your logbook." I thanked him. At least I felt somewhat vindicated for the gear up in that it wasn't my piloting, it was my messed up mind. I knew then that I either needed to become happy in my marriage or get a divorce, one of the two.

The more I thought about it, I was lucky it happened in the amphib. At least that hadn't damaged the prop and the engine, just a couple of keel strips and my pride. It could have happened just as easily in 46Quecbec or worse yet the 421. And that would have cost a lot more than $800 bucks!

I said a silent, "thank you God" for the cheap lesson and vowed to not let this divorce affect my flying anymore.

After the check ride with Mr. Olson, and lunch, I flew the 180 41Kilo down to Moose Lake and picked up Don Bean from Don Bean Mobile Homes, and we flew down to Flying Cloud airport to look at a Cessna 210 N3796Y. Don liked the 210 so he bought it and flew it back to Moose Lake. I flew 41Kilo back to Duluth. I was tired; it had been a long day. Gene was still at the office when I got back and was happy that everything that day had gone well for me. And he handed me an envelope with 100, one dollar, bills in it. I liked working with Gene he was good to me! Plus, I wouldn't have to beg the wife for coffee money in the morning now either! We went over to the Officer's Club and celebrated my successful check ride and sale. I didn't bother calling home.

When I got home it was after suppertime and the kids were in bed. The wife wanted to know why I hadn't called. I said, "Why?" We talked that night and I told her my check ride had gone well and that the examiner had said to get my divorce over with. Then I told her I had decided that I was either going to get what I wanted and needed out of this marriage or we're going to get a divorce, because I'm not flying with this garbage on my mind anymore. I told her I had given this situation a lot of thought since the gear up and I've determined that flying airplanes was more important to me than this marriage to her is. "And," I said, "I'm sick and tired of these, "bolts out of the blue", like my mother thinks your bored, he can be an SOB, I might burn the gravy, your afraid I'm having an affair, bla, bla, bla." I said, "I wished I had packed my bags after the first one because apparently that was just the tip of the iceberg!" I said, "If you want to have an affair you go right ahead, I don't really give a damn! And I'm not wasting any more money on marriage counselors.

Either you and I are going to see eye to eye and meet each others needs or it's over." I said, "I'll give this marriage six months and if I'm not happy with you, I'm gone. It's going to be that simple." I had decided it's time to either sink or swim, and when I get in that mood, things are going to change in a hurry. She was crying and said she wanted to keep the marriage together. Then we went upstairs and made love and fell asleep in each other's arms. We were both physically and mentally exhausted.

Chapter Thirty

I took the next day off. I had seen Earl King a few days earlier and he had told me about a 1973 Thunderbird he had down at his shop in Superior. I took Ginger and drove my Mustang down to Earl's reconditioning shop and looked at it. It was a beautiful gold color with a brown vinyl top and a brown leather interior, like brand new I thought. Earl had been one of my students and had gotten his private license from me back in April 1972. We'd had fun flying together and had become friends. He had also repainted the door on the Mustang after Ginger had scratched it. I asked him how much he wanted for this, "old beat up Thunderbird that he probably got out of a junk yard and threw a quick paint job on it and now wants to dump it off on me to get my pristine Mustang, in trade." Earl just smiled and gave me a figure that I thought was fair. I knew he'd do that. Of course I had told him I'm just a poor flight instructor turned poor aircraft salesman and if I go through a divorce I'll need a job polishing cars for him. And I said, "If I get it home and the wife bitches at me, you might have to take not only my Mustang, but the wife in trade too!" I took Ginger and drove the Thunderbird down the highway a few miles and back and was hooked, so to speak. Ginger had her head out the window and must not have heard me when I asked her how she liked it but, she didn't even look at me. I think she was just happy to have her ears flopping in the breeze. So when I got back I wrote Earl a check and he said he hoped it was good.

I said, "Just make sure you put it in the bank before I get divorced." I took Ginger for a ride out to the hunting area and we went for a nice walk in the woods. As usual, she had a great time hunting partridges. And I had a great time not shooting at anything. When we got back to the car I let Ginger in the riders side and before I closed the door I kneeled down, gave her a hug and said, "I love you Ginger, did I ever tell you I'm sorry I hit you in the butt with my shotgun?" She must have understood me because she licked my face again, as if to say, "I forgive you stupid." Again I thought, someday I'd like to have a wife with a disposition like my dog has!

By the time I got back the wife and kids were home. They must, have seen me and Ginger pull into the driveway because when I hit the garage door opener they were all in the garage by the time the door got up! The kids were all excited about the new car and couldn't wait to sit in it. The wife was even kind of excited about it. I loaded everyone in and we went for a ride out the Jean Duluth road a few miles then I stopped and let the wife drive it back.

Later that night the wife said, "Great move Hubbell, all of our relatives and friends already think we live on "snob hill". I've got a new car and now you've got a Thunderbird. What am I going to tell them?" I said, "Tell them to eat their hearts out. Or else, to spend years and a lot of money getting their private, commercial, float, instrument, multi-engine, instructor, glider and a multi-engine Airline Transport rating and some sales experience, and then come sell airplanes with me. And then fly through the fog and ice in all kinds of airplanes seven days a week." That was the end of that subject. I mixed her a drink, extra strong and led her upstairs. Like I always figured, candy's dandy, liquor's quicker! (I hate myself when I'm like that though.)

I've often wondered why God made the world where us men will crawl to get what we want. The animals don't crawl like us men do to get some sex. They don't buy jewelry and clothes or wine and dine the females. They just pick out a female and hop on! I think I'll ask God if I can come back as a lion or maybe a white tail buck in my next life. They've got it made! All fall, all a white tail buck does is lock horns with another buck now and then and jump the does. They don't even ask her *"Was good for you,"* or nothing. They don't even care! I'll bet they jump a100 does a month for a few of months or so and after that they go hang out by themselves in the swamp or woods someplace. They don't have to listen to the doe complain because she's getting fat and keeping them awake all night, or buying cribs and booties and stuff. The doe gives birth in the spring and the buck doesn't even have to pay the bill, buy clothes, food, provide shelter or listen to the fawns bawl at night, or nothing! He just lays on a hill in the sun, watching the fawns running around and doesn't even give a damn which ones are his. Sounds like a good life to me! Yup, I'm coming back as a white tail buck in my next life!

Chapter Thirty One

Don Bean had called me and said the 210 had a little hydraulic fluid leaking out of the valve assembly behind the center pedestal. He was really nice and said he'd be glad to pay for fixing it if I'd come get it and bring it up to our shop and back. I said I'd do that and flew my favorite 180 N7541Kilo down to Moose Lake to get it. Don met me at the airport and we pulled the 210, N3796Yankee out of his hanger and put 41Kilo back in it. Fifteen minutes later I was landing back in Duluth.

The next morning, July 17th, 1976, Dick Larson and I flew a new 172 N9915Quebec up to Grand Rapids to look at a 1958 Cessna 175. I let Dick fly the 172. I figured he needed some 172 time a lot more than I did.

The man that owned the 175 had passed away and we were selling it for the estate. Gordy had the keys for the airplane and hangar so we got those from him and went out to look it over. It was original and nice. It hadn't been flown much in the last few years either. In fact, the shop at Grand Rapids had just done a fresh annual on it a couple of days ago so we could sell it. I had never flown a 175 either, so was kind of anxious to see how it performed. We pulled it out of the hangar and did a preflight inspection and spent a few minutes looking through the manual. I told Dick to take the left seat and I read the checklist as he started it up. There wasn't much wind to amount to anything, but we still taxied down to the end of 34 to give 76Bravo time to warm up and for us to have a little more time to become familiar with the instruments and radio's, etc. I read the checklist as Dick went through the run up. When he was done I made a call on unicom and we taxied out onto the runway. I told Dick to feed the power to her kind of slow and steady. I like to apply the power on the roll so the engine has some cooling air flowing over it as it's putting out more power and heat. It didn't take very long and that 175, was off the ground and climbing like the proverbial homesick angel! Boy was that thing climbing! We went up and leveled off at 4,500 feet and let it accelerate up to it's cruise speed and then throttled back and adjusted the mixture. It was a geared engine so you had to get use to it cruising at a higher rpm than a normal 172. And of course, with 175 horsepower compared to 150hp in the 172, there was no comparison in performance! I looked over and Dick was smiling so I knew I just about had this months, two house payments in the bank! When we landed, Dick said he liked it and wanted to buy it! I told Gordy I was going to leave the 172 there for them and Dick and I would fly the 175 back to Superior and do the paper work and then I'd send the estate a check for the airplane.

Dick was doing a great job flying the airplane. After landing back at Superior, we put it in his hangar and I signed his logbook so he could get some insurance lined up. Then Dick and I went to his bank and he got me a cashier's check and we stopped for lunch and did the paper work. After all that he drove me back up to Halvair.

The shop had repaired the hydraulic leak in the 210 so I called Don and said I'd be in Moose Lake in twenty minutes. He said he'd meet me at the airport. By the time I got there, Don had the hangar door opened so we pulled 41Kilo out and put 96Yankee back in. Then I got in 46Kilo and flew that back up to Grand Rapids and brought the 172 back to Duluth. I made it home in time for supper even!

I had been teaching Ginger some tricks in my spare time. At first I had taught her to roll over, left and right, then to turn around, left and right. And to sit and stay. And then I would have her sit and stay and I'd put a piece of pancake on her nose and walk away. She'd sit and stay and of course her eyes were glued on that pancake. I'd go out into the living room where she could still see me, all the time saying, stay, stay, stay. Then I'd say, OK and snap my finger. She'd flip that piece of pancake up and catch it and gulp it down. I got her where I could eliminate saying Ok and just snap my fingers and she'd flip it up and gulp it down. I think they call that, classical conditioning, or something. Then I replaced the pancake with a small piece of a hot dog right out on the end of her nose. That was almost too tempting for her at first. I'd have to stand in front of her and keep repeating, stay, stay, stay and then snap my finger, and that piece of hot dog was gone! I finally got her where I could say sit, stay and put a piece of hot dog on her nose and keep repeating sit, stay, sit, stay as I walked out of the room. When I was out of her sight I'd snap my fingers and she's flip it up and gulp it down. Ginger became very popular with the neighborhood kids for doing her tricks. Just about every Saturday if I was home the kids would be saying, "Mr. Hubbell, can Ginger do her tricks?" So I'd have them come into the living room and sit in a circle on the floor. There would be 6-8 kids. Then I'd point to the kitchen and tell Ginger to go, sit and stay. I would do that with verbal and hand signals. After a while I could do it with just hand signals. Ginger would go out into the kitchen and sit and stay looking at me. I thought, hmmm, I wonder if I can get the wife to sit and stay by snapping my fingers, better yet to lay and stay? Hmmm, just a thought? So once Ginger was out in the kitchen, sitting and staying, I'd hide a piece of hot dog in one of the boys pants cuff or under someone's collar. Then I'd snap my fingers and Ginger would come in and her nose was going like a vacuum cleaner, as she'd check each kid out to see who had the hotdog. The kids of course would be giggling like crazy as she sniffed them. Ginger was a great dog. All the kids loved her. I loved her too.

The next month was a good month in the airplane business. Gene was selling and I was selling, life was good!

On August 24, 1976 Gene and I went to a Cessna meeting down at Delavan, Wisconsin at the Lake Lawn Airport and Lodge. I flew my favorite 180, 7541Kilo down there. Gene didn't really like to fly tail draggers so I did most of the flying and demo'ing them. The Cessna meetings were always informational and motivating. Not that I needed any motivating with two house payments to make! Another nice thing about Cessna meetings is that I got to meet other dealers that I had only talked to on the phone. I met Tom Kelly and his wife Cheryl there. Tom was from Chicago and had sold a lot of new Cessna's. In fact, he got the award for selling the most new single engine Cessna's and Gene said that he wins that award almost every year. He and Cheryl kind of specialized in 172's and 150's.

Cessna always put on a great banquet and social hour. We were only there one night. I didn't feel like calling home though. I had lost that feeling in the last year. I hoped it would come back someday, but wasn't banking on it.

The meeting ended at noon on the 25th so we got ready to come home. Gene had made arrangements for one of the Cessna people from Wichita to fly a new 185 N80136 up to the meeting so we could pick it up there and save the expense of going to Wichita to get it. Pretty smart thinking on his part I figured! It was a "no radio" airplane so I flew that home and Gene flew 41Kilo back.

On the way back I went up to 6,500 to get on top of the haze. It was beautiful up there. Once again, I'm looking down and wondering, what do people do that don't fly? I can't imagine going through life without flying airplanes. I thank God my dad had a couple of Champs when I got out of the Airforce or I might never had made that "y" in the road of life. It's amazing how the "y's" in the road of life have effected my life. What if I hadn't met and talked to that guy at the paper mill and found out that he was making $350.00 a month and I had just started and I'm making $350.00 a month. Would I still be working there? If I hadn't joined the Air Force I'd never met Johnson and gone to Texas, Okinawa and Washington, DC. And if I hadn't married the wife I probably would have stayed in the Air Force. Would I have gotten shot down over Vietnam? Hmmm, what if there hadn't been a fire extinguisher on the forklift at the match mill? Would I have burned the whole mill down? Would I be a lot happier if I hadn't married the wife? I figured most of the "Y's" in life had been good to me so far. With the exception of my marriage, I'm happy, healthy and having fun. I guess I can't ask for much more than that! But having two house payments was bothering me a little. I needed to get that problem resolved. I need to get the wife resolved too, I thought. If I can get that house sold and the wife figured out, I'd have a pretty good life I figured!

I didn't even need to look at a map to find my way back to Duluth. I've always thought, I've got the instincts of a homing pigeon! I knew there was some restricted airspace near Camp McCoy so I just pointed "136" northwest toward the Mississippi River and intercepted that just below La Crosse.

Then I flew the river upstream a little and then pointed "136" about 340 degrees, assuming I'd have a little wind out of the west. I got lucky and passed just off to the west of Eau Claire and of course I recognized Rice Lake from landing there so many times when I was flying for Northland Homes. And it's not long in the 185 and I can see Lake Superior from that altitude. I landed at the Park Point airport and called the tower at Duluth to coordinate my no radio landing with them. That was the only problem with bringing no radio airplanes back from the factory at Wichita. I'd always have to land at Cloquet to give them a call. But that only took about ten minutes. Sometimes it was late though and I'd be very tired.

On the morning of September 9th I flew another 185 N1748 Romeo up to Grand Rapids. I got into a 172 N9603Hotel and flew that down to Mora and demo'd it to Bill Fisher from Fisher Motors. Bill didn't jump on it so I flew it over to St Paul and demo'd it to Nick Nichol's. Nick didn't jump on it either so I flew it back to Duluth.

Chapter Thirty Two

I called back down to Casa Grande and talked to the realtor again. I told him I don't understand why he hasn't sold my house. "It's a hell of a nice house in a hell of a nice neighborhood," I said, "and the price is fair." My listing agreement had expired with him and I had told him that I would still pay him a commission if he sold it, but it's been over a year, in fact fourteen months now. I told him all he's done is gotten a guy and his family living in it and I'm not even getting any rent. Hmmm, how do I know, maybe the guy's his brother in law or something, I'm thinking.

I must have been tossing and turning the night of September 23rd, 1976 because the wife nudged me about 6:30 on Friday morning, the 24th and wanted to know what was wrong. I said, "I'm concerned about the house deal in Casa Grande. In fact, let's get up and get packed; we're going to Casa Grande." She said, "We're going to Casa Grande today?" I said, "Yes, we're going today. If I didn't want to go until tomorrow, I'd tell you tomorrow." I can be a little cranky until I have my first cup of coffee. I said, "I'll have to go over to the office for a while and talk to Gene about the deals I've got going and to give him my prospect notes so he can talk to my customers while I'm gone." I said, "You make arrangements with the neighbors to take care of the kids for a week or ten days." She asked, "How are we going to get there, are we flying commercial?" I said, "No, we're going to drive." I knew she'd like that because she liked to drive the "T" bird. She started getting the kids up and was telling them what was happening when I left the house. I stopped by the Chalet on the way to the airport and had breakfast. Gene was already at the office when I got there so I told him I needed to be gone for a while to go see what the deal was with my house in Arizona. Gene knew that I had been bothered by that situation and he was very understanding and wished me a safe and successful trip. Tom Halvorson, the Vice President of Halvair, arrived just as I was about to leave the office and I told him I was going to be gone for maybe ten days to go to Arizona and find out what the deal was with my house down there. He asked how I was going to get down there and back? I said, "I'm going to drive my Thunderbird." He said, "I can't afford to have you gone that long, take the 180, 41Kilo. It's yours just pay for the gas." I said, "Thanks a lot Tom, that'll be a heck of a lot nicer than driving!"

When I got back home I told the wife that Tom had offered me to take my favorite 180 to Arizona. I think she was a little disappointed because she wasn't that great of a flyer anyhow. Every time I would pull the carburetor heat out and the engine changed pitch she'd about bail out. I must have told her 25 times why it does that and it still alarms her. It would tick me off a little that she didn't have very much confidence in me. She had proven that again when I soloed Tim on his sixteenth birthday in Casa Grande and she didn't want to stand by me in case he crashed. Hmmm, maybe I should have divorced her then? I wouldn't have landed that 180amphib gear up if I had done that. Hmmm, had I taken a wrong "Y" in the road of life?

We had 41Kilo loaded up and off the ground by 9 am. The weather was perfect all the way to Arizona so I had decided to fly the trip VFR. I flew from Duluth direct to the Gopher

VOR on the northwest side of Minneapolis. About 20 miles northeast of the VOR I gave Minneapolis approach control a call to check in. The controller gave me a transponder code and said to squawk ident. I dialed in the code and pressed the ident button. The controller said he wasn't receiving my ident and to call him when I was about ten miles from Gopher. So when I figured I was about ten miles from the Gopher VOR I called approach again. He asked me to ident again. He said he still wasn't picking up my ident and to call him about five miles away from the VOR. So when I figured I was five miles from Gopher I called him again. He still wasn't getting my ident. He said to call him when I was over Gopher. I could look down and see the Gopher VOR, so when I was just about right on top of it I called the approach control guy again. He said to ident and I did, but he still wasn't receiving my ident. So just for the hell of it I said, "Can't you see a yellow and white Cessna 180 right over the Gopher VOR on your radarscope?" He kind of laughed and said, "I'm sorry sir, we don't paint pictures." He must of thought I was a real hick and of course I couldn't blame him! I figured he'd have a good time at lunch telling the rest of the controllers about the guy, who thinks they get pictures of airplanes on their scopes!

It was such a beautiful clear day I just figured I'd fly southwest for about four hours and then land someplace for fuel. The wife had packed some coffee, sandwiches, bananas and cookies so we had plenty to eat along the way. I made the first fuel stop in Kearny, Nebraska. I don't think we were on the ground much more than a half an hour and we were topped off and back in the air! I just climbed out on the same heading that had gotten me this far. A little less than four hours later we were coming up on Santa Fe, New Mexico. I remembered Santa Fe from the time I had flown Roy Lee up there to get some turquoises to make jewelry. We landed there and topped off with fuel and took off and headed southwest. We had about 430 miles to go to Casa Grande, just about three hours I figured.

I knew the scenery was breathtaking from Albuquerque down to Show Low having, flown that with Roy Lee in the 210. So when I got west of Albuquerque I dropped down for a little terrain flying. I slowed up to about 120mph and was about 300 feet above the ground and just weaving between the buttes and generally heading southwest. I pointed out the VOR on top of the butte above us to the wife when we went past St Johns. The wife wasn't saying much. I wasn't sure if she was just enjoying the ride or to, scared to talk, so I climbed up to an altitude where she got her color back. The view was still magnificent! We couldn't get over how many different colors there were!

I figured we had another hour and a half before we'd get to Casa Grande. So I climbed up to 4,500 and slid my seat back a little and trimmed 41Kilo up and just "neck reined" her with a little rudder now and then. The wife poured me a cup of coffee and handed me a few chocolate cookies. I thought, it doesn't get much better than this, what do people do that don't fly? I can't imagine going through life without flying airplanes. Just this trip for instance, taking off from Duluth, Minnesota this morning and enjoying the view of the woods and the lakes, and pretty soon the open farmland of south-western Minnesota, South Dakota, Nebraska and then the high desert of Colorado and now this spectacular view of New Mexico. We even saw a few caves that looked like people might have lived in them many years ago. I still can't help but asking, "Why me God, Minnesota farm boy Les Hubbell, who am I to be able to do this? What have I ever done to deserve to be able to do this?" I feel so humble. I know that I am so very lucky to be able to do this. I thanked God that my Dad had two Champs when I came home from the Air Force, or I might never have learned to fly. Pretty soon I could see Phoenix off to the west and Tucson to the south. It was a beautiful clear day, or course just about every day in Arizona, was a beautiful clear day, I remembered. I dialed in the Casa Grande VOR and got a good signal.

It wasn't very long and I could see the cars on Interstate 10 running between Tucson and Phoenix and Casa Grande straight ahead!

In another 15 minutes I was in the pattern at the Casa Grande airport. I couldn't help thinking again, what do people do that don't fly? We had left Duluth, Minnesota at 9 am this morning and now about 1500 miles and 11 hours later, we were landing at Casa Grande, Arizona. And the early settlers were lucky if they made seven miles a day with their horses and wagons I had read someplace. Hmmm, if my mental math is right, they'd been over two hundred and ten days getting here!

The wife had called Herb and Joyce at the store from Santa Fe while I was getting 41Kilo fueled and told them we were on our way down there. Herb had said he'd leave his car at the airport for us, and Joyce would make reservations at the Francisco Grande. I landed and taxied in and sure enough, there was Herb's Mercury Grande Marquis parked by the building. I got the 180 tied down and we grabbed our bags and loaded them in the Mercury and headed out to Herb and Joyce's house. They were expecting us and it was really good to see them again. Herb mixed us all a drink to celebrate our safe trip. The wife said that she wasn't too sure a few times, about how safe the trip was, and then she told them about having to look up the see the VOR when we went by St

Johns. I said, "Hey if you ain't living on the edge you're taking up too damn much space!" Herbie and I toasted to that!

We'd had a long day so we headed out to the Francisco Grande. We were both very tired and slept well, not waking up until 9 am our time the next morning. We had a leisurely breakfast and then drove to a car rental place in town and rented a car. The wife drove the Mercury to the store and I drove the rental car. The store looked good. I think Herb and Joyce were having fun running it.

I called Harper from the store and made arrangements to meet with him at 9 am on Monday. Then I called the realtor and told him I was in town and would like to meet with him and the guy that's living in my house at 10 am Monday morning. He said that would work for them.

We had coffee with Herb and Joyce at the store and then the wife and I drove out to take a drive-by look at the house and to visit Bill and Marjorie next door. They were glad to see us again. I noticed there wasn't even a for sale sign in front of the house. I thought, hmmm, maybe it is the realtor's brother in law living there? I asked Bill and Marjorie if there had ever been a "for sale" sign in the yard. They said there had been one until the people moved in. I asked them what the people in the house were like and how old they were, etc. They said they didn't see them out much, but they were older couple and kept to themselves and had very little company.

We had a couple of beers with Bill and Marjorie for old times sake. They had been really nice neighbors.

There wasn't much I could do after that until Monday morning except visit with Herb and Joyce, and take them to lunch at the Pizza Corral or the Grande.

On Sunday morning I let the wife sleep in and I drove out to Maricopa to see if they were flying any gliders. It was a nice morning and they had gliders coming and going. My instructor wasn't working there anymore I found out. I went in and said hi to Les Horvac and his wife. Of course Horvac still remembered me. I asked him if I could rent a glider or am I going to have to take an instructor with to get recurrent because I haven't flown one since I was here a year and three months ago. Horvac just looked at the schedule and assigned a glider to me. It was fun to get in a glider again. I felt like it had been yesterday! The tow went good and I found enough lift to stay up for forty, five minutes!

On the way back I stopped by the Casa Grande airport and had 41Kilo topped off with fuel and added a quart of oil. I gave her a good looking over.

I drove back out to the Grande and had dinner with the wife in the Grande's restaurant. I made sure she had a couple of drinks and then I asked her if she felt like taking a "nap?" I said it had been a long trip and you're probably still tired, maybe you should have another drink. Like I always figured, candy's dandy, liquors quicker!

After our "nap" we drove back out and visited with Bill and Marjorie some more. And then we drove over and visited with Roy Lee and his wife for a while. Then we drove back over to Herb and Joyce's and sat around their pool and visited for a while. Then Herb said it was their turn to take us out for supper. I said the Pizza Corral is good enough for me, and the wife agreed. So we loaded up in Herb's Mercury and went over to the Pizza Corral. Herb had driven Mercury Marquies as long as I'd known him. He always swore that was the best car ever made.

By the time we were done eating pizza and drinking beer it was about 8 pm. I said, "Do you know who I'd like to see while were here?" Herb said, "No, who?" I said, "I'd like to see those people that came in and bought all their furniture and appliances from us when they moved here. I said, "Remember we had them out to our house for steaks and drinks the evening we had delivered everything to them." I said, "Sam and Brenda were their names." I asked if they had seen them lately, they said they hadn't. I said, "Let's drive over and see if they're home." After a few beers we didn't even think about calling them, we just drove over and rang the doorbell. Brenda came to the door. She was glad to see all of us! She said, "Come in, it's so good to see you again." So we went in and sat at the kitchen counter and Brenda set us up a beer. She said, "I'll go wake Sam up, he will want to see you guys." I said, "No, don't wake Sam, I know he goes to work about 3 am, so let him sleep." Brenda said, "No, he wouldn't forgive me if he found out you were here and I didn't wake him." So she went and woke Sam up. Pretty soon he came out of the bedroom all groggy with his hair all messed up. He said, hi and sat down and looked at me through blurry eyes and said, "What brings you back to town Hubbell?" I said, " I came down to see what the hell is going on with my house." Brenda just about went into orbit! She said, "What's the matter with your house." I said, "A guys living in it and suppose to be buying it, but I'm not getting any money, so my attorney and I are meeting with him and his realtor in the morning at 10 am." Brenda said, "We'll buy it, we'll buy it, won't we Sam!" Poor Sam is sitting there, barely awake not knowing what's going on! She said, "I told Sam that night we were out there that, if you guys ever sold that house I wanted it, and before we knew anything it was sold." She said, "If it ain't sold, we'll buy it! We'll pay you

$500.00 more than the other guy if we can get it, won't we Sam, won't we Sam!" Poor Sam, he still isn't awake. I said, "You don't have to pay $500.00 more than the other guy, if you want it, I'll sell it to you for the same price." She said, "Give them a deposit Sam, hurry up!" "How much of a deposit do you want Les," Sam asked, still not awake enough to know what the hell's going on. I said, "Give me a two thousand dollar deposit and I'll get you the house if I can." It turned out Brenda was pregnant again and they only had two bedrooms and didn't have room to add on a third bedroom on their lot. So Sam wrote me out a check for two thousand dollars.

I let the wife sleep in Monday morning and went down to the restaurant and had breakfast. I was at Harper's office right at 9 am and true to form, there was Harper leaned back in his chair with his cowboy boots up on the desk, reading the morning paper. He said, "Good to see you Hubbell, what's new?" I said, "I sold my house last night, that what's new." He sat up and said, "Well, now we got trouble!" I said, "How do you figure that?" He said, "Doesn't that guy in the house have a contract on it." I said, "Hell no, that expired six months ago! He wants to rent it now and I'm not in the renting business." He picked up the phone and called the realtor. He said, "Hey, does your guy want to rent that house or buy it?" Apparently the realtor said his guy wanted to rent it so Harper said, "We'll be over there in fifteen minutes." Then I told Harper about my deal with Sam and Brenda and how bad she wants the house. And I said, "Now Harper, when we get over there I want to collect six months back rent, cash, from this guy at $400.00 a month. And if he can't pay it I want him moved out and off my property by 4 o'clock this afternoon. If he can pay the back rent and needs 30 days to find some place else to move to and pays another months rent, I'll go along with that. And I want to go out there after this meeting to check the house for damage. If there is any damage I'll want that repaired too."

So we got in my rental car and drove across town to the realtor's office. The realtor was really friendly, of course. Then he introduced us to the guy who was living in my house. He was Mexican and about 55 years old I figured. He looked like a real gentleman and turned out to be a hell of a nice guy. He was very apologetic about how the deal had gotten screwed up because first the bank had approved him, he said, and then after he moved in they raised the down payment higher than he could come up with. We sat down and Harper told them what I wanted. The guy said, "That's no problem, I can go home and get the cash." Harper asked him if he needed another month and the guy said he would appreciate being able to do that. So he got in his car and drove out to the house and came back within 30 minutes with $2,800 in cash and gave it to me. The realtor had his secretary type up the agreement and a receipt and I signed that. I suspected that was part of the money he had saved up for the down payment. Harper and I shook hands with those guy's and went back to his office. I told Harper I'd send Sam and Brenda over to see him and asked him if he would make sure all the paper work got done right for them and me, and then send me a bill. I paid Harper $100.00 for what he had done today and left.

I drove out to the house and rang the doorbell. The man answered the door and let me in. He was still apologizing for me having to come down there and get this settled. He introduced me to his wife. She was equally apologetic too and told me I was welcome to inspect the house. I walked through the house. It was immaculate. They obviously loved the house. It was as neat and cozy as could be. I ended up feeling sorry for them. If I hadn't committed it to Sam and Brenda I would have done what ever I could have to help them buy it after I saw how nice they had kept it and what decent people they were.

I drove back out to the "Grande" and picked up the wife and we drove back into town and went over to visit Sam and Brenda. Sam worked an odd ball shift, like from 3 am to 11 am so he had just gotten home shortly before. They were all excited when I told them the house was going to be theirs. Then I told them about the people in the house and how nice they were and how nice they had kept the house. I suggested that maybe they should have them come over and look at their house. (I never heard whether that worked out or not.) I gave them Harper's telephone number and said he would handle the paper work and bill me for it. And then we drove over to the Pizza Shack and celebrated their new house with a pizza and a couple of beers! We dropped them back off at their house and went back to the store to visit with Herb and Joyce. They were both busy with customers so I told them we were leaving in the morning and we would like them to come out to the "Grande" for supper with us about seven. They said they'd like that.

We drove back out to the Grande and had a drink to celebrate that the house deal was finally over with! Then I looked at the wife and said, "You look really tired and I'm really, really tired after a strenuous day of negotiating the house deal, maybe we should take a nap? She said, "Is that all you can think about, is sex?!" I said, "No, sometimes I think of flying too. In fact, sometimes when I'm flying I think of sex too." She said, "You better not be thinking of flying when were having sex!" So we went back up to the room and, took a nap.

We were waiting in the restaurant when Herb and Joyce arrived. They'd had a very good day in the store so I bought a round of drinks to celebrate that! Then Herb bought a round to celebrate that our house deal was done. I was thinking of buying a round to celebrate that I'd had a good nap, but didn't think the wife would appreciate my humor so I let it go. Besides, I was thinking of having another nap after supper so didn't want to ruin my chances. We had a nice supper and visit with Herb and Joyce and said goodnight early because we were going to make an early takeoff and head back to Minnesota in the morning. I checked us out of the Grande after supper with Herb and Joyce so all we had to do in the morning was to load up and leave. The wife had picked up some coffee and rolls and some other snacks for the return trip. We were still full from having eaten supper with Herb and Joyce anyway so we just loaded up and headed out to the airport at 6:30 our time. I stopped at a Circle K along the way and got us a cup of coffee.

I had made arrangements with Herb to pick up the rental car and return it for me. He said he and Joyce would take care of it before they went to the store in the morning. (Little did we know that would be the last time we would see Herb. He died August 16, 1979)

I parked about twenty feet in front of 41Kilo with the lights on and while the wife was loading the lunch I put the bags in the luggage compartment. I gave 41Kilo another good preflight and drove the car over and parked it and left the key on top of the rider's side front tire like I had told Herb I would. 41Kilo started right up and I taxied out, did a run up and took off at 7 am into a clear but dark sky. The stars were brilliant. I went up to 7,500 ft and headed northeast toward Santa Fe. Just to be on the safe side, I called center and got flight following, just in case. I figured we should have about a 10 mph tail wind so we'd be back in Santa Fe in about two hours and fifteen-twenty minutes. I've always liked flying in the dark too. It always seems more peaceful. The stars up above and lights on the ground and the sound of the engine, it's peaceful to me. I still remember the night I was flying the Twin Comanche across northern Wisconsin one night though for Northland Homes. I think Joe and I were going to Ironwood, Michigan. It was snowing lightly, the stars were out and there were farm lights on the ground. I was getting a case of vertigo every time I'd look out the windshield, so I quit looking out the windshield until we were near Ironwood. I'd never had that before.

It wasn't very long though and I could see signs of the sun coming up from 7,500 ft. It seemed like it went from dark to light in just a few minutes. Almost like turning a switch on!

We were near Santa Fe right about two hours and twenty minutes later as I had guesstimated. I had a lot of fuel left, the oil pressure and temperature were in the green and we were making good groundspeed, so I asked the wife if she needed a bathroom or is she good for another hour and twenty minutes and we'd land at Pueblo, Colorado. She said she was good to go so I turned to the north and headed for Pueblo. From Santa Fe I flew north in the same valley between two mountain ranges that we'd come down in. There were a couple of good peaks along the way. Not too far north of Santa Fe the map showed a 13,000footer and farther north, a 14,000footer. The scenery was beautiful. The wife even liked it! I flew north up to an airway going from Las Cruses to the east through another valley. When we popped out of that valley we were out on the high desert and it was clear sailing to Pueblo.

I called Pueblo approach about 25 miles out. At ten miles he handed me off to the tower. I applied carburetor heat so slow and then pushed it back that the wife didn't even notice it. I figured it was so dry out here there wasn't much chance of getting any carburetor ice today any way. We landed on runway 27. I had learned in the Air Force to leave the mixture leaned out when you land at these higher elevations or the engine will flood out. When I called ground I asked him if there was a restaurant on the field and he directed us toward Flower aviation down on the west end of the airport. By the time I taxied to their ramp there was a girl in short shorts and halter top waving at me. I thought, hmmm, I think I'm going to like this place. Before I shut down there was a fuel truck pulling up. The girl in the short shorts was rolling out a carpet on the wife's side. Smart girl, I thought. We walked over to Flower Aviation. The FBO was full of large plants and some exotic birds flying around, parrots I think. They had a nice restaurant so we decided to have lunch now and then just snacks the rest of the way home. We ate and picked up a couple of cokes and candy bars and paid for the fuel. Then I picked up the phone and called Flight Service. The weather was good VFR all the way to Duluth he said. And we should still have about a ten knot tailwind up at 7500 ft, I figured.

On the way in I had noticed some interesting airplanes and a train off the south side of the parking lot so we walked over there. They had a couple of planes that I hadn't ever seen before. They also had a train engine with two big jet engines in it that looked like it was designed to run on compressed air in a U shaped channel. We spent about thirty minutes looking around and then I realized we still had a long ways to go yet so we better get the show in the air.

I drained the tanks and kicked the tires and we got in to start up. I only had the mixture halfway out when I started up and taxied back out to runway 27. I realized we were at 5,000 feet elevation but I knew 41Kilo still wasn't going to waste much time getting airborne as light as she was. So I requested and got a midfield departure. I did a run up and wiggled the ailerons and rudder and checked the elevator and called the tower and said I was ready to go and requested a right hand turn out to the north. He cleared me for take off and I pulled out onto runway 27. I made a last check to see if everything was in the green and looked at the wife to see if she was in the pink and buckled in. I brought the power up to 2300 rpm's and leaned the mixture out until the rpm's started dropping and then richened it out until it was smooth and just a little more and went to full throttle. It wasn't very long and the tail wheel was lifting off the runway and not much longer and 41Kilo was telling me she was ready to fly. The airspeed was just getting into the green so I applied a little back, pressure and we broke ground. I liked 41Kilo, she didn't spend much time fooling around on the ground. And when she got in the air she was ready to climb. None, of that sinking feeling you get with some underpowered airplanes. I made a right turn to 005 degrees and climbed up to 7,500. I figured I'd just fly north until east of the Front Range airport at Denver and then turn to the northeast. Both the wife and I were enjoying looking at the mountains, as well as the high desert. I don't think I had ever seen her actually enjoy flying before, like she was now. We were getting along pretty good on this trip I thought, but I didn't know what she was thinking. I didn't ask her either. I guess I had made up my mind anyway that if I get anymore, "bolt's out of the blue" or "knives in the ribs", as I called them, I'm leaving. I'm tired of the hassles and I'm not going to go through much more of it. I had also made up my mind, that if I'm not happy with this woman, I'll go find another one. In fact, I had thought of going to that woman's apartment in Casa Grande to see if her TV needed adjusting. I looked over at where she lived as I drove out to the house to inspect it. But I thought, the wife and I are doing OK for now so I won't rock the boat. I would have never thought that I'd be thinking of cheating on my high school sweetheart? But I am. I know my marriage isn't right when I'm thinking that. I'm not sure even that any other woman would even want to make love with me either. Maybe I should keep what I've got? I don't know, maybe all women are like this?

I pointed out Colorado Springs to the wife and told her that was also Peterson Air Force Base where I used to go when I was a flight engineer for the Vice Chief of Staff's Office. "If we weren't in a hurry to get home, it would be fun to land there and stay at the Antlers Hotel," I told her. "And we could walk down to the bar that I used to go to and listen to some good country music, if it was still there. But we've been gone a week already so I better get back to work," I said. I turned northeast about five miles before the Front Range airport just to avoid any traffic that might be on final for 27 there. I headed directly to the Akron VOR and then straight to O'Neill, Nebraska for fuel and a pit stop. "There sure isn't much to see out here after looking at the mountains," the wife said. I said, "Yes that's true, but you don't have to worry about hitting anything either! And if the engine quits we've got all kinds of open range to land on." I slid my seat back and found a coke and a candy bar to nibble on. The air was smooth, so I just neck rained 41 Kilo for the next 15 miles or so. I could look down at the ground and tell we were moving along pretty good. It's hard to time yourself across anything because they don't have roads or fence lines every mile like we do back home. There was just a big open range down there. We were getting close to O'Neill and I was thinking of making a run for Duluth. I figured I could probably make Duluth nonstop and have maybe forty five minutes of fuel left. And then I thought what if I lose this tail wind? And what if the Duluth weather goes down? Then I thought, it only takes a half an hour or forty five minutes to land and get topped off and plus we would get to walk around a little and use the bathroom. Besides, I needed another coke, I told the wife. She said she did too. I told her I needed something else too. She rolled her eyes and said, "I wonder what that could be?" "A candy bar," I said.

I checked the oil, the exhaust stack and the belly of the airplane and walked around it to see if any parts were about to fall off, while the guy was refueling 41Kilo. The wife had gone into the building. I walked into the building and used the bathroom. The wife had gotten a couple of cokes and candy bars out of the machine. I paid for the fuel and we, "loaded up and headed out". I climbed up to 5,500 ft and trimmed 41Kilo out. I was glad we had stopped. Now there was no problem if we had to go someplace other than Duluth. I figured we'd be about two hours and forty five minutes getting to there. The weather was perfect. I told the wife it isn't very often you can cover that many miles without having to deal with some weather. I'm trying to be nice to her, but I know I'm still kind of pissed inside over that amphib deal. That wouldn't have happened if I had been a happy camper, I figured. And when I think about it, I've never really heard a kind, appreciative or complimentary word from her. Boy, Johnson sure got lucky, I thought.

We're back in familiar territory now. I don't even have to look at a map any more. I pointed out Sioux Falls off the right wing to the wife. I told her, "That's where your Dad and

I had gone to pick up Aunt Cora after Lawrence had died."
Then I saw Brookings and pretty soon Marshall, and
Willmar. I told the wife, "I'm sure glad Tom let me use 41Kilo
or we'd been five long days just driving down there and back.
I said, "I'd rather take a beating behind a bar than drive that
far." She just looked at me. We flew right between Willmar
and Litchfield and then right smack over St Cloud. It was
starting to get dark now. I still made out the Milaca airport
and saw the lights of the Moose Lake airport. It had been a
good trip but I was anxious to get home and see the kids and
Ginger and to sleep in my own bed. I called Duluth
approach over Cloquet. The wind was out of the west so they
were using runway 27. About 5 miles out approach handed
me off to Duluth tower and he wasn't busy so he cleared me
to land runway 27. I three pointed 41Kilo right on the numbers and made the diagonal turnoff and the tower said to,
"taxi to Halvair." They were familiar with 41Kilo. I'd been
in and out of Duluth with her many times. It was good to be
back. I parked 41Kilo on a tie down and we walked in and
used the bathrooms. I drove the "T" Bird out on the ramp so
we could load it up with our luggage and stuff. There wasn't
anyone at Halvair but the line kid. I asked him to top off
41Kilo and put the bill on my desk and I'd pay it in the morning.

The wife called the neighbors and told them we were back
and we'd be there in about 30 minutes.

We drove home and went next door and got the kids and
Ginger and thanked the neighbors. I told them I wouldn't
charge them anything for taking care of my kids. The wife
was going to send them a thank you card with some money
in it to cover their additional food expense.

It had been a great trip! I got my house sold, collected $2,800 in rent and had a great visit with Herb and Joyce, Bill and Marjorie, Sam and Brenda and Harper.

And I sure appreciated Tom Halvorson letting me take the Cessna 180 41Kilo that saved about 5 days of driving! And I hate having to drive much more than 50 miles!

The only problem with coming back to Duluth was, now I have to face the reality of what am I going to do about my marriage? I love my wife and kids but I'm not happy with our marriage. Something is missing. I keep telling myself, that she's just not very demonstrative, but she's a good mother, she keeps a good house, she's a good cook, she manages money good, and she never turns me down for sex. (Unless she has her period.) But it still bothers me that I couldn't get a hug and kiss when I come home, because she might burn the gravy. And why my dog is always happier to see me than my wife is? Am I expecting too much, I ask myself? Should I be happy with things the way they are? Most of my friends have wives that are also good housekeepers, good with the kids, good cooks and money managers, and they still take time to welcome their husband home. I'm thinking, hmmm, I'm 39 years old already! Do I want to spend the rest of my life with a woman that doesn't respect me, doesn't have any confidence in my instructing, and isn't glad to see me when I come home? I'm still puzzled as to why she said, "you're just afraid I'm having an affair," when she was in Hawaii. Why would she say that? Was she having an affair? Why would she say that? I've never suspected or accused her of having an affair. Why would she say that then? I don't know, maybe I don't want to know? Hmmm, I wonder if I took her back to the grocery store and told Carl she's spoiled, if he'd take her back?

Continued in Book Three

This book is dedicated to
Gene Berg
Destin, Florida
If it wasn't for Gene recruiting me into aircraft sales in
August of 1972 I wouldn't have had all the fun
I've had in life!
Thanks Gene!

Leslie V. Hubbell
"Your Average Aircraft Salesman"

I Give:
Thanks and credits to my editors:
Don and Barb Scherbing, Monticello, MN
John Cartier, Duluth, MN
My cousin, Milea O'Brian, Outing, MN

I Give:
Thanks and credits for the pictures to:
John Cartier: for all the pictures of 42Joliet, Tan-Tar-A
Lodge etc.
Jay Frey: for the picture of 372 lifting off the dolly.
Ken Bellows: for the picture of 372 on the
glacial lake in Alaska
Mrs. Reimers: for the two pictures of Mr. Reimers
Tom and Becky Prior: for the pictures of Becky and
me and 86 Delta.
Ted Micke: for the glider picture
Tom Halvorson for letting me use 41Kilo to go to
Casa Grande and back!

And last, but certainly not least, I give thanks and credit
to God for my
health and happiness.